Escape from Work

JAPANESE SOCIETY SERIES
General Editor: Yoshio Sugimoto

A Social History of Science and Technology in
Contempory Japan, Volume 2
Shigeru Nakayama

Gender and Japanese Management
Kimiko Kimoto

Philosophy of Agricultural Science: A Japanese Perspective
Osamu Soda

A Social History of Science and Technology in
Contempory Japan, Volume 3
Shigeru Nakayama and Kunio Goto

Japan's Underclass: Day Laborers and the Homeless
Hideo Aoki

A Social History of Science and Technology
in Contemporary Japan, Volume 4
Shigeru Nakayama and Hitoshi Yoshioka

Scams and Sweeteners: A Sociology of Fraud
Masahiro Ogino

Toyota's Assembly Line: A View from the Factory Floor
Ryoji Ihara

Village Life in Modern Japan: An Environmental Perspective
Akira Furukawa

Social Welfare in Japan: Principles and Applications
Kojun Furukawa

Escape from Work: Freelancing Youth and the Challenge to Corporate Japan
Reiko Kosugi

Social Stratification and Inequality Series

Inequality amid Affluence: Social Stratification in Japan
Junsuke Hara and Kazuo Seiyama

Intentional Social Change: A Rational Choice Theory
Yoshimichi Sato

Constructing Civil Society in Japan:
Voices of Environmental Movements
Koichi Hasegawa

Deciphering Stratification and Inequality: Japan and beyond
Yoshimichi Sato

Social Justice in Japan: Concepts, Theories and Paradigms
Ken-ichi Ohbuchi

Gender and Career in Japan
Atsuko Suzuki

Status and Stratification: Cultural Forms in East and Southeast Asia
Mutsuhiko Shima

Globalization, Minorities and Civil Society:
Perspectives from Asian and European Cities
Koichi Hasegawa and Naoki Yoshihara

Advanced Social Research Series

A Sociology of Happiness
Kenji Kosaka

Frontiers of Social Research: Japan and beyond
Akira Furukawa

Modernity and Identity in Asia Series

Globalization, Culture and Inequality in Asia
Timothy S. Scrase, Todd Miles Joseph Holden and Scott Baum

Looking for Money:
Capitalism and Modernity in an Orang Asli Village
Alberto Gomes

Governance and Democracy in Asia
Takashi Inoguchi and Matthew Carlson

Escape from Work

Freelancing Youth and the Challenge to Corporate Japan

Reiko Kosugi

Translated by

Ross Mouer

Trans Pacific Press

Melbourne

First published in Japanese in 2003 by Keisō Shobō as *Furiitaa to iu ikikata*.
This English language edition published in 2008 by
Trans Pacific Press, PO Box 120, Rosanna, Melbourne, Victoria 3084, Australia
Telephone: +61 3 9459 3021 Fax: +61 3 9457 5923
Email: tpp.mail@gmail.com
Web: http://www.transpacificpress.com

Copyright © Trans Pacific Press 2008

Designed and set by digital environs, Melbourne, Australia. www.digitalenvirons.com

Printed by BPA Print Group, Burwood, Victoria, Australia

Distributors

Australia and New Zealand
UNIREPS
University of New South Wales
Sydney, NSW 2052
Australia
Telephone: +61(0)2-9664-0999
Fax: +61(0)2-9664-5420
Email: info.press@unsw.edu.au
Web: http://www.unireps.com.au

USA and Canada
International Specialized Book
Services (ISBS)
920 NE 58th Avenue, Suite 300
Portland, Oregon 97213-3786
USA
Telephone: (800) 944-6190
Fax: (503) 280-8832
Email: orders@isbs.com
Web: http://www.isbs.com

Asia and the Pacific
Kinokuniya Company Ltd.

Head office:
Shin-Mizonokuchi Bldg. 2F
5-7 Hisamoto 3-chome
Takatsu-ku, Kawasaki 213-8506
Japan
Telephone: +81(0)44-874-9642
Fax: +81(0)44-829-1025
Email: bkimp@kinokuniya.co.jp
Web: www.kinokuniya.co.jp

Asia-Pacific office:
Kinokuniya Book Stores of Singapore Pte., Ltd.
391B Orchard Road #13-06/07/08
Ngee Ann City Tower B
Singapore 238874
Telephone: +65 6276 5558
Fax: +65 6276 5570
Email: SSO@kinokuniya.co.jp

ISSN   1443–9670 (Japanese Society Series)

ISBN   978-1-876843-44-1 (Hardcover)
ISBN   978-1-876843-45-8 (Paperback)

The National Library of Australia Cataloguing-in-Publication entry

Kosugi, Reiko.
    Escape from work: freelancing youth and the challenge to corporate Japan.

    Bibliography.
    Includes index.
    ISBN 9781876843441.

    1. Self-employed – Japan. 2. Work – Social aspects – Japan.
    3. Youth – Employment – Japan. I. Title. (Series:
    Japanese society series).

306.360952

Cover illustration: Young people in a shopping area in Tokyo. Photo supplied by the author.

Contents

Figures

Tables

Preface

The Japanese version of this volume was first published in 2003 as *Furiitaa to iu Ikikata* (The lifestyle of the casual labor force). As a researcher focusing on the school-to-work transition, it seemed to me that in the second half of the 1990s a noticeable change could be detected in how newly graduated young people were making that transition. In 1997 I formed a research team that visited a number of schools and enterprises to ask about what was happening. We also began to look at some of the statistical data relevant to understanding change in the school-to-work transition. It became obvious that the number of high school graduates not making the transition into the labor force immediately after graduation had increased and that a large number of students were not participating in the placement activities organized by their schools. The term that was used to describe these youth was "*furiitaa*". On the one hand, the term came to be a shorthand for young Japanese in lowly paid casual work that offered little in terms of job security. For many of the *furiitaa* the barrier between where they were and the world of full-time regular employment had suddenly become insurmountable. At the same time, because the term also embodied a reference to "being free" and fed the belief that any stint in the casual labor force would be a temporary detour, many found solace in being labelled "*furiitaa*" when facing the challenge of hurdling that barrier. This nuance or twist in the meaning associated with being a "*furiitaa*" fostered in some *furiitaa* a sense of optimism regarding their own economic future.

Following those early explorations, the research team undertook several rounds of interviews with *furiitaa* and administered to them quantitatively oriented surveys. Through that multi-dimensional approach we gradually came to gain an overall picture of what was happening in terms of changing employment practices and social change and the impact of the "*furiitaa* phenomena" on the way the labor market for new graduates was evolving. The data was compiled through a team effort involving a number of persons organized under the auspices of the Japan Institute for Labour Policy and Training, and some of the research reports that emanated from that research team are mentioned in the list of references appearing at the end of this volume. As a member of the research team, I was also able to view the data from my own vantage point, and this volume is one outcome of that activity.

As Japan moved into this century another phenomenon became apparent, the increase in the number of young people characterized by NEET (meaning "not in education, employment, or training), and in 2005 we began to study that particular group of young people as a distinct group. In 2005 I was able to compile another volume, *Furiitaa to Niito* (The casual labor force and the NEET phenomenon). The long first chapter in that volume has been included as Chapter Five in this English volume.

By June 2007 the employment situation for young Japanese had improved considerably as the economy continued to recover rather spectacularly from the Heisei Recession which began in the early 1990s. The labor market for university graduates was very buoyant in the Japanese spring of 2007, and one could say that the new graduates found themselves in a sellers' market. Nevertheless, for young Japanese who become *furiitaa*, the door to full-time regular employment remains closed for the most part, and the need for policy initiatives to deal with the aging population of *furiitaa* has become a big challenge for the present government.

Whether we can learn something from the situation facing these young persons in Japan that has a greater relevance to youth in other countries remains to be seen. It is nonetheless clear that policies have been instituted in many other countries to facilitate the movement of such youth into the regular labor force. The situation of youth in a number of European countries is considered briefly in comparative perspective in the seventh chapter of this volume. In any case, it is clear that the way in which Japanese society is organized has been greatly affected by the emergence of the *furiitaa* as a new kind of quasi social class. If this small volume can in someway contribute to the broader discussion of these issues in a comparative perspective, the author would be more than pleased.

In closing I would like to acknowledge the assistance of Professor Ross Mouer of Monash University as the translator and the encouragement of Professor Yoshio Sugimoto as Director of Trans Pacific Press in Melbourne. The first stimulus came from Professor Sugimoto who opened the door which made publication possible. Then came the assistance of the translator, Professor Mouer, in providing advice on many points through a series of detailed questions for each chapter as he progressed through the translation. I trust that the volume is highly readable in its slightly altered format and look forward to receiving feedback from a wide audience outside Japan

Reiko Kosugi
June 2007

1 The Free Worker

Toward a definition

The word "*furiitaa*" first appeared in the late 1980s. *Furomu A*, a magazine with advertisements for casual part-time employment, created the word for its advertisements. The term soon caught on and became a widely recognized type of employment in Japan's labor market. At first the term "*furii arubaitaa*" (free casual worker) was used. The term "*arubaito*" came from the German word for work, "*arubeit*", and gained usage in Japan as a term referring to the work done on a part-time or seasonal basis mainly by university students seeking some extra spending money. The English suffix "-er" (as "-*aa*") came to be added to indicate someone (an *arubaitaa*) who did *arubaito*. However, in the process of making a movie, a film producer shortened the term to "*furiitaa*".

As the term became more accepted in the Japanese lexicon, it came increasingly to have a distinct meaning as a label for young people who were unable to find employment upon graduating from school or university, and who then drifted into a more-or-less permanent lifestyle which could be sustained on *arubaito*. This was a departure from the norm, which was that all Japanese males and most females would find regular permanent employment upon completing their education. The image created by this term was of a young person boldly choosing to struggle in some form of casual employment while they worked toward some goal – a path difficult to follow when bound by a commitment to the corporate employment or to the other full-time on-going employment associated with being a regular employee (*seishain*). Figure1.1 shows the types of employment status that existed in the late 1980s.

By the turn of the century the term had come to embrace a number of subtle nuances, some stretching the meaning in opposite directions. The reality is that "*furiitaa*" means different things to different people. One reference is to young persons who choose to live life in a somewhat capricious manner, free from doing any

Figure 1.1: Employment statuses in contemporary Japan

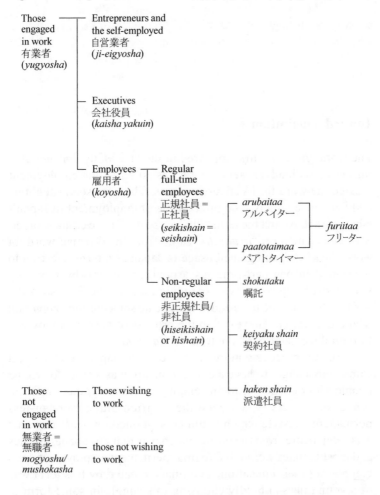

work at all. Another is to young persons who want full-time regular employment, who are unable to find a suitable position, but who are nevertheless doing *arubaito* in a kind of holding pattern until the right job comes up. It is also used to refer to artistic types doing casual work because they have to eat while waiting for their next gig or breakthrough. One married woman aged 40 once wrote to a major newspaper, claiming that her regular job was as a *furiitaa*. In general the term refers to any person doing *arubaito* who is not a student. Many school teachers use the term when talking about former students who graduated without a clear idea as to whether they will get a permanent job or go on for more education. Used in this way the term refers to a new departure from a way of life that has been the norm in Japan since the end of the war in 1945. More broadly speaking, then, the term is also used to refer to anyone who does not become a regular company employee (*seishain* or *seiki shain*). This includes all part-time workers, those working on fixed term contracts and those who do *arubaito* and are not enrolled as a student.

In order to compile its statistics, the government defines *"furiitaa"* as someone aged between 15 and 34.[1] The term was further circumscribed to indicate only those who are hired as *arubaitaa* or *paatotaimaa*. Moreover, married women were excluded; in the case of men, the term was restricted to those who had been doing such work for less than 5 years. For those without work, it is limited to those who are neither studying nor engaged in housework and who desire to be employed as *arubaitaa* or *paatotaimaa* (Rodosho 1991: 177–178). The Ministry was still using the same definition nearly a decade later in its labor white paper for 2000 (Rodosho 2000: 150–153). However, elsewhere in the conduct of some surveys *"furiitaa"* is defined as "those aged under 30 who are neither a student nor a regular employee (*seishain*), and not engaged as a housewife" (Rikuruto *Furomu A* 2000: 2) or as "persons not enrolled in school who are without permanent employment but engaged in some kind of casual (*rinjiteki*) or part-time (*paatotaimu*) work" (Nihon Shokugyo Kyokai 1991: 131).

The grouping shown on the far right in Figure 1.1 may be designated as "the *furiitaa*". For this volume the *"furiitaa"* are defined first as young people who are not students and are not employed as regular employees (*seishain*). Nearly everyone would agree with that as a starting point. It is also easy to understand the logic behind separating out housewives who work as *paatotaimaa*. Many of the issues faced by the *furiitaa* are also experienced by the other non-regular employees shown in Figure 1.1 – dispatched workers, *shokutaku* and other contracted employees who are normally given status as company personnel. Moreover other data suggests that most persons defined as *furiitaa* according to the criteria given above regard themselves as *furiitaa*. In this book we will be focusing attention on persons aged 15–34 who are not married women. Among that population are the *furiitaa* who include both (a) those who are employed as *paatotaimaa* or as *arubaitaa* and (b) those who are unemployed but still wanting to work.

The prevalence of the *furiitaa* in Japanese society

The Ministry of Labor's White Paper for 2000 (Rodo Sho 2000: 177) uses data gathered in 1997 through the *Employment Status Survey* (Shugyo Kozo Kihon Chosa) that is regularly administered by the Somu Sho (the Ministry of Internal Affairs and Communication). The *Employment Status Survey* is an officially designated survey that has been conducted since 1956. It has been carried out every five years since 1982 and is completed by over 400,000 households that include some 1.1 million individuals. According to that survey, in 1997 there were 1.73 million *furiitaa* who fit the Ministry's own definition that was mentioned above (Table 1.1). It is important to remember, however, that the Ministry of Labor omits from its figure those who have worked continuously as *furiitaa* at the same firm for over five years. It is also important to remember that the large number of students who also work on an extended basis as *arubaitaa* is not captured in this survey.

Three findings stand out. First, in percentage terms the increases were largest between 1982 and 1987 (60 percent) and then again between 1992 and 1997 (57 percent), with the later increase being greater in absolute terms. Second, females have fairly consistently accounted for about sixty percent of all *furiitaa*. Third, it is clear that the number of *furiitaa* continued to rise at a steady pace following the survey in 1997.

An age profile of the *furiitaa*

Young people in their early twenties account for the largest number of *furiitaa*. According to the 1997 *Employment Status Survey*, when we include only those aged below 35 and exlude married women, 45 percent of all male *furiitaa* and 50 percent of all female *furiitaa* were aged 20–24. However, when taken as a proportion of all persons employed as *furiitaa*, the proportion accounted for by those in their early twenties falls. It is important to remember that many married women and many other persons also in casual employment are not included in the above figures. Accordingly it is not necessarily the case that there is an overly pronounced tendency for young persons to be so employed. Table 1.2 shows the overall importance of such employment for different age groups. The figures show that part-time work and *arubaito* is most prevalent among male employees aged 65 and above. Nearly 30 percent are so employed. About half of all married women aged between 35 and 65 are so employed. For

Table 1.1: Estimates of the number of furiitaa: 1982–2001 (1000s)

| | Number of *furiitaa* | | |
Year	Females	Males	Total
1982	320	270	590
1987	530	410	960
1992	610	490	1,100
1997	1,000	730	1,730
2001	1,450	1,060	2,510

Note: The figures for 1982–1997 are taken from the tri-annual reports of the Sorifu Tokei Kyoku on the *Shugyo Kozo Kihon Chosa (The Employment Status Survey)*. The figures for 2001 were data supplied to the researchers by the Somu Sho (Ministry of Internal Affairs and Communication) in 2006.

Source: Nihon Rodo Kenkyu Kiko (2005), p. 107.

Table 1.2: Percentages of employees in casual employment by age group in August 2006

| | | Females | |
Age group	Males	Unmarried women	Married women
15–24	15.9	17.4	53.8
25–34	4.3	23.1	41.3
35–44	2.2	32.2	51.6
45–54	2.4	42.7	50.5
55–64	9.8	53.6	50.8
65+	30.4	24.2	41.2
Average for all age groups	6.3	21.1	49.1

Note: The denominator for the calculations is all employees excluding those in executive positions. The numerator consists of the sum of all *arubaitaa* and *paatotaimaa* excluding those who are not students.

Source: Somusho Tokei Kyoku (2006a). The figures were not published, but were supplied to the researchers by officials at the Somu Sho (Ministry of Internal Affairs and Communication). They can now be downloaded from http://www.stat.gv.jp/data/dt/zuhyou/600500.xls.

unmarried female employees the proportion in part-time and casual jobs increases with age until 65.

When considering labor force participation rates by age group, the changes are conspicuous. Until the early 1990s it was basically middle aged and older workers, especially married women, who were concentrated in part-time work and other non-regular employment. In 1991 the *Special Survey of the Labor Force* revealed that only 7.0 percent of males and 8.6 percent of females were casually employed

(Somu Sho 1991: 66–69). However, the amount of casual employment
among this age group rapidly increased during the 1990s. To
highlight the characteristics of this new category of workers, it
has been useful to confine our attention to males and to unmarried
females aged under 35.

The context in which young people became *furiitaa* was very
different from those contexts in which middle-aged and older
persons were being channelled into doing *paatotaimu* and *arubaito*.
In the 1990s young males and females in their early twenties both
entered such employment at a rapidly accelerating rate. From their
late twenties onwards, however, men and women started to behave
very differently in this regard. Men previously in casual employment
moved rather quickly into full-time regular employment in their
late twenties. At the same time, women moved in the opposite
direction, shifting from full-time regular employment to casual
employment as they aged. It is difficult to believe that young women
are not aware of these facts; when young women decide to position
themselves in the *furiitaa* labor market, they almost certainly do so
with expectations that are quite different from those of their male
counterparts.

One further point might be made regarding young males. Table
1.2 shows that in 2006 only 4.3 percentage of young men aged 25–34
were working as *furiitaa*. However, that figure was only about 2
percent until the mid-1990s, and it has moved up at a steady but
gradual pace since then. Moreover, Hori's (2002) analysis of the
Employment Status Survey revealed clearly that the proportion of
older males working as *furiitaa* has also risen overtime. As Chapter
Eight argues, this trend among these slightly older workers deserves
careful attention when thinking about the future of work in Japan.

The educational background of *furiitaa*

Table 1.3 shows for 2006 the results of a survey taken each year by
the Ministry of Education concerning the paths taken by graduates at
different levels in the education system. It is clear that the proportion
of tertiary graduates who became unemployed is larger than that for
secondary school graduates. In addition to those who were expecting
to be unemployed, an additional 19,000 senior high school graduates,
5000 junior college graduates and 17,000 university graduates
reported that they would be employed in temporary work. There is
a high probability that graduates who become unemployed and enter
temporary work will become *furiitaa*.

Table 1.3: *Numbers and percentage of those becoming unemployed upon graduation in March 2006*

Highest completed level of education	No. graduates without employment	% graduates becoming unemployed	% graduates entering the labor force
Senior high school	140,000	10	62
Junior college	20,000	19	32
University	120,000	22	38

Source: Monbu Kagaku Sho (Ministry of Education, Culture, Sports, Science and Technology), *Gakko Kihon Chosa (Sokuho)* (Early Tabulations from the Basic Survey of Educational Institutions), as taken from *http://www.mext.go.jp/b.menu/ toukei/001/0608015/005/sy0034.xls*, and *http://www.mext.go.jp/b.menu/toukei/ 001/0608015/006/hi0038.xls*

Because we have fairly reliable statistics on what students do upon graduation, we can obtain a fairly detailed picture of what is happening. The number of high school graduates who were unemployed increased by 56,000 or 56 percent between 1992 and 2002 and then began to decline. Among university graduates, however, the number who were unemployed or only temporarily engaged rose over 400 percent during the same period. This suggests that the number of university graduates who became *furiitaa* increased extremely rapidly during the 1990s.

Table 1.4 draws on data from the *Employment Status Survey* and gives us information on the educational background of the *furiitaa* population. The survey classifies the graduates as coming from (i) a middle school, (ii) a senior high school, (iii) a two-year junior college or specialized training college, or (iv) a four-year university. The data from this survey allows us to look at the number of *furiitaa* as a percentage of graduates without work, indicating that *furiitaa* account for a declining percentage of those without permanent employment as the level of education increases. Looking at a breakdown of the *furiitaa* population by level of education, the figures in Table 1.4 show that university graduates accounted for 11.1 percent of *furiitaa* in 2002; that graduates from junior colleges and specialized training colleges accounted for 20.8 percent; and that junior and senior school graduates accounted for 68 percent. Several factors account for this distribution. First, those with higher levels of education move more quickly from temporary or casual employment into permanent regular employment than do high school and middle school graduates who have fewer opportunities to gain such employment. Second, there are many more secondary

Table 1.4: The educational background of the furiitaa: *1982–2002*

	Middle school graduates	Senior high school graduates	Graduates of junior colleges and specialized training colleges	Four-year university graduates	Total for all *furiitaa* (%)	Total number of all *furiitaa* (10,000s)
1982	20.5	52.7	16.3	10.6	100.0	590
1987	29.5	56.6	15.1	8.7	100.0	960
1992	19.6	56.4	16.2	7.9	100.0	1,100
1997	14.4	54.5	20.9	10.2	100.0	1,730
2002	15.4	52.6	20.8	11.1	100.0	2,510

Notes:
1. The definition of *"furiitaa"* used here is persons aged 15–34 who are not attending an educational institution but are employed as *paatotaimaa* or as *arubaitaa*. It also includes those in that age group who are unemployed, not going to school and not doing housework but who desire to be employed as a *paatotaimaa* or *arubaitaa*.
2. The term "graduates" refers to the highest level of school completed. For example, those who did some of the senior high school curriculum but did not finish senior high school are tabulated as junior high school graduates.
3. The data reported here comes originally from the annual reports of the Somu Sho's Tokei Kyoku on its *Employment Status Survey* (Shugyo Kozo Kihon Chosa).

Source: Rodo Seisaku Kenkyu-Kenshu Kiko (2005), p. 108.

graduates than tertiary-level graduates. Third, because universities are less thorough in gathering their statistics, it is possible that some of their graduate *furiitaa* "slip through the net" and are not counted.

Our understanding of the situation is improved if we look at the prevalence of *furiitaa*-type employment by level of education. Table 1.5 shows clearly that the percentage of males and females engaged in such work drops dramatically with a rise in the level of education attained. This is particularly true for those aged 25–34. It is also the case that many of those who obtain only a junior high or senior high education will find themselves working as *furiitaa*.

Returning to the third reason given for the small proportion of *furiitaa* who were university graduates, we should note that many university graduates seek employment on their own and do not go through their university's placement office. If they do not report back to their universities, they are often recorded simply as being without a recognized position (*i.e.*, as not being in the labor force). Having said that, one must also note that many universities, especially the private ones, pay a lot of attention to making sure their graduates are employed. At such institutions it may well be

*Table 1.5: The relative concentration of young employees in part-
time and casual work by age and gender in 2001 (%)*

Level of education completed	Males	Unmarried women	Total for males and unmarried women
15–24 years old			
Middle school or senior high school	17.4	30.3	22.9
Junior college or higher technical college	17.6	14.9	15.7
University	10.6	8.9	9.8
Total for age group	15.9	21.1	18.5
25–34 years old			
Middle school or senior high school	5.6	29.9	11.2
Junior college or higher technical college	3.8	12.8	8.7
University	2.9	10.2	4.7
Total for age group	4.3	17.4	8.4

Note: The denominator for the calculations is all employees excluding those in executive
positions. The numerator consists of the sum of all *arubaitaa* and *paatotaimaa*
excluding students.

Source: Somusho Tokei Kyoku (Ministry of Internal Affairs and Communications,
Bureau of Statistics)(2006), Rodoryoku Chosa Yosai Shukei (The Detailed Tabulations
of the Labor Force Survey), as provided on http://www.stat.go.jp/data/roudou/2006q/
dt/zuhyou/600500.xls.

that the number of those "slipping through the net" is actually rather
small. Nevertheless, even if university graduates do enter the labor
market as *furiitaa*, they are very likely to move rather quickly into
permanent full-time employment as company employees. At the
other end of the educational spectrum are those with only a middle
school education (a category which includes all of those who drop
out of high school). They are not only more likely to find themselves
in *furiitaa*-type employment, but are also more likely to linger in
such employment for a much longer period of time.

The geographical distribution of *furiitaa*

As Table 1.6 shows, the prevalence of *furiitaa* varies spatially from
one prefecture to another. With the exception of Okinawa, the highly
urbanized prefectures have the highest percentages involved in
furiitaa-type employment. This outcome reflects the different way
in which the urban and rural economies are structured. The lowest
rates are found in the rural prefectures where manufacturing plays a

more central role. The urban economy requires more flexibility and hence the greater use of casual labor. Between 1997 and 2002 the percentage of *furiitaa* in the labor force has risen in all of Japan's geographic regions. Using data from a survey conducted in 2004 and 2005 by the Office of the Cabinet, Nishimura (2006: 146–142) argued that the use of *furiitaa* is not just an urban phenomenon, just as unemployment is not just a rural phenomenon. In the background is the spread of the service economy and its impact on employment.

On the supply side, human relationships seem to be much more fluid in urban Japan, allowing for greater choice and less pressure to have full-time permanent work. A further influence is the increasing gap between the better high schools and the ones that offer less opportunity. To the extent that the latter schools are "abandoned" by the system, they are likely to become a constant source of semi-educated graduates who are much less able to compete for the full-time regular positions. Over time a kind of class culture emerges, and *furritaa*-type employment comes also to be associated with those from a lower socio-economic lifestyle. Reflecting on the fact that the percentage of senior high school graduates who become *furiitaa* is lower in rural areas despite the overall increase in the extent to which schools have become stratified, Hori (2003: 70–77) argued that rural graduates are more likely to look at other options

Table 1.6: The prevalence of furiitaa *in selected prefectures: 2002 (%)*

Prefecture	Males aged 15–34	Unmarried females aged 15–34
Okinawa	15.3	26.7
Kyoto	13.6	23.1
Osaka	12.1	25.8
Tokyo	11.9	19.6
Miyage	10.8	24.5
Fukuoka	10.5	23.1
Ishikawa	6.2	16.5
Fukui	5.5	17.7
Yamagata	5.4	18.2
Toyama	4.7	15.5

Note: The numerator is the number of *furiitaa* using the definition given above for this column. The denominator is the number of employed persons in the labor force excluding those in management positions, married women and those enrolled in an educational institution.

Source: Rodo Seisaku Kenkyu Kenshu Kiko (2005), pp. 125–126.

when they cannot find permanent full-time employment. He also noted that rural schools have been more persistent in pushing graduates into regular full-time employment. The rural schools function differently and that is reflected in the outcomes for their graduates.

Types of *furiitaa*

The *furiitaa* can be further classified according to how they come to be *furiitaa*. A sketch of their different backgrounds can give an overall picture of the *furiitaa* as a set of composite individuals. The number of young Japanese becoming *furiitaa* suddenly jumped in the mid-1990s. A look at the subjective dimension can help explain that phenomenon.

In 1999 the Nihon Rodo Kenkyu Kikan (Japan Institute of Labor) initiated a research project on patterns of labor force participation among young Japanese. Part of that study involved a series of interviews with 97 persons who were, or had been, *furiitaa*. The interviews were conducted in the summer and fall of 1999. (For more information, see Nihon Rodo Kenkyu Kiko 2000: 20–21). Each of 97 individuals was interviewed for at least one hour about the reasons and the background behind their becoming a *furiitaa*, their thoughts for the future and their past experience in the education system. In 2000 final year senior high school students were interviewed and in 2001 a random sample of young people in metropolitan Tokyo were studied. A fourth component of our study involved the analysis of the returned survey sheets from the Somu Sho's *Employment Status Survey*. Based on a qualitative assessment of that data, the typology appearing in Table 1.7 was created.

Those that fit into the first two types might collectively be referred to as "the moratorium type". They are the types who postpone choosing a work career. Some do so because they cannot find a career they want to enter. Some do so because "for the time being" they want to weigh up their options before continuing their education; they choose neither to study nor to work full-time. This group of individuals includes those who become *furiitaa* immediately after graduating from school, university or other institution; those who dropped out of their school, college or university; and those who were going to a university entrance exam preparation school after not doing well enough in their final year at school but then for one reason or another decided not to sit for their designated entrance examination. It also includes those who obtained a proper job upon

Table 1.7: A classification of furiitaa *by the reasons they gave for being so employed*

Major category	Sub-category	Description	Number of cases
The social dropout (moratorium type)	1) School dropout	Received education without any vision of their future, often dropping out of school (or university) along the way	29
	2) Work dropout	Left other work without a clear plan or idea about the type of regular employment they preferred	9
The dreamer	3) The artist in pursuit of a means to express themselves	Accepted part-time or casual work as a means of establishing themselves in performance or other artistic fields	16
	4) Artisan in an open market apprenticeship	Accepted part-time or casual work (*e.g.*, as a cake decorator, baker, or bartender) in an area where skill is required but formal apprenticeships are non-existent or hard to find	11
Those in *furiitaa*-type work because of external circumstances	5) *Furiitaa* who are seeking regular employment	Those doing *furiitaa*-type work in a kind of holding pattern until they find work as a regular employee (*seishain*) or who are near to achieving that status working for a labor dispatch firm	11
	6) *Furiitaa* who are filling in time	Persons working to pay off school fees or to otherwise accomplish some short-term goal in terms of earnings, but with a clear idea that full-time regular employment will be sought once some intermediate (*e.g.*, educational) goal is achieved	13
	7) *Furiitaa* who are dealing with personal issues	Those choosing such work as a means of coping with their own illness or another illness in their family, with failure of a family business or with some issue in their interpersonal relationships	6
Other			2
Total			97

Source: Nihon Rodo Kenkyu Kiko (2000), p. 5.

graduating but then quit for some reason and became employed as a casual worker. For many of these *furiitaa* casual employment was seen as a means of filling time while they planned for their next attempt at regular employment.

The second major category consists of the "dream seekers". They have a clear vision of what they want to do and often it is outside the world of the standardized salaried employee (the "*sarariman*"). To achieve their goal they often have to finance their own training. Sometimes that is done by taking on any work that is possible; sometimes this type is fortunate to find work in an artistic tradition or trade as a kind of informal apprentice. Here we are talking about finding a path into an artistic field. Many interviewees mentioned their dream of playing in a band, becoming a dancer with a performance or entertainment company. Others sought after a qualification as a cake decorator, a hair dresser or a script writer.

The third major type includes a range of persons who feel they are employed as *furiitaa* "under duress". There are individuals who would prefer a different employment status but are making do as a *furiitaa* until some variable in their life changes. Many sat a company entrance examination, but were not hired. Some are actively applying to companies for work as a regular full-time employee. Others have given up hope of obtaining employment as a regular full-time company employee, but still wish they could become one. Some wanted to be further educated but were unable to continue their education owing to their family's circumstances; they are employed as *furiitaa* in order to save enough by themselves to attain an educational goal "down the track". Some left school or university to help out with a family business, but were then stranded when the business become insolvent. These types found themselves dropped back in the open labor market at a time when the better jobs were unavailable. Their placement as *furiitaa* might be chalked up to bad luck and unfortunate timing.

The preceding three paragraphs give a rough indication of the major categories that emerged from the above-mentioned interviews. Table 1.7 shows how each grouping could be further broken down to obtain seven sub-groupings. A closer look at the reasons young people enter *furiitaa*-type employment may well assist us in our efforts to understand the behavior of those in this emerging labor market. With these distinctions in mind we will consider that behavior further in the chapters which follow. The next chapter looks briefly at the processes by which young people make the transition from school to work. The next two chapters then examine more closely the context in which secondary graduates (Chapter Two) and tertiary graduates (Chapter Four) become *furiitaa*. Chapter Four shifts attention to aspects of the work performed by *furiitaa*. The chapters forming Part Two introduce the voices of those we interviewed. Chapter Five illustrates the variety of contexts from which the *furiitaa* emerge in terms of the categories shown in Table 1.7. Chapter Six discusses ways in which the labor market for *furiitaa* might be evolving.

Part Three concludes with a brief survey of the situation in other countries (Chapter Seven), some policy recommendations (Chapter Eight), and some thoughts on how Japanese society itself might be changing at the beginning of this century (Chapter Nine).

2 Difficulties in Finding Permanent Employment

From being a new graduate to doing casual labor

The annual hiring of new graduates each April is given wide coverage in the Japanese media. Because it has been the practice for firms to give priority to the hiring of new graduates, and then for many employees to stay with their initial employers for an extended period of time, a special labor market has emerged, and the contracting of labor in that market has come to capture the interest of many citizens as an index measuring how the national economy is performing and how successive cohorts of young people are likely to fare financially in the future. Accordingly, the way that market evolves over the 6–12 months before a cohort graduates is carefully scrutinized in the media. Terms like "the ice age" quickly gained coinage in the media and became a common way of describing the employment outlook facing the cohort which graduated in the late 1990s and early part of this century.

Most *furiitaa* in the study by the Japan Institute of Labor were working as *furiitaa* because their application to one or more firms for full-time regular employment had not been successful. It seems they were simply unfortunate to enter the labor market at a time when positions for new graduates were being frozen or even reduced. From the middle of the 1990s the demand for new graduates suddenly declined. This is shown in the statistics on the labor market compiled by the Ministry of Labor and then by the Ministry of Welfare and Labor after the restructuring of the national bureaucracy at the beginning of this century (Kosei Rodo Sho Shogugyo Antei Kyoku: from each year's report). As Table 2.1 shows, in March 1992 firms wanted to hire 1670 thousand new graduates whereas the figure was only one seventh that number at 220 thousand a decade later in March 2003. By 2006 it had recovered to 290 thousand. During that ten years from 1992 the number of graduates seeking work also dropped, though not by nearly as much as demand had dropped. Accordingly, the index of labor demand,

Table 2.1: Job offerings and the index of labor demand for high school graduates

Year	A Number of job offerings for high school graduates	B Number of high school graduates seeking jobs	C The index of labor demand A/B
1990	1,342,898	522,527	2.6
1991	1,606,159	519,790	3.1
1992	1,673,057	500,568	3.3
1993	1,377,057	442,786	3.1
1994	934,075	376,648	2.5
1995	642,613	331,516	1.9
1996	536,175	304,091	1.8
1997	517,763	288,090	1.8
1998	517,822	272,296	1.9
1999	359,938	228,991	1.6
2000	271,667	201,346	1.3
2001	276,118	203,692	1.3
2002	242,926	184,135	1.3
2003	218,604	172,731	1.3
2004	224,984	173,171	1.3
2005	258,050	176,403	1.5
2006	293,520	179,683	1.6

Source: Kosei Rodo Sho Shokugyo Antei Kyoku (as taken from annual reports). This data may also be downloaded from: http://wwwdbtk.mhlw.go.jp/toukei/kouhyo/indexkr _31_2.html

the major statistic the government uses as a measure of labor market tightness, declined for new graduates from over 3.0 to under 1.5. The index is calculated by dividing the number of job offers by the number of job seekers.

Because the government does not carry out a similar survey of the market for college and university graduates, we need to refer to the survey data produced by the job marketing company Recruit (Rikuruuto Waakasu Kenkyujo: from the annual reports). Its survey suggests that in March 1992 there were 740 thousand job offers for university graduates seeking full-time regular employment, a figure that had dropped to 400 thousand in March 2000 before rising to 570 thousand in 2002 and then to 700 thousand in 2006. Recruit's research produced an estimate showing that over the same period the index of labor demand for university graduates fell from 2.41 in 1992 to 0.99 in 2000 before rising to 1.33 in 2002 and then to 1.60

in 2006. For two-year junior college graduates the index fell from 1.22 (with 200 thousand job offers) in 1992 to 0.51 (with 50 thousand job offers) in 2002, a very stringent situation in which there was only one job for every two graduates seeking work.

In this regard we cannot simply look at the index of labor demand and jump to conclusions about one market necessarily being more difficult or challenging than another for those seeking to enter the labor force. In the case of high school graduates, firms must advertise their position through the government-run Public Employment Security Office (PESO) (Shokugyo Antei Jo). Before approaching schools with their job offers, firms must first take their job offer form to PESO and receive its stamp of approval. This means the figures on the market for high school graduates are more accurate than those concerning the market for the graduates from Japan's tertiary institutions. The data obtained by the private surveys of Recruit are not as comprehensive as the data collected by PESO as there is little compulsion for firms and individuals to reply to the private body. Assuming that its survey has the same bias over time, the Recruit surveys provide valuable insight into longitudinal trends. However, the basis on which the Recruit data is compiled for the tertiary sector is very different from that compiled by the government on the secondary sector. Nevertheless, the findings of the Recruit Research Institute are corroborated by those from other surveys administered by other employment companies and by several of the newspapers, including Japan's major financial review (the *Nihon Keizai Shimbun*).

Here I have tried to indicate how severely the employment situation had deteriorated for graduates during the 1990s before recovering considerably in the first decade of this century. While this is important to keep in mind, it should not affect the general conclusions regarding the processes by which young Japanese come to work as *furiitaa*. Regardless of the data used, it is clear that from the mid 1990s firms had become much less likely than before to hire graduates straight out of secondary schools and tertiary institutions. Many firms hold their entrance exams for prospective graduates in mid to late September each year, and then are allowed to inform potential graduates about the success or otherwise of their application for employment on 1 October. The annual reporting of schools to PESO occurs at the end of September each year. It then calculates an index of offers made which becomes a measure of the success rate of all applicants in their efforts to gain employment. The index at the beginning of the 1990s was about 70 percent. By the first few years of this century it had fallen to 30 percent. After the first round of offers are made in September, many students sit for a second and even a third round of examinations at other companies. Gradually more jobs are offered and, in theory, each student comes to be offered some kind of position by the time they graduate the following April. All job offers are contingent on the student graduating in March.

In recent years the index has been gradually rising from the end of September until it reaches about 90 percent by the time each cohort of students graduates. Many of the remaining ten percent who are not to be hired have little alternative to entering the labor market as *furiitaa*. Until the early 1990s the index rose to 98 or 99 percent by the end of March. In other words, it used to be the case that nearly all graduates had a permanent job waiting for them upon graduation. However, the situation began to change in the 1990s, and today some ten percent of graduates do not have such employment waiting for them. This is a big change in just over a decade. The result is that there is now a pool of surplus labor which flows into the market for casual employment.

One source of insight concerning this phenomenon may be found in the reports made by schools to the Bureau for Employment Security in the Ministry of Welfare and Labor (Kosei Rodo Sho Shokugyo Antei Kyoku 2002). With regard to university graduates, the Bureau surveys students at the beginning of October, about six months before they graduate (when companies can officially announce their employment offers), and then again at the beginning of April (just after they graduate). Sixty five percent of university students graduating in March 2002 had received offers of employment by 1 October 2001, the date on which the first round of job offers begin to be made. The figure had risen to 92 percent by April 2002. For women graduating from junior colleges, the figures were 37 and 90 percent respectively; for males in higher technical colleges (*koto semmon* gakko), 92 and 98 percent; for students in specialized training schools (*senshu gakkko*), 33 and 83 percent. Males both in technical colleges and in universities seem to do rather well in gaining employment by early October, six months before they graduate. Other students find it takes more effort and a longer wait before their jobs are firmed up. About ten percent of university graduates and twenty percent of college students remained unemployed upon graduation.

The survey of persons seeking work is conducted each year in July, September, November, January and March among students who are in their final year and will graduate the following April. At each juncture the Bureau for Employment Security publishes the number of job seekers and job offers. Over the period during which the surveys are implemented, the index of labor demand goes up. How actively students look for work is the key on the supply job. That in turn is influenced by the efforts that school teachers make on behalf of their students and by the various mechanisms that are in place to facilitate the matching of job seekers and prospective employers in the labor market. If the rate at which employment is being offered falls to low levels, the Bureau initiates job fairs and school visits in locales where the market is least buoyant. One change that has occurred over time can be seen in the way the number of job seekers fluctuates over the eight-month period leading up to graduation. Each year in the early 1990s the total number of students indicating a desire for full-time regular employment upon graduation steadily increased from July to the following March just before their graduation. From 1993, however, that figure begins to decline over those eight months.

Among the students who were to graduate in March 2002, 250 thousand reported that they had been hunting for regular employment in July 2001. That number steadily dropped until it settled at about 180 thousand by the time that cohort was graduating in March 2002. In other words, about 70,000 students (nearly 30 percent) had withdrawn their application for employment during the eight-month period. This means that a significant proportion of the students who initially wanted employment had either altered their employment strategy (*e. g.*, seeking work through relatives or other avenues outside the system), or had decided not to seek employment at all. There would probably be a good number who thought they would find employment through a personal connection, were unsuccessful in that move, and then withdrew from the labor market altogether. In these trends we can perhaps see how companies began to cut back on the number of persons they would hire following the first contractions of the economy in 1992 – contractions which resulted in students being more tentative about seeking employment. After testing the waters briefly as a final year student in July, many seem to have become a bit disappointed with their prospects and would have prevaricated, in the end deciding for one reason or another not to seek regular employment at that time.

Since the early 1990s the number of final year high school students has steadily declined each year. There is probably a process whereby the students in one year pass on to the next cohort their knowledge and experience concerning the way in which the overall labor market is working. At the same time it is also likely that a subtle interplay in the market between the supply side and the demand side exists as students and employers each try to guess how the other will behave.

We do not have the same kind of detailed information about the behavior of students in Japan's tertiary sector. However, most observers are certain that the same interplay exists at that level. It was clear in the early years of this century that between 10 and 20 percent of students were graduating without any promise of employment. Many third-year students began the process of looking for employment in July, but found the process too gruelling and decided to withdraw from "the race for regular jobs". To the extent that this tentativeness on the part of students comes to reflect, and to be reflected in, caution on the part of employers, we have a dynamic which can only contribute to a further expansion of the market for *furiitaa*.

Changes in the labor market for new high school graduates

Along with the drop in demand for new senior high school graduates has come a shift in the type of employee wanted or in the type of work being offered. To better understand what is happening, we might briefly look at employment offers in areas where the drop in the number of students seeking work has been noticeable and at students for which data on the change in the job content have been collected. Job offers are sent by firms to schools only after they have been sent to PESO and it has given approval to the firm. Accordingly, PESO is able to maintain official records of such job offers. The Bureau of Employment Security (*i.e.*, Kosei Roso Sho 2002 and earlier the Rodo Sho 1992) has published data which allows us to compare the situation in March 2002 with that in March 1992. We referred to that data earlier in noting that the number of job offers had fallen over the decade to one seventh of the 1992 level. A closer examination of that data reveals that the decline was most pronounced in Japan's largest firms. This meant that the demand for new high school graduates came to be mainly from Japan's smaller employers. In 1992 29 percent of final year students had found employment in a large firm by the time they graduated. That figure fell to 15 percent by 2002. Over the same period the percentage finding work in small firms with fewer than 29 employees doubled from 11 to 22 percent. This shift was particularly pronounced among female students.

By job content, the demand dropped for clerical office workers and technicians. It increased for service workers and for production process workers. In 1992, among those who found work 42 percent did so in office and technical positions. That figure had fallen to 25 percent by 2002. Over the same period, the percentage going into service-related occupations increased from 7 to 15 percent; those taking positions as production process workers, from 32 to 43 percent. To conclude, the overall drop in the number of job offers and job seekers was accompanied by a shift away from the large-scale sector and white-collar work.

The changing times are reflected in the kinds of job offers which flow into each school. Of course, the preceding discussion is about overall national averages. Depending upon each school's location and the surrounding economy, the changes would have come through in different ways. Also, the situation in which each school finds itself and the mechanisms at work to connect job seekers with job offers interact to create a specific kind of labor market at the secondary level. At the university level, we can obtain a picture of what is happening from the overall statistics. It is more difficult to grasp from those figures a clear idea about what is happening in the labor market for secondary school graduates. In the next section, however, we might consider what happens in the market for high school graduates from a micro-economic perspective.

The employment process for final-year high school students

Nearly all high school graduates seeking employment do so through their schools. The process may be briefly described as follows. First, firms formulate their needs, and send position descriptions to PESO. Once they receive approval from that body firms send their position descriptions to the schools from which they hope students will apply. They may deliver the announcements in person, send them in the mail or communicate the information in another way. They do not approach students directly, but rather ask schools to recommend appropriate students. Until recently firms were not allowed to approach students directly by advertising in newspapers or other media until about one month before the students graduated.

The reality was that the market for graduates tended to be dominated by the school sector in ways that made it difficult for firms to take the initiative to approach students directly. Upon receiving the requests from companies for them to recommend students for employment, the schools would advise students of the opportunities for employment upon graduation, and then invite them to indicate an interest in the various positions on offer. It is often the case that students would consult carefully with their homeroom teacher and with the teacher responsible for looking after their well-being. Students who wanted other employment would usually be carefully counselled on their options.

Once students had their applications in, with each student applying for just one company, the students would all go off to their nominated companies and sit for the first round of entrance examinations (which were on 16 September in 2002). Students who fail the entrance examination to the company that was their first choice are allowed to apply to another company. It is expected that those who are successful in the first round will accept employment with that company. The accepted practice is for each student to be recommended to only one company. Many schools maintain an internally recognized standard. Such schools will not recommend students who fall below that standard. This is done to maintain the integrity of their recommendations. The school's status is enhanced to the extent that it can be assured that the more prestigious or reputable firms will return each year asking for it to recommend a certain number of its graduates for the firms to hire. Often a relationship develops between a school and an employer to the extent that the school knows it can each year place a set number of students with that employer, and the employer is happy to hire the students merely on the strength of the school's recommendation. In many cases, the practice was for a school to nominate students for specifically designated employers, and to have its recommendation honored. More established vocationally oriented schools obviously want to develop their ties with the more established firms, and *vice versa*. The customary embargo on firms prevents them from having their entrance exam before the middle of September. However, once the exam is held, it is common for offers to be made by the end of September to some 70 percent of all students who want employment upon graduation the following March.

In 2003 the proportion of job applicants who received confirmation notices for employment had shrunk to 30 percent, and a good many students were left to face graduation without regular employment in hand. The *kyujinbairitsu* is now below 1.0, meaning it is no longer the situation that there is at least one job somewhere for each student. So tight had this particular labor market become by the first few years of this century.

The above figures are national averages. It is important to remember that there is considerable variation from one area to another. The drop in demand for high school graduates occurred first and most noticeably among Japan's largest employers. That demand had been spread far and wide across all geographic regions. When it dropped, many local economies were exposed. In many rural areas two facets of larger social changes were becoming apparent. First, older children were traditionally expected to remain at home or close by to look after their parents. As families shrank in size, a larger proportion of students consisted of first-born children. To lure these students away from the family home, a considerable incentive was required, and only the large firms could offer such an incentive. While some regions had a solid local economy, often based around one or more localized industries (*jiba sangyo*), the employee benefits were not enough to entice many of the graduates from less well-off locations to places where the jobs were more readily available. Many more graduates than in the past were coming to accept casual employment which would allow them to remain nearby their family of origin. The result has been increasing variation in the labor market from one local region to another.

The widening gap in terms of access to the shrinking number of "good jobs" was visible not only in terms of geographic regions. It also became apparent in terms of the schools supplying the new graduates. Many of the firms which continued to hire graduates narrowed the range of schools from which they would accept graduates. When cutting the number of new graduates to be hired, firms gave priority to maintaining ties with the schools that had supplied them with the better graduates over an extended period and had developed an on-going and close relationship with such schools. New schools without such a history and those with only a generalist curriculum were especially hard hit.

To offset the decline in job offers being made by Japan's large, more prestigious firms, schools and PESO sought to locate new sources of demand, and these "new" employers have come to account for an increasing proportion of the jobs on offer. They are mainly very small or even medium-sized firms which previously had not participated in the labor market for new graduates. This has resulted in a huge shift in expectations, and today's graduates can no longer expect to choose from among a large supply of stable jobs as had once been the case when the same firms would return year after year as the major players in the market for such graduates.

For a long time, the best graduates from each school could expect to receive a good offer of employment from a good firm based on their academic performance and their record of near-to-perfect attendance. As long as the old system remained in place, a certain level of expectation was maintained within each school. Students studied hard to get good marks with the expectation that would be rewarded with a good job at the end of their final year at school. As long as the system worked, most students would remain motivated throughout their three years in senior high school. However, once the customary link between schools and the labor market was broken, the consequences could be felt throughout the secondary school system, and many students suddenly lost the urge to study.

Senior high school students would have a good deal of information about the employers that each year hired new graduates from their school. So too did the schools themselves and those responsible for counselling the students. Teachers were in a position to advise students and comment on their aptitudes in ways that would facilitate the largest possible number of students obtaining suitable employment. However, in many cases they know almost nothing about the new employers coming into the market. In recent times the percentage of new employees who leave their employer shortly after being employed has increased. One reason for that lies in the mismatches that frequently occur when graduates take on employment about which they have not been properly briefed or informed.

From regular employment to casual employment

Although there has been a tremendous shift in the demand for new high school graduates, the mechanisms which supported the established practices associated with the channelling of students to designated employers remain in place. This means that many involved in the market for new graduates have continued to go through the same motions which worked in the past. There is now room to question whether those very same procedures have evolved in ways that function to produce a steady flow of students into the growing pool of *furiitaa*. Some insight into how this is occurring may be gleaned from a survey conducted among third-year high school students in the greater Tokyo metropolitan area in January 2000 by the Japan Institute of Labor (Nihon Rodo Kenkyu Kiko: 2000b).

Fifty-two high schools in Tokyo, Kanagawa, Saitama and Chiba were approached. Thirty-six schools offered a general comprehensive curriculum; eight were technical high schools; and eight were commercial high schools. A total of 7930 final-year students were surveyed (with 6855 useable responses for response rate of 86.4 percent) along with 52 teachers responsible for the student's placement with an employer upon graduation. Fifty two percent of all the students surveyed had wanted regular employment at some time during their final year in high school. However, by January of their final year only 27 percent had received an offer of employment. Of the other 25 percent, 11 percent had withdrawn from the search for employment through their school before the placement activity (*shushoku katsudo*) began in July, eight percent had with their school started placement activities but then withdrew, and six percent had continued to look for work although they had not yet received an offer. The remaining students never began the search. Their goals did not include permanent regular employment. As Table 2.2 shows in columns A and B, about 40 percent of students who had dropped out of placement activities during their final year planned to continue their education. A much smaller percentage (9.4 and 7.5 percent respectively) had no plans at all.

Twelve percent of high school students were planning to work as *furiitaa*. Half of those students had been looking for work during their final year, but had given up some time between April and the following January. This leads to a further question: what is the difference between those final year students searching for work who received offers and those who did not. The data in Table 2.3 provides some information on some of the traits and behavior of those two groups. The likelihood of receiving a pre-graduation offer is shown to vary by the students' major field of study and by gender. Male students doing studies related to manufacturing and graduates of either gender who were in commerce were much more likely to receive offers of employment. Fewer than half of those doing the generalist course of study received offer. Moreover, a particularly small proportion of female students doing their studies in manufacturing had received an offer. Finally, many of the students doing a generalist course who had not received offers by January had given up their hunt for regular employment.

The widening gap between schools in terms of those that were approached by potential employers and those that were not was mentioned above. In this regard, Table 2.4 shows the extent to which students at schools varied in their employment success rate

Table 2.2: Changes in the plans of final year high school students who believed they would not enter full-time regular employment

Path chosen before graduation	Students who believed they would not enter full-time regular employment				All students
	A	B	C	D	
Plans to continue education at a specialized training school or other similar institution	20.3	25.8	40.8	39.0	23.7
Plans to continue education at a specialized training school or other similar institution yet to be decided	6.6	5.0	6.9	6.5	4.3
Plans to continue education at a specific university or junior college	8.0	10.6	21.9	24.3	13.9
Plans to continue education at a specific university or junior college unclear	5.8	2.3	8.2	14.3	7.8
Plans to be a *furiitaa*	40.7	40.5	17.2	11.6	12.0
Plans to be in a family business or working as an entrepreneur	5.1	5.9	0.6	0.8	1.2
Other plans	2.5	2.0	1.3	0.8	0.8
No plan at all	9.4	7.5	3.1	2.6	2.6
No answer	1.6	0.5	0.0	0.1	0.2
Total	100.0	100.0	100.0	100.0	100.0
Number of students (N)	513	442	319	3274	6,855

Notes:

Path chosen before graduation: path chosen by final-year high school students in January before their graduation in March 2000.

A: Students who looked for work in their third year, but then later decided not to look for regular employment upon graduation.

B: Students who decided the previous April that they would not look for regular employment upon graduation.

C: Students who decided in their penultimate year not to look for regular employment upon graduation.

D: Students who never intended to seek regular employment upon graduation.

Source: Nihon Rodo Kenkyu Kiko (2000b), p. 56.

according to the ranking their school had in terms of the demand from stable employers for their graduates. Schools were ranked according to an index derived by dividing (a) the number of job offers they received from a stable employer over the past ten years by (b) the number of students enrolling for the school's placement activities on the 1 April 1999. The schools were then grouped into four quartiles based on the score they achieved according to that

Table 2.3: Breakdown of students receiving and not receiving an employment offer by course of study and by gender in January 2000

	Students who received offers	**Students who did not receive offers**		**All students**	**Number of students**
		Students who continued in employment placement activities	**Students who withdrew from placement activities**		
Students in generalist courses					
Males	49.0	15.7	35.3	100.0	826
Females	47.1	15.5	37.4	100.0	885
Total	47.6	15.6	36.8	100.0	1816
Students taking a commercial curriculum					
Males	62.9	11.4	25.7	100.0	226
Females	67.2	12.1	20.7	100.0	547
Total	65.2	11.8	22.5	100.0	810
Students taking a manufacturing or industrial arts curriculum					
Males	73.7	7.5	18.8	100.0	805
Females	41.8	25.5	32.7	100.0	69
Total	70.8	8.7	20.5	100.0	955
All students	57.8	12.9	29.3	100.0	3,262

Note: The figures represent the percentage of students in each group who at one of three junctures in their final year had wanted to find full-time regular employment. The entire sample included 6855 students, of which 3593 had not wanted to have such employment upon graduation. The remaining 3262 had wanted employment.

Source: Nihon Rodo Kenkyu Kiko (2000b), p. 58.

index. Table 2.4 shows how students at the schools in each quartile fared in terms of their search for regular full-time work. It is clear that a much higher percentage of students at the more prestigious schools (those with an ability to maintain a stable and predictable demand for their graduates) (Quartile I) received more employment offers than did students at less prestigious schools.

Table 2.5 shows the extent to which academic performance (as self-assessed by each student) and the student's attendance record (also self-reported) affect the likelihood that a graduate will receive an offer of employment. Poor attendance and low levels of academic achievement result in a markedly decreased likelihood that a student will receive an offer of employment. Poor outcomes at school also increase the likelihood that students who do not get an offer will drop out of the school's employment placement activities altogether

*Table 2.4: Percentage distribution of students by placement out-
comes and by the type of school they attend*

	Type of school by quartile			
	Quartile I	Quartile II	Quartile III	Quartile IV
Students who received an offer	69.3	51.8	55.6	46.2
Student who had not received an offer but continued to participate in employment placement activities	10.3	13.1	13.3	19.8
Students who had not received an offer and withdrew from placement activities	20.4	35.1	31.1	34.0
Total (%)	100.0	100.0	100.0	100.0
Total (N)	978	604	843	429

Notes:

1. Type of school by quartile: based on the level of prestige the school commands in the labor market between 1990 and 1999.

2. Information from 2834 schools was examined. For each school the number of firms that had offered more than one graduate a position upon graduation each year from 1990 to 1999 was divided by the number of students who wanted full-time employment in 1999. The resultant quotient was used to categorize schools into one of four groups, with those in Quartile I having the highest quotient and those in Quartile IV having the lowest.

Source: Nihon Rodo Kenkyu Kiko (2000b), p. 79.

(column C in Table 2.5). In the background is fact that schools base their decision on how strongly to recommend each student to a good employer upon each student's marks and record of attendance. Students who do poorly in those regards will be counselled early on that their chances of getting an offer are considerably diminished from the start.

In these regards it is also instructive to note that the students in the group with the worst attendance and poorest grades in the manufacturing stream did better in obtaining job offers than did those in the group with the best attendance and academic achievement in the generalist course of study.

The conclusion to be drawn in those regards is that while the gap between well performing schools and poorly performing schools is widening, schools maintain the practice of differentiating among students who are conscientious and achieve and those who are not and do not. In some schools with underachieving students, then, a much higher percentage of students are unlikely to receive a job offer. It is reasonable to speculate that such schools are an important source of *furiitaa*.

Table 2.5: Labor market outcomes by days absent and performance

A. By days absent from school

Days absent from school	Students who received offers	Students who did not receive offers		Total (%)	Total (N)
		Students who continued in employment placement activities	Students who withdrew from placement activities		
General Curriculum					
0–10	53.5	14.1	32.5	100.0	1,100
11–20	35.8	16.2	48.0	100.0	265
21+	26.6	24.6	48.8	100.0	203
Commerce Curriculum					
0–10	70.3	11.0	18.8	100.0	538
11–20	57.1	11.4	31.4	100.0	105
21+	38.1	20.6	41.3	100.0	63
Manufacturing/Industrial Arts Curriculum					
0–10	73.0	7.3	19.7	100.0	644
11–20	61.7	13.1	25.2	100.0	107
21+	59.7	12.9	27.4	100.0	62

B. By academic results

Academic results	Students who received offers	Students who did not receive offers		Total (%)	Total (N)
		Students who continued in employment placement activities	Students who withdrew from placement activities		
General curriculum					
Consid. above average	58.1	9.9	32.0	100.0	191
Slightly above average	52.1	15.2	32.6	100.0	309
Average	47.1	16.3	36.6	100.0	481
Slightly below average	45.6	18.1	36.2	100.0	309
Consid. below average	36.7	17.3	46.0	100.0	313
Commerce curriculum					
Consid. above average	76.0	8.0	16.0	100.0	100
Slightly above average	69.5	8.4	22.0	100.0	1,554
Average	66.0	15.5	18.6	100.0	194
Slightly below average	66.2	9.0	24.8	100.0	133
Consid. below average	50.8	16.7	32.6	100.0	126
Manufacturing/industrial arts curriculum					
Consid. above average	75.2	4.3	20.5	100.0	117
Slightly above average	73.5	6.6	19.8	100.0	166
Average	73.8	6.3	20.0	100.0	240
Slightly below average	68.1	9.9	22.0	100.0	141
Consid. below average	60.0	15.5	24.5	100.0	155

Source: Nihon Rodo Kenkyu Kiko (2000b), p. 77.

Changing employment practices and the new graduates

At the beginning of this Chapter I stated that the interest of firms in hiring new graduates had dropped considerably. There are several reasons for this. The most obvious factor is the recession of the 1990s. However, if that were the only cause we would expect the demand for new graduates to rise again. However, if the source of the decline is rooted in fairly significant structural changes in the economy and in the society at large, then we must look elsewhere for explanations.

A recent survey of 513 firms which had until recently employed new high school graduates revealed that 47 percent had stopped hiring such graduates sometime in the 1990s. The largest number of firms (48 percent of those that stopped hiring) mentioned the worsening economic climate (*i.e.,* the recession) as the major reason. Forty-two percent answered that they were hiring tertiary graduates for work that had previously been done by secondary school graduates. A further 20 percent of the firms indicated that they were setting a much higher standard in their operations and needed to limit their hiring of full-time regular employees to the more educated. Another 19 percent claimed they were shifting work to casuals, and 17 percent replied that their firm had come to believe that high school graduates were underqualified for the work they needed done.

The most commonly cited reason for cutting back on the hiring of new high school graduates was the worsening economy; the other four reasons have to do with structural change and transformation in how work itself is organized.

Here it is useful to distinguish between considerations related to new graduates in general (such as the decision to casualize all work) and those which are specifically related to attributes of new high school graduates in particular (such as a change in the nature of the work for which new high school graduates were hired in the past).

In 1995 Nikkeiren (The Japan Federation of Employer Associations) published a report entitled "Japanese-Style Management for a New Era". On pp. 31–33 it introduced the view that Japanese firms would need increasingly to augment (a) established employment practices which had customarily included a commitment to long-term employment guarantees and the hiring of staff and operatives as regular permanent employees (*seiki shain*) with (b) an array of short-term or temporary employees who would not be treated as regular permanent employees. The report proposed that firms judiciously consider the right balance between three types of employee: (i) employees who will require skills which can only be acquired through a long future within the firm (*choki chikuseki noryoku katsuyogata*); (ii) workers with a high level of narrowly defined technical or professional skill (*kodo senmon chishiki katsuyogata*), and (iii) those who will constitute a very flexible and easily adjusted labor force for the firm (*koyo ju-nangata*). The first type consists of employees who are hired immediately upon graduation from a secondary or tertiary institution. It is expected that this type of employee will spend their entire career with the same firm. This group, then, would form the core labor force at each firm and be most likely to be hired as *seiki shain*. The second type was the highly educated specialist. Annual salaries for a fixed term (say, three to five years) were recommended for those employed in this group. The third group was seen as consisting of employees without a high level of skill requiring extensive training or education. The employment status recommended for this group was as *paatotaimaa* or *arubaitaa*. The idea behind this proposal was that society itself was rapidly changing in unpredictable ways along with globalisation and that a certain amount of flexibility was needed in managing employment in an increasingly complex economy. At the same time the report argued that the new approach in the determination of employment status would be in line with the already occurring bifurcation of the labor force into those who enjoyed regular permanent employment as *seiki shain* and those who did not.

Other reasons for the decision of firms to limit their hiring of high school graduates also come to mind. One might be the competitiveness of those with work experience in more open labor markets. Given the high unemployment rate, many workers with previous experience are more pliable than in the past. They also do not require the same orientation to working life that new graduates do. Many smaller firms will see that as a significant cost savings.

This factor connects to the declining academic level of high school students who make themselves available in the labor force upon graduation. In February 2000 this was noted in an editorial in one of the country's leading newspapers for businessmen:

> Urgent attention must be directed to the problem of new high school graduates. Their willingness to work and their level of skill are both matters for serious concern. From the viewpoint of the enterprise, four concerns are often raised in the following order of importance: (i)

insufficient general knowledge; (ii) issues with regard to attitude and manners; (iii) deficient communication skills, and (iv) the weakness in terms of basic learning skills for acquiring further knowledge. The four concerns might be summarized as don't know, don't understand, can't do, and can't read. As long as reforms are not introduced to overcome these shortcomings, it is likely that the drop in demand for new high school graduates will continue unabated. (*Nikkeiren Taimusu*, 14 February 2000, p. 1).

The challenges facing Japan's schools cannot easily be met. The demand is not only for higher skill levels. It is also for better mannered graduates with a stronger work ethic and more "common sense". It may be that the pliable new graduate who was easy to mould to the company's needs is now a relic of the past.

Unemployment and youth's decision to work as *furiitaa*

Although the unemployment rate for Japan's young people began to improve in 2002, with changes occurring in the way in which work is organized it remained at three times the level recorded for persons aged 40–54. What kind of young people are the unemployed? We can use the detailed tabulations from the Labor Force Survey which average the monthly returns for 2005. As the tabulations in Table 2.6 indicate, the unemployment rate for those aged 15–24 is higher than the rate for those aged 25–34. This is true for males and females. For both age groups and gender groups (*i.e.,* in all four quadrants in Table 2.6), the rate is slightly lower for graduates from higher technical colleges and specialized training schools than it is for university graduates. Nevertheless, tertiary students as a whole have a much lower unemployment rate than do secondary school graduates. The special supplementary survey administered in August 2000 separated out the middle school graduates from the senior high school graduates. In that year the unemployment rate for males and females aged 15–24 and having only a middle school education was over 20 percent (Nihon Kei-eisha Renmei and Tokyo Kei-eisha Renmei 2000 as reported in *Nikkeiren Taimusu*, 24 February 2000, p. 2). The evidence is that the unemployment rate is highest for poorly educated young people in Japan. This is consistent with the claim that employers are wanting to employ graduates with more skills and sophistication, attributes often acquired through further education both in terms of overall knowledge and human relationships.

Table 2.6: *Unemployment rate for males and females aged 15–34 in 2001 and 2006, by level of education*

A. August 2001

Level of education	Males			Females		
	A Gainfully employed	B Fully unemployed	Unemployment rate 100B/(A + B)	A Gainfully employed	B Fully unemployed	Unemployment rate 100D/(A + B)
15–24 years old						
Middle school & high school	171	27	13.6	125	19	13.2
Junior and technical college	44	4	8.3	101	7	6.5
University & graduate school	45	4	8.2	38	1	2.6
Total	260	35	11.9	265	28	9.6
25–34 years old						
Middle school & high school	421	30	6.7	234	19	7.5
Junior and technical college	130	5	3.7	197	15	7.1
University & graduate school	302	10	3.2	101	6	5.6
Total	853	46	5.1	533	40	7.0

B. August 2005

Level of education	Males			Females		
	A Gainfully employed	B Fully unemployed	Unemployment rate 100B/(A + B)	A Gainfully employed	B Fully unemployed	Unemployment rate 100D/(A + B)
15–24 years old						
Middle school & high school	147	21	12.5	116	22	9.5
Junior and technical college	35	4	10.3	78	5	5.6
University & graduate school	39	5	11.4	36	2	5.7
Total	221	30	12.0	230	22	9.5
25–34 years old						
Middle school & high school	409	29	6.6	232	19	1.7
Junior and technical college	125	5	3.8	206	13	4.8
University & graduate school	284	12	4.1	128	6	4.8
Total	818	46	5.3	566	38	5.7

Note: Fully unemployed = Number who are fully unemployed / (Number who are gainfully employed + Number who are fully unemployed).

Source: Somu Sho Tokei Kyoku (2005a), Detailed Tabulation. Available at http://www.stat.gov.jp/data/roudou/2005n/dt/index.htm

The pattern of unemployment shown in Table 2.6 is remarkably similar to that of the *furiitaa* labor force. However, a careful comparison reveals that the unemployment rate for males aged 15–24 is higher than that for girls, although young girls in the same age bracket are more likely than males to be employed as *paatotaimaa* or *arubaitaa*. There are more opportunities for young women to engage in that sort of employment. In any case, the higher rate of participation in casual employment helps to account for the lower unemployment rate in Table 2.6 for women aged 15–24. The choice, then, for many young persons is to be unemployed or to work as a *paatotaimaa* or as an *arubaitaa*. With the drop in the number of jobs being offered to young graduates, Japan's youth are likely to face an increasingly difficult time in the nation's labor markets. It is especially difficult for those with lower levels of education who end up in casual employment to make the shift to regular full-time permanent employment as s*eiki shain*.

From the point of view of the labor market, an increasingly high premium is being placed on each individual's plasticity and an ability to learn new things. In the past buyers in the labor market viewed the pliability of new graduates favourably. It is said that many employers preferred to employ new graduates as a blank slate rather than persons with previous experience who might be locked into different work habits. (A summary of this commonly held view may be found in Tanaka 1980: 371–380.) As the economy moves into the high tech industries and as competition from abroad increases, however, the need for enterprises to adapt also increases at a rapid pace, and many employers have been turning away from young graduates who do not have enough demonstrated skills and concomitant attributes and who therefore come into the labor market still requiring a considerable period of costly in-house or on-the-job training.

3 Those Who Don't Become Employed

Postponing the decision to work

The survey mentioned above found that about one half of the high school graduates who were to become *furiitaa* had initially sought full-time regular employment during their final year in school. Although the increase in the number of *furiitaa* owes in good measure to the drop in the amount of regular full-time employment being offered to senior high graduates, by the end of the 1990s we can also detect a significant shift in the outlook of new graduates who each year choose not to enter the labor market.

Our 1998 survey asked students to reflect back over their three years in senior high school and to recollect their career orientations at several different points in time (Table 3.1). Many graduates either had not thought carefully about their options or had found the array of options too confusing.

Among those who initially sought employment but then became *furiitaa* were students who, in the final analysis, could not make up their minds about what to do upon graduation. That involves, first of all, a decision whether upon graduation they will continue their education or enter the labor force. The annual employment cycle for school graduates revolves around the company tests which begin in mid-September. Accordingly, students need to start firming up their choice of prospective employers once their third and final year of schooling starts at the beginning of April so that by July or August they can enrol to sit the exams at their employers of choice. Table 3.2 shows the proportion of final year senior high school students that are proactively involved in the search for full-time regular employment, an activity known as "*shushoku katsudo*", at three points in time from April to October. Of particular interest is the percentage of students engaged in none of those activities (such as reading through the descriptions of job openings supplied by firms or consulting with teachers about their employment options).

Among those who later obtained a job offer by January, very few had been completely idle during the July to August and the

Table 3.1: The change in the employment choices made by furiitaa-*bound students while in their final three years in senior high school (% of sample)*

	Seeking regular full-time employment	Seeking more education			Confused or had not thought about employment upon graduation
		Seeking entry to a specialized training college	Seeking entry to a junior college	Seeking entry to a four-year university	
When in years one or two	25.2	25.2	2.6	6.9	32.8
In April or May of their final year (year 3)	33.7	20.3	1.6	2.9	28.1
In July or August of their final year (year 3)	30.3	14.5	0.7	1.8	27.0
Percentage of students who fell into one or more of the above categories	49.5	39.2	3.6	9.0	53.5

Note: The percentages given above were calculated from the author's re-tabulations of the original data. This data was based on the responses of 822 senior high school students who at the end of their final year anticipated they would be *furiitaa* upon graduation.

Source: Nihon Rodo Kenkyu Kiko (2000a), p. 57.

Table 3.2: The percentage of final-year high school students who took no positive action related to their future upon graduation the following March

	Students who had received a job offer	Students who had not yet been offered employment but were continuing to look	Students wanting employment who changed their mind and did not have a job offer	Students who had done nothing to find employment but changed their mind
April–May	43.1	49.2	41.5	55.9
July–August	6.3	19.2	10.9	33.0
September–October	9.9	19.7	19.5	43.7

Source: Nihon Rodo Kenkyu Kiko (2000c), p. 60.

September to October periods. Successful students had been busy narrowing their choices, visiting the premises of prospective employers, and sitting for the exams that firms conducted. This is the peak time for such activity. A good number of the third-year students who had not received an offer by the end of January (when the survey was administered) indicated that they had done nothing to find work during the period from July to October. Among those who had not engaged in any of the activities associated with job hunting a very large number had changed their initial decision to look for employment, deciding instead to focus on other matters. One could say that work as a *furiitaa* was the only option open to many of those who had failed to look for work during their final year at school. Many had simply not been able to make up their mind, and January arrived for those students before they could free themselves from their indecision.

Many of the students who either had decided outright not to look for employment or had somehow let the time slip by were from the non-academic generalist stream of studies (*futsu-ka*). The data for our study came from two types of schools – academic high schools whose mission is to educate students who would go onto university and those educating students who were to pursue other avenues. The latter set of schools produced students who went in various directions upon graduation. Some went to four-year universities; others, to junior colleges and specialized training colleges; still others, into permanent and casual employment. Nearly all of the graduates from some vocational high schools became employed. At the academic high schools most of the students will be looking forward to attending a four-year university. Students at these types of schools find themselves in a milieu where they don't have to think hard about their options upon graduation. It's simply taken for granted that most will proceed along the path followed by earlier cohorts who passed through their school. However, graduates from a generalist curriculum tend to go in many different directions, and later cohorts who attend generalist schools have a much less concrete idea as to the possible careers they might pursue. For many of them the choice of what to do is much less obvious, and the resultant indecision leaves them not knowing what to do, and they become *furiitaa* by default.

If we return to Table 3.1, we can see that the largest number of *furiitaa* come both from students who had wanted employment and from those who had not given the matter much thought and were undecided as to what to do. Classmates who planned to advance to a four-year university or a junior college were much less likely to end up as *furiitaa*. Few change their preference to enter a university or to obtain regular full-time employment

Next came the group of students who initially planned to go to a specialized training college upon graduation. Many students who initially wanted to get into a specialized training college changed their minds and became *furiitaa*. This may reflect the fact that entry standards are low at many technical colleges. Such institutions are often seen by prospective students as being an easy choice. They usually do not require much commitment on the part of students who are not performing well, are lacking confidence, or are otherwise undecided. Low standards mean many high school graduates can still get in if they change their mind after first becoming *furiitaa*.

A clear difference can be seen as early as the first or second year of high school between (a) the few students who intend to progress to a four-year university or a junior college and (b) other students who plan to enter the ranks of the *furiitaa*. Nevertheless, the number of university and junior college graduates who become *furiitaa* has increased rapidly during the four years between 1998 and 2003. In other words, going on for further education does not close the door on obtaining work as a *furiitaa*, and those with a tertiary education are discussed below in the next chapter.

The difficulty of finding "the job one wants to do"

The survey undertaken by our research team at the Japan Institute of Labor in 200? asked third-year high school students about their plans after graduation. Students were asked to place themselves in one of eight categories according to their thinking in January of their final year (about two months before they would graduate): (i) going to university or junior college, entrance accepted, (ii) going to university or junior college, but the exact university is not yet decided, (iii) going to a specialized training college, entrance accepted, (iv) going to a specialized training college, but with the college still undecided, (v) planning to work, employment offer accepted, (vi) planning to work, but employer still undecided, (vii) having no idea as to the future after graduation, and (viii) planning to become a *furiitaa*. Students were also asked a number of questions concerning their orientations toward work. The findings from a cross-tabulation of the two assessments are given in Table 3.3.

Compared with the other students in their cohort, those who plan to become *furiitaa* are distinct in several ways. First, they do not want to settle into one job; instead they prefer to gain experience doing a variety of jobs. Second, they are clearer in wanting to avoid working in areas in which they feel they have no aptitude. The data in Table 3.3 also suggests that they appear to be much less likely to value having a high income or job security. Among the eight groups this group's positioning in terms of these orientations is most similar to that of those who have no idea as to the direction they wish to follow.

Those findings probably reflect the attitude of some youth who want a job in which they can express themselves and fully utilize their talents. Many who feel that way might see "shopping around" in the labor market as the best way of locating the position most suited to their own combination of skills and personality. In another survey conducted by the Japan Institute of Labor (Nihon Rodo Kenkyu Kiko 2000b), young people who had already become *furiitaa* were interviewed. When talking about their motivation in becoming *furiitaa*, those who were interviewed mentioned their desire to find work they liked doing and suggested they were simply in a kind of "holding pattern" while looking for that ideal job.

About forty percent of the students interviewed used the phrase *"yaritai koto"* to indicate that they had something else that they wanted to do which could not be achieved through full-time regular employment. They saw being a *furiitaa* as a positive thing – a good means to accomplish a clearly defined goal. However, they were at the same time negative when it came to being a *furiitaa* who did not have a goal in mind. In terms of their self-image, having a goal for which being a *furiitaa* was only a means was quite important, and they seemed to distinguish clearly between *furiitaa* with a goal and *furiitaa* without a goal.

Students who plan to become *furiitaa* and those who have no plans at all for working have a similar profile. It seems that students who are still without a plan in the January just before graduation are likely to graduate having neither found full-time employment nor gained entrance for further education. They tend first to find *arubaito* and then become *furiitaa*. Students who are unable to decide clearly on a full-time job or on further education seem to become locked into working as a *furiitaa*.

When these students say there is something else they would like to be doing, what is it that they have in mind? High school students in our survey gave concrete examples of what they meant by "something else". The answers revealed a slight gender-based difference. Many of the boys without a clear path to follow indicated that they were interested either in the entertainment industry – joining a band or becoming a dancer – or in a career in sports as a boxer or a racing car driver. While many girls were attracted to the entertainment industry, they also seemed on the whole to mention more frequently an interest in acquiring down-to-earth skills for being a bartender or a waiter.

Table 3.3: The likelihood of following a particular path after graduation and ten orientations toward work

Orientation toward work	Rank order of groupings based on their post-graduation plans							
	1st	2nd	3rd	4th	5th	6th	7th	8th
1. I want to experience different kinds of work rather than doing just one job for a long time	F 3.22 a	Q 3.05 a	Y 2.94	W 2.87	X 2.86	Z 2.85	V 2.83	K 2.82
2. I do not want to do work that I am not suited to do	F 3.46 a	Z 3.35 b	X 3.34 c	Y 3.34	Q 3.33	W 3.28	K 3.26 a	V 3.19 b, c
3. I want to become famous	F 2.61	X 2.61	Y 2.55	W 2.55	Q 2.54	V 2.50	Z 2.50	K 2.41
4. I prefer to enjoy life at a leisurely pace and don't want an overly demanding job	Q 2.68	F 2.58	V 2.56	X 2.51	Z 2.50	Y 2.50	W 1.98	K 2.39
5. I've not thought too much about how I will be living in the future	Q 2.45 a	Y 2.09 a	V 2.08	F 2.07	X 2.06	Z 2.01	W 1.98	K 1.96
6. I want to develop a higher level of technical knowledge and skill	X 3.80 a	W 3.68 b	Z 3.54 a, c	Y 3.53 d	V 3.34 b, c, d, e	F 3.21 e	Q 3.17	K 3.16
7. I want to have a life outside of my work	Z 3.63	V 3.60	Y 3.57	X 3.56	W 3.56	F 3.54	K 3.49	Q 3.47
8. Earning a high income is more important than my relationships with other people	V 3.21	Z 3.19	Q 3.18	W 3.18	Y 3.18	X 3.15	F 3.07	K 3.05
9. I want to be engaged in work which is useful for other people	X 3.27 a	Z 3.25 b	W 3.20 c	V 3.18 d	Y 3.17 e	K 3.08 a, f	F 2.93 b, c, d, e, f	Q 2.80
10. I want to have a job which provides a high degree of certainty	Z 3.62 a	V 3.62 b	X 3.52 c	K 3.52 d	W 3.52 e	Y 3.45 a, b, f	Q 3.33	F 3.28 c, d, e, f

Notes:

1. Students were asked to indicate how strongly they agreed with each of the statements concerning their orientation to work. Answers indicating a high degree agreement were given four points; those who felt some level of agreement were given three points; those indicating scepticism, two points; and those indicating strong disagreement, one point. The average was then calculated for students in each group based on the likely path students would follow after graduation. Groups were then ordered according to the average score given the students in each group, with the column labelled "1st" indicating the group with the highest score.
2. Each of the eight groups is identified in each box as follows:
    Z: university decided

    Y: university undecided
    X: technical college – decided
    W: technical college – undecided
    V: work – have offer
    K: work – undecided
    Q: no idea
    F: *furiitaa*

3. Reading across each row, the lower case alphabet letters indicate a difference in scores that is significant at the .05 level. The group signified with an "a" to the left has a significantly higher score than the group to the right with the same "a". Because the groups are rank ordered by their scores, the higher score signified by the first "a" would also be significantly higher than the scores of all other groups even further to the right of the group with the second "a".

Source: Nihon Rodo Kenkyu Kiko (2000b), p. 158.

The reasons for wanting to become a *furiitaa*

Students who were planning to become a *furiitaa* were asked in our survey to indicate the most important reason they wanted to become a *furiitaa*. The results are given in Table 3.4. Looking at the second column from the right, it is obvious that the most important reason most frequently chosen by the respondents was "I've got something I want to do that cannot be achieved through regular full-time employment" (22.8%). The next reason most commonly ticked was that they could not find work for which they were suited (14.9%). These two reasons reflect an outlook in which the students have a dream of doing something different in the future. Those citing the costs of further education or an inability to find a good job (each about 8 percent of the overall sample) tended to see work as a *furiitaa* simply as the work they were stuck with.

    In these regards, there seems to be a considerable difference between male and female students. More males than females gave as a reason for becoming a *furiitaa* their desire to do something that could not be achieved through regular full-time employment. Female students were approximately twice as likely to give reasons that had to do with the suitability of the work or the employer. I suspect that female students were more likely to have had difficulty finding employment in the months leading up to graduation and were hence more likely to feel that their only option was to work as a *furiitaa*. Chapter Two provided an overview of the path followed by high school students who initially wanted full-time permanent employment but then changed their minds. At each of the points in time that students were surveyed about 40 percent of all students who had been looking for such employment decided to "give up" and

Table 3.4: *Percentage distribution of high school students by the reasons cited for wanting to become a* furiitaa

| Reasons | Distribution by the Reason Cited as Being the Most Important | | | | | Distribution of all students against most important reason cited | Distribution of all students for all reasons that were cited |
| | By gender | | By course of study | | | | |
	Male	Female	Generalist	Commerce	Industrial arts		
I've got something I want to do that cannot be achieved through full-time regular employment in a company	28.7	18.8	21.9	24.8	26.0	22.8	33.8
I don't know what type of work I'm most suited for	17.9	12.7	14.8	16.5	12.3	14.9	38.3
I cannot yet afford the cost of further education	6.4	9.0	8.1	8.3	6.8	8.0	41.4
The current situation at home makes it difficult to continue my education	3.7	6.0	5.6	1.5	4.1	4.8	22.5
I could not find a suitable employer	5.4	10.4	7.2	11.3	11.0	8.3	40.1
I could not find an employer who would hire me as a regular employee	1.4	4.2	2.5	5.3	2.7	3.0	12.4
I prefer to have more free time than would be allowed if I were a full-time regular employee	4.1	7.4	6.0	9.0	2.7	6.2	42.8
I want to avoid the stress associated with being a full-time employee	0.0	0.2	0.2	0.0	0.0	0.1	16.8
I want to easily be able to change the work I do in a manner not allowed full-time employees	0.7	0.5	0.4	0.0	2.7	0.5	18.6
For the time being all I want is some income	5.1	7.2	8.5	0.0	1.4	6.3	43.1
The pay for *furiitaa* is better than that earned by full-time regular employees	0.7	0.5	0.4	0.8	1.4	0.5	9.1

My academic record is not good enough to continue my education	4.4	1.4	2.3	1.5	6.8	2.6	26.8
I do not want to go on for further education	3.4	3.2	4.1	1.5	0.0	3.2	27.6
I am happy to be a *furiitaa* as long as I can do the work I like	4.1	9.3	6.9	10.5	4.1	7.2	33.2
I am rather close to someone who is working as a *furiitaa*	0.0	0.2	0.2	0.0	0.0	0.1	9.2
Other reasons	6.4	6.0	5.5	6.8	6.8	5.8	4.7
No Answer	7.8	3.0	5.6	2.3	11.0	5.6	1.0
Total	100.0	100.0	100.0	100.0	100.0	100.0	100.0
(N)	296	432	567	133	73	773	773

Source: These figures are re-tabulations which were calculated using data from Nihon Rodo Kenkyu Kiko (2000a), p. 110.

seek work as *furiitaa*. However, there was a considerable difference
between male and female students in that regard; nearly 50 percent
of females did so while only 30 percent of male students did so.
When it became difficult to find full-time regular employment
female students tended to opt for work as a *furiitaa* whereas males
sought to find a place in a specialized training college or other type
of post-secondary school. Table 3.4 shows that female students were
much more likely than their male counterparts to conclude that
further education was too costly and veer toward work as a *furiitaa*.
This reflects not only realities in the labor market, but also the social
circumstances in which women find themselves – expectations
which give them different options and surround them with different
expectations.

To fully appreciate the thinking of those who gave up the hunt
for full-time regular employment, it is not enough to look only at
the tick put against the most important reason for doing so. It is
most likely that each student approached their decision with several
considerations in mind. Accordingly, each respondent was asked
also to tick other considerations that had weighed on their mind
when they decided to accept work as a *furiitaa*. The result when all
considerations are included is shown in the second column from
the right in Table 3.4. This presentation gives us a different picture.
The most common cited reasons were the desire for an immediate
income stream and the desire for more free time than what is
afforded most full-time regular employees. Each was ticked by over
40 percent of the respondents.

To identify clustering among the 15 reasons displayed in
Table 3.4 a principal component analysis was performed using
Varimax rotation. The search found five factors around which
clustering occurred, and the results are given in Table 3.5. The
first cluster consisted of the reasons associated with the absence
of the stress associated with permanent full-time employment.
The students citing those sorts of reasons could be said to have a
concern for maintaining options or a measure of freedom in their
everyday life. A second cluster could be said to revolve around
the economics of proceeding on for further education. The third
cluster was established by the two reasons that related directly to
issues involved in obtaining a suitable offer from an appropriate
employer. The fourth cluster was constituted by a set of four reasons
suggesting that some form of work was preferred to further study.
The final cluster could be said to revolve around a commitment to
doing something other than would be provided by full-time regular

employment or by further education. The reasons attached to this cluster related to uncertainty about one's aptitudes; few respondents identifying with this cluster ticked "wanting to do something else". Here the signal being registered may actually have been pointing to a desire to do something else when the respondent did not know what that something was.

In the preceding discussion, five general orientations were identified as possibly providing an overall framework shaping the decision of students to work as *furiitaa*. In the following two sections of this chapter implications flowing from the first two clusters are examined further.

The preference for more free time and less stress

Both the first and the last cluster concern the psychology of students who ticked one of the associated reasons. Among the reasons for becoming a *furiitaa*, having something else they wanted to do was most frequently ticked. This was mentioned in this chapter. "Wanting more freedom and less stress than they would otherwise have in regular full-time employment" did not elicit much comment from the students who chose that as a reason for becoming a *furiitaa*. This was so even though many students who became *furiitaa* cited it as a very important reason for becoming a *furiitaa*. Nevertheless, the responses point to a desire to "get outside or to escape from 'the system'". To examine that desire more carefully, the researchers examined the principal component scores generated by factor analysis to see if those having that predisposition responded in a predictable manner to other questions in the survey.

One relationship highlighted by that analysis was with the way in which students assessed the *furiitaa*. Many had a positive image of the *furiitaa*, agreeing that *furiitaa* had gone out and looked for a lifestyle suited to their own personality and/or needs. Others agreed that "it was no big deal being a *furiitaa* as most soon found regular employment" or that "*furiitaa* were to be envied because they were working to achieve their dreams." Students who thought favourably about the *furiitaa* were inclined to be *furiitaa* themselves, believing that avenue would allow them to work freely in a relaxed manner.

There was also a correlation with how students who became *furiitaa* wanted to work in the future. Those who planned to work as *furiitaa* for an extended period until their late twenties were significantly more likely than others to be wanting to work as *furiitaa* or not to work at all when they were thirty. The factor

Table 3.5: Values derived from a factor analysis of orientations leading to the various reasons for wanting to become a furiitaa

Reasons	First factor Desire for freedom to do "one's own thing"	Second factor High cost of further education	Third factor Difficulty of finding a job	Fourth factor Dislike of studying	Fifth factor Another goal in mind – cannot achieve through full-time regular employment
Cluster 1					
I want to easily be able to change the work I do in a manner not allowed full-time employees		0.001	0.105	0.005	0.146
I want to avoid the stress in working with others that is associated with being a full-time employee		-0.024	-0.042	0.064	0.186
I prefer to have more free time than would be allowed if I were a full-time regular employee		0.030	0.000	0.234	-0.053
The pay for *furiitaa* is better than that earned by full-time regular employees		0.062	0.030	0.187	-0.191
For the time being all I want is some income		-0.015	0.374	0.095	-0.115
Cluster 2					
The current situation at home makes it difficult to continue my education	-0.032		0.005	0.007	-0.031
I cannot yet afford the cost of further education	0.075		0.025	-0.026	0.044
Cluster 3					
I could not find a suitable employer	0.065	0.043		0.161	0.022
I could not find an employer who would hire me as a regular employee	0.015	0.015		-0.102	0.057

Cluster 4					
I do not want to go on for further education	0.152	-0.200	0.069		-0.125
My academic record is not good enough to continue my education	0.034	0.045	-0.046		0.312
I am happy to be a *furiitaa* as long as I can do the work I like	0.139	0.094	0.281		-0.170
I am rather close to someone who is working as a *furiitaa*	0.212	0.042	-0.066		0.201
Cluster 5					
I don't know what type of work I'm most suited for	0.081	0.073	-0.026	0.066	
I've got something I want to do that cannot be achieved through full-time regular employment in a company	0.086	0.134	-0.435	-0.059	
Dispersion	2.140	1.503	1.498	1.468	1.240
Explanatory Power	0.143	0.100	0.100	0.0098	0.083

Note: Another goal in mind – cannot achieve through full-time regular employment = Another goal in mind which cannot be achieved through full-time regular employment

Source: These figures are re-tabulations which were calculated using data from Nihon Rodo Kenkyu Kiko (2000a), p. 110.

analysis found that the link was particularly strong among female respondents. A further linkage was found with the students who had a good experience doing *arubaito* while still in high school. Many students reported positively that they had worked as *arubaitaa* longer than other students, had acquired considerable self-confidence through that experience, and believed they could upon graduation live independently on earnings as an *arubaitaa*. They expressed the view that a regular full-time job would be boring. Those with these orientations were probably looking for some kind of freedom from the stress that is associated with life as a salaried employee – stress generated by having in some way to take responsibility for some aspect of the firm's overall performance or by not being able to freely decline overtime or to freely utilize accrued leave whenever they wanted to do so.

Those with the outlooks described just above tended to view being a *furiitaa* positively and to have an aversion to working as a full-time regular employee or even to work itself. My own personal view is that this type of student wants to avoid the responsibilities and other trappings that go with being a full-fledged adult member of society. I suspect this outlook is one that underlines the need for the individual to have more time before taking on the commitments associated with full involvement in the labor force. In that there is likely a wish to have a longer adolescence, to continue to enjoy the freedoms associated with life as a student or teenager a bit longer. This tendency seems to be particularly strong among the female students who responded to our survey. Many of these young women have a fairly concrete image of themselves as future mothers who as middle-aged women will work part-time while also looking after their families. Part-time work will come with a low level of responsibility and without the pressures of having to demonstrate the commitment commonly associated with building a future career with their employer (*e.g.*, by doing overtime or by taking the initiatives that lead to promotion). In some ways materialistically oriented female students have quite a realistic vision of the future. Of course as high school students they have not yet begun to think through thoroughly the consequences of being a mother and/or a housewife. However, when they want to postpone the assumption of roles associated with being a "real member of the labor force", they can come up with a number of "excuses". They might claim that they'd never really thought seriously about becoming a career woman. Or they might answer that they are happy to do any job they enjoy since they plan to quit work anyway once they become married.

When assessing the motivation of students who decide to become *furiitaa*, gender cannot be overlooked. It is useful, in my view, to distinguish between two related but distinct events in the lives of most women. One is the move to find a recognized occupation (as a *shokugyo-jin*) while remaining economically independent from their parents. The other is marriage and the acceptance of a situation in which they are economically dependent on their husband, an approach which goes along with an acceptance of role specialization and the husband being the main breadwinner. Aware of their likely future as middle-aged housewives, many female students might well feel little resistance to the suggestion that they work as a *furiitaa*. The decision to work as *furiitaa*, avoiding stress and enjoying their work life until marriage, makes perfectly good sense for many female students.

Because male students are socialized to accept a gender-specific role as the breadwinner and to assume full-time regular employment so they can fulfil that role, male students are less likely to see the *furiitaa* as a positive role model. While some male students are attracted by the desire to have freedom and to experience as little stress as possible in their lives, the proportion of males citing that kind of sentiment as a reason for becoming a *furiitaa* was smaller than for the female sample. There is more resistance to the idea that life as a *furiitaa* might offer positive outcomes, and less likelihood that being a *furiitaa* will be justified on those grounds. For males planning to become *furiitaa*, having an end goal – an alternative career – in mind was important. Here we should note that a good number were not sure as to what they would end up doing, but were nonetheless committed to a career in music or to being involved in the entertainment industry in one way or another. For many the dream to succeed in such a competitive industry where success depended on one's own popularity was more like a childhood fantasy. Even if there was a well thought-out plan, this inclination still represented a departure from the safer and more accepted route to life as a fully employed salaried employee or company man.

The high cost of further education

For some students the cost of further education was seen as a barrier preventing them from realizing the future they would like. Table 3.4 shows that 8 percent ticked the high cost of education as the main consideration lying behind their decision to become *furiitaa*. However, 41 percent indicated that it was a consideration. To a marked degree each student's financial situation as a senior high school student is a given and quite beyond their control. This finding is consistent with a large body of literature in recent years which puts forward the view that socio-economic background is a major factor enhancing educational outcomes for students.

Chapter Two reported that about 40 percent of students who initially wanted to find full-time regular employment and then changed their minds would look for work as *furiitaa* (Table 2.2). Another option for students who turn away from regular full-time employment was to add to their educational qualifications by entering a specialized training college or other type of post-secondary school (about 30 percent) or a university or junior college (over 10 percent). It would seem that many who reassess their prospects in the labor market come to see value in furthering their education. However, a good number who want to invest in that manner find their options severely limited by financial constraints. Gender is again important. Whereas 50 percent of female students who stop looking for permanent employment had worked as *furiitaa*, only 30 percent of males had done so. We can surmise that the expectations of parents for their offspring depend on gender. Below are two typical responses from female respondents who replied to the open-ended invitation for comments:

> When I failed to get into the specialized training college of my choice and decided to study something else, I found I did not have enough money to pay the fees and my parents recommended that I work as a *furiitaa*. If I can get a subvention from the government, I will be able to make ends meet, even without any money from my parents. Just to get this far with my studies I've had a hard time emotionally and have had to struggle financially. However, after having done all that I will still not be able to afford to continue my education even though I studied really hard. (a third-year female student at a generalist high school)
>
> Even now, after deciding to become a *furiitaa*, I still want to go to a specialized training college and will not give up. I will carry on and save my money so I can do so. (a third-year student at a generalist high school)

In our interviews with the *furiitaa* themselves, it was common for them to emphasise the fact that they were working as *furiitaa* only for a set period to save enough to cover the costs of attending a college. We also met young *furiitaa* who had moved beyond the need to work as *furiitaa* to become *furiitaa* working with a commitment to building their own future through their own efforts. We also found that many *furiitaa* would talk about only one of their reasons for becoming a *furiitaa* even though a number of considerations were actually influencing their thinking in that regard. There is no easy way to generalize about how each of these young individuals ended up deciding to become a *furiitaa*.

The lifestyle of students who decide to become *furiitaa*

The lifestyle of students during their years in senior high school also gives us clues as to why some plan to become *furiitaa*. Our survey sought to obtain information about each student's attendance at school in their final year, their marks in academic subjects, their participation in extra-curricular activities, and the extent to which they engaged in *arubaito*. Table 3.6 compares the responses of students planning to be *furiitaa* with those of the other students. The first difference that stands out is the much higher rate of absenteeism among the students who are planning to work as *furiitaa*.

Given the way the employment guidance system currently functions in Japan's high schools, students with poor attendance and poor academic records have trouble getting their school's recommendation which is necessary if they are to sit for a company's entrance examination. By 2002 the employers' demand for high school graduates had fallen to one seventh that recorded in 1992. The company job offers are opened by the schools in July each year. By 2002 the number of positions being offered was only half the number of students who had indicated an interest in being involved in the school activities designed to help each student search for employment. As mentioned above, half of the students who plan to become *furiitaa* at the end of their final year were signed up to look for employment the previous July, nearly nine months before their graduation. During the intervening months many of those students had become pessimistic about their chances of obtaining a satisfactory offer of employment and had decided to change direction. While they came to verbalize that decision in ways that linked it to a desire for greater freedom and less stress or to a preference for a career outside the corporate sector, in the background was the tightness of the labor market for new high school graduates.

Table 3.6 shows a clear difference between the students who become *furiitaa* and the others in their cohort in terms the rate at which they participate in extra-curricular activities (section C in

Table 3.6: The distinguishing lifestyle of the students who planned to become furiitaa

A. Percentage distribution of students based on academic performance

	Considerably above average	A bit above average	About average	A bit below average	Considerably below average	No answer	Total	(N)
All students	14.8	20.3	28.0	17.4	16.2	3.3	100.0	6,855
Furiitaa-oriented students	6.4	9.9	21.3	24.0	33.8	4.6	100.0	822

B. Percentage distribution of students based on attendance

	Number of days absent					
	≤ 10 days	11–20 days	≥ 20 days	No answer	Total	(N)
All students	71.9	14.0	10.2	3.9	100.0	6,855
Furiitaa-oriented students	47.8	23.5	24.2	4.5	100.0	822

C. Percentage distribution of students based on participation in extra curricular activities

	Students who participated	Students who did not participate	No answer	Total	(N)
All students	42.5	54.6	2.9	100.0	6,855
Furiitaa-oriented students	25.2	70.9	3.9	100.0	822

D. Percentage distribution of students according to their experience in doing *arubaito*

	Students with work experience as an *arubaitaa*	Students with work experience as an *arubaitaa* during the school term	Total possible for each item	(N)
All students	81.9	64.9	100.0	6,855
Furiitaa-oriented students	90.1	76.6	100.0	822

Source: Nihon Rodo Kenkyu Kiko (2000b), pp. 119–121..

the table) and in the number of hours they spend doing *arubaito* (Section D). Although 80 percent of all students had at some time engaged in *arubaito*, the figure was even higher at 90 percent for those who were to become *furiitaa*. This difference also held with regard to doing *arubaito* outside the summer holiday period and other breaks in the school year. A closer look at the responses of students planning to become *furiitaa* revealed that many were working 4–5 hours a day, 4–5 days a week. In other words, even as senior high school students many were working as *arubaitaa* 20–25 hours a week.

The prevalence of *arubaito* is likely to vary from one geographic area to another and from school to school. It is likely that students in rural areas will have fewer opportunities to do *arubaito* than their counterparts in the more densely populated urban areas. It is also likely that few students attending high schools that prepare them for the university entrance examinations will engage in *arubaito*. Because this survey was limited to urban high schools that did not prepare students for those examinations, it is most likely that the percentage of students in our survey who were doing *arubaito* was above the national average for their age cohort. Nevertheless, the important point is that the vast majority of students who plan to become *furiitaa* have had experience working as *arubaitaa*.

Students who work 20 hours a week are like part-time employees. Students engaged in such part-time work are more likely to be absent from school or to arrive late to class (Section B). In a very real sense these students are at best only part-time students even though they may be enrolled as full-time students. However, once they graduate their half-time commitment to school is no longer required, and it is easy for them to continue with their *arubaito* and make the transition into becoming long-term *arubaitaa* (in other words, "*furiitaa*"). Mentally they are already in the frame of mind to accept such employment. When we asked such students about their thoughts on having been an *arubaitaa*, over thirty percent indicated that the experience had given them confidence that they could make a living doing such work on a longer-term basis. In this response we can see how their early experience as *arubaitaa* paved the way for some students to view life as a *furiitaa* as a viable option by opening their eyes to other choices they could make in terms of work and lifestyle.

At the same time, the types of work high school students can do as *arubaitaa* are limited. Most firms require some measure of skill, and on-the-job training is necessary to do many of the jobs they have. Few firms have jobs into which inexperienced high school students can easily be slotted. Most jobs of that sort are to be found in convenience stores, fast food outlets, and relatively inexpensive family-oriented restaurants. Employers may plan to train their *arubaitaa* to do specific tasks as required, but probably will not have the time or manpower to train such employees in the overall operations or flow of work. One may talk about students learning skills on-the-job, and advancing into a relevant trade, but in reality that would occur in only the smallest number of cases. It may be that some occupationally relevant knowledge is acquired by doing *arubaito*. But how useful that knowledge is in a very competitive labor market is questionable. Rather, it is likely that many *arubaitaa* end up learning only that life as a regular full-time salaried employee can be very boring, offers little time to do the things one wants to do, and creates stress. It is likely that the passing glimpse students get of the workplace through casual employment may well predispose them to wanting to adopt the lifestyle of a *furiitaa*. For them the world of work becomes a choice between the good life as a relatively free and happy-go-lucky *arubaitaa* and the hard life as a stressed-out employee with little free time.

The income of a high school *arubaitaa* paid on an hourly wage is about 50,000 yen per month. This income is not negligible in contemporary Japan. It is certainly enough to allow many students to imbibe the youth culture that permeates much of Japan. Although students doing such *arubaito* may miss classes and fall behind in their studies (Section A), many become active purveyors of the youth culture that is so popular among many young people in Japan. Once into that culture, it is easy for students to re-invent their future in ways that link into finding work within that culture. Such work is by its very nature often casual.

Students who develop a lifestyle around such part-time work have come to account for a sizeable proportion of the graduates from urban high schools providing a generalist education for those who are not planning to go on for further education. Here we should note the view that through the education system Japanese society is being re-stratified in its more densely populated urban areas. It is likely that the students who are heavily into *arubaito* are concentrated into certain types of high schools which are socio-economically marked. It is in this way that the decision to become a *furiitaa* becomes linked to the broader processes of social reproduction and re-stratification.

4 University Graduates as *Furiitaa*

More unemployed university graduates and more *furiitaa*

The number of unengaged university graduates who upon graduation seek neither full-time regular employment nor further study is increasing. The increase began with the recession in the early 1990s. According to the *Basic Survey of Educational Institutions* (*Gakko Kihon Chosa*) which is conducted annually by the Ministry of Education (now the Ministry of Education, Science and Technology), the number of new university graduates who became unengaged (*mugyosha*) rose nearly five times from 25,000 in 1992 to 120,000 by 2002.

Several factors account for this increase. One is the declining demand for graduates fresh out of university. Over the same period form 1992 to 2002 the number of such graduates gaining employment dropped from 350,000 to 310,000. Compared with the market for senior high school graduates, the decrease in the demand for university graduates has been relatively small. At the same time the increase in the number of such graduates has been huge. In 1992, the number of graduates from four-year universities was 440,000. This had risen to 550,000 over the decade to 2002, an increase of 110,000. One could say that the decade had produced a glut in the number of high school and university graduates coming onto the market.

The other noticeable increase over that period is in the number of students who upon graduation enter a postgraduate program of study, up from 30,000 in 1992 to 60,000 in 2002. This in part reflects the increased demand of businesses for individuals with higher technical skills and knowledge; employers have become much more selective over time. The labor market had tightened considerably, and there had become a surplus of high school and university graduates in the labor market.

Given the inability of the labor market to absorb new graduates at the present time, the drive for further education serves only to postpone the entry of many individuals into the harsh world of today's labor market. Even if this surplus in the supply of labor can be attributed to the downturn in the business cycle during the Heisei Recession of the 1990s, the hard debates will centre around the extent to which the higher education system will be able to impart the skills needed by business in the near future.

The transition to regular full-time employment

Although the number of university graduates becoming unengaged persons (*mugyosha*) increased greatly during the 1990s, as we saw in Chapter One the number of graduates who became *furiitaa* did not increase to the same extent. This probably reflected the fact that many graduates who might have become *furiitaa* would have done so for only a very short period of time. In this chapter we consider how university graduates made the transition from doing *arubaito*, other part-time work or non-engagement to being a regular full-time employee (*seishain*). To obtain an overall understanding of the situation, one must look at how new graduates plan and then actually progress with their careers. There are a few studies which have done that.

With regard to secondary school graduates, in 2000 the Ministry of Education surveyed graduates who were one year out from graduation and those who were three years out (Kokosei no Shushoku Mondai ni Kansuru Kentokai 2001). The survey targeted about 2000 graduates who had graduated without full-time regular employment or plans for further education. The goal was to approach 4–6 students each from 400 schools: 2–3 who had graduated one year earlier and 2–3 who had graduated three years earlier. In the end the survey was mailed to 2000 individiuals and 924 valid responses were returned. The results were that 15 percent of the graduates had found full-time regular employment during the first year after graduation; while 57 percent were employed as *arubaitaa* or as part-timers. Ten percent were unemployed; and another 5 percent had gone on for further education. Ten percent were employed as dispatched workers. For those who were three years out from graduation the figures stood at 43, 39, 11, 5 and 2 percent respectively. The data showed there was a tendency for these young persons to make the transition from non-engagement through *arubaito* to full-time regular employment.

An earlier survey of school graduates who had graduated in 1988 was administered in 1990 by the Japan Institute of Labor (Nihon

Rodo Kenkyu Kiko: 1992). It found that about thirty percent of those who were employed as *arubaitaa* or as part-timers upon graduation had shifted to full-time regular employment during the 32 months after graduation.

Based on those kinds of findings, it is safe to conclude that approximately 30–40 percent of graduates without full-time employment who do not progress to a tertiary institution upon graduation are likely to have found full-time regular employment within three years.

What about university graduates? In late 1998 the Japan Institute of Labor surveyed four-year university graduates who had graduated in March 1995. The survey was mailed to 11,945 persons who had graduated in March 1995 from 106 faculties at 45 national, local public, and private universities. It was administrated between December 1998 and February 1999. Valid responses were received from 3,421 individuals representing a 30% rate of return; 357 envelopes were returned by postal service stamped "forwarding address unknown", and 181 surveys were returned with unusable answers. The survey in Japan was part of a larger comparative research project for which the European component was coordinated by Professor Ulrich Teicher at the University of Kassel in Germany. The European Survey was conducted as the European Community's Targeted Socio-Economic Research. The survey was administered in the following eleven countries: Austria, Czechoslovakia, Finland, France, Germany, Italy, Norway, Spain, Sweden, the Netherlands and the United Kingdom. About 30,000 surveys were returned. The European surveys were administered at about the same time as those in Japan. The results of the Japan survey may be found in Nihon Rodo Kenkyu Kiko (2001a).

Among those who were neither regular employees (*seishain*) nor students upon graduation, the survey found that about half of women graduates and two thirds of male graduates had become regular full-time employees during the subsequent 44 months (Nihon Rodo Kenkyu Kiko 2001a). Based on this data it seems that unemployed university graduates are more likely than their high school counterparts to make the transition from casual work or non-engagement to full-time regular employment over the first 3–4 years following graduation. The remaining portion of this chapter will consider the process by which university graduates become *furiitaa* and the process by which they make the transition to regular full-time employment.

Non-engagement, being a *furiitaa* and one's university

The findings from the 1998 survey reveal that about sixty percent
of the university graduates were in full-time regular employment,
whereas those in casual work or who were non-engaged accounted
for only about 20 percent of those who returned the survey (Tables
4.1–4.4). Most of the remaining students had continued their
education in one way or another. These findings are almost identical
to those obtained by the Ministry of Education.

These tables give us some inkling as to the characteristics
associated with graduates who are non-engaged or who work in
positions other than those provided to full-time regular employees.
The proportion of female graduates in the two relevant categories is
somewhat larger than that for their male counterparts (25 percent to
17 percent). Table 4.2 shows that a high percent of male and female
graduates in faculties of science, fine arts and education were not in
full-time regular employment. For males not in tenured employment,
the faculties for medicine and the fine arts were conspicuous.
Although many graduates in medicine were counted in the statistics
as remunerated casuals, they were working as paid interns and were
receiving further training before finding permanent employment
as doctors. Only a small proportion of the males and females who
graduated from an engineering faculty seemed to follow this path.
The same was true of male graduates from science, economics
and commerce, areas commonly noted as having the most sizeable
gender differentials.

Table 4.3 shows that the tendency for graduates to works as
furiitaa also varied according to geographic location, a finding
in line with the data that we introduced in Chapter Four on senior
high school graduates. The percentage of graduates who became
unengaged or work in positions which were not regarded as full-
time permanent employment was particular high in Hokkaido and
Northeastern Japan, with a noticeable difference between male
graduates (22.8%) and female graduates (38.7%). The figures are
much lower in the two most densely populated areas (the Kanto and
Chubu regions). Here we can see the effects of living in a rural area
where the local economy is much less dynamic and good jobs are
harder to acquire. In this regard, it is said that university graduates
are employed to work in the head office and senior high graduates in
the local branches. However, the main offices of Japan's largest and
most stable employers are usually situated in the large urban centres.
Nevertheless, many of the graduates from universities that are

Table 4.1: The percentage distribution of March 1995 university graduates by type of engagement immediately after graduation

Engagement status upon graduation	Male graduates	Female graduates	Total
Full-time regular employment	61.2	59.2	60.2
Self-employed	0.8	2.1	1.4
Graduate school	15.8	7.8	12.0
Other educational institutions	2.6	3.5	3.0
Casual employment	9.3	13.9	11.5
Non-engagement	7.9	11.0	9.4
Other, no answer, missing value	2.4	2.4	2.4
Total for all students	100.0	100.0	100.0
N	1,808	1,613	3,421

Note: 'Immediately after graduation' means the situation during the first month following graduation.

Source: Nihon Rodo Kenkyu Kiko (2001a), p. 47.

Table 4.2: The percentage of March 1995 university graduates who were unengaged one month after graduation but had found full-time regular employment after 44 months by the type of faculty from which they graduated

Faculty	Male graduates	Female graduates
Humanities and Arts	25.0	27.5
Law	22.7	18.6
Economics and Commerce	17.8	22.2
Other Social Sciences	23.3	32.8
Science	9.6	25.0
Engineering	6.5	4.9
Agriculture	8.1	20.0
Health and Medicine	30.4	18.8
Home Economics	–	18.2
Fine Arts	38.5	38.3
Education	26.0	32.3
Other	19.4	26.8
Average for all students	17.2	25.0
N	1,808	1,613

Source: Nihon Rodo Kenkyu Kiko (2001a), p. 49.

studied in Japan's peripheral rural areas have a strong predilection to work near their family and in the locales where they grew up and have established networks. This natural outlook is reinforced by the move toward smaller families in which a larger proportion of the children are the eldest son, a factor which motivates a large proportion of rural graduates to consider their responsibility to look after aging parents and the family farm. While generally local economies lag behind urban economies in a way that is reflected in the demand for labor in rural communities, and this factor seems not to have been as severe a damper for university graduates as it has been for senior high graduates, there continues to be significant variation in this regard from one geographic region to another.

The relative academic standing of an institution also seems to influence the choices that students make. Table 4.4 provides a breakdown first by each institution's legal status, depending upon whether it is a national university, a local public (prefectural or city university) or a private university. Private universities may be ranked according to the academic rigor required in their entrance examinations, with Type I institutions having the highest standards. Those with the lowest standards have been labelled "Type IV private universities". Type IV private universities have the highest percentage of graduates who became non-engaged or employed on a casual or part-time basis (24.3% of males and 40.0% of females). Type III private universities (27.5% of males), Type II private universities (23.1% of males) and local public universities (37.3% of females) also produce such graduates. The results for publicly funded local universities may be influenced by the small sample size and the fact that many of those institutions have established programs in the fine arts and in the performing arts – areas that traditionally produce graduates who do not seek full-time permanent employment with one of the large, well-known corporations. As one might expect, the less demanding private institutions are most likely to have a large proportion of graduates who do not enter "standard employment" upon graduation.

Students know that firms will consider gender and the name of their university when recruiting new graduates. The above discussion clearly indicates that gender and the institution one attends influence the way students perceived their own marketability in the labor market for new graduates and, consequently, the decisions they make as they prepare for graduation and possible entry into the labor market. At the same time, as was the case with senior high school students, the tightening of the labor market since the early 1990s has

Table 4.3: The percentage of March 1995 university graduates who were unengaged one month after graduation but had found full-time regular employment after 44 months by the geographic location of the university from which they graduated

Geographic location	Male graduates	Female graduates
Hokkaido and Northeastern Japan	22.8	38.7
Kanto Region	13.8	19.3
Central Japan	15.4	20.9
Kansai Region	18.0	25.1
Western Honshu and Shikoku	16.9	26.3
Kyushu and Okinawa	18.1	27.3
Average for all students	17.2	25.0
N	1,808	1,613

Source: Nihon Rodo Kenkyu Kiko (2001a), p. 49.

Table 4.4: The percentage of March 1995 university graduates who were unengaged one month after graduation but had found full-time regular employment after 44 months by the type of university from which they graduated

Type of university	Male graduates	Female graduates
National	12.7	20.7
Other public	15.5	37.3
Private—category I	13.4	18.3
Private—category II	23.1	18.9
Private—category III	18.8	27.5
Private—category IV	24.3	40.0
Average for all students	17.2	25.0
N	1,808	1,613

Note: Private universities were divided into four categories based upon the difficulty of entrance, from "1" for the most difficult to "4" for the easiest to enter.

Source: Nihon Rodo Kenkyu Kiko (2001a), p. 49.

also remained as the most significant background factor for university students as they approach graduation.

Becoming a *furiitaa* and employment placement activities

While the decline in the demand of employers for new graduates was shown to be one factor accounting for the increased number of high school graduates who become *furiitaa*, it was also clear that the outlook and preparation of those individuals also influenced their outcomes in the labor market upon graduation. Here we will shift our attention to consider those concerns as they relate to university graduates.

Unlike secondary students, final-year university students must take a good measure of responsibility for making their way into the labor market. In the past employers would work through the placement office at each university in a manner similar to that which occurred at the secondary level. It was common for employers to narrow down the range of universities from which they hoped to recruit new employees, and to send job offers only to a set number of institutions. At the same time, it was common for firms to accept for employment those students that a designated university recommended. Students often knew ahead of time the firms to which they would be recommended even as they began their search. "Free searching", which involved students and firms approaching each other on their own without the intervention of university placement offices, began in the 1970s. Firms came to indicate their general job requirements in large employment catalogues that included basic information on firms. The catalogues were distributed directly to the potential graduates. It was then up to students to do their homework, obtaining additional information and approaching firms. Before long that approach became the norm for students graduating in the humanities and social sciences. For those in the hard sciences, the intervention of academic staff and the placement activities organized by each faculty remained important. However, here too the opportunities for free job searching have increased, and that approach is gradually also becoming the norm for science students.

Given these changes in the labor market for university graduates, the seriousness with which they looked for work in their final year becomes an important factor determining their employment outcome. We can ask about the number of companies or government agencies approached, about the time in their final year when they started to look for employment, about the tests they sat (for qualifications or licences to be teachers, public servants, or publicly certified professionals) and about other activities they under-took to find employment. Regardless of whether they worked in the public sector as civil servants or in the private sector as employees, those who were employed full-time without a contracted period were labelled "*seishain*" to form a statistical group that could be compared with other graduates who became "unengaged individuals" or "*furiitaa*".

Table 4.5 shows that there is a clear correlation between actively looking for employment and finding it. In recent years we have commonly been told that the number of university students who do not search for work is increasing. We can now see the consequences in terms of the higher percentage of graduates who find themselves in non-regular and casual employment or with no work at all.

Another way of arranging the data shows us the percentage of all students who took steps to find employment but were unsuccessful. The calculations reveal that 17 percent of male students and 24 percent of female students who looked for work were ultimately unsuccessful. These figures tell us that simply wanting to work is no longer an accurate indication of success in the labor market as in the past. This is especially true for female students.

A closer look at how students went about their search for employment reveals a difference between those wanting employment in the private sector and those looking to the public sector as civil servants or as teachers. A large percentage of those looking in the private sector were successful, whereas a smaller percentage of those looking to the public sector had been successful. The non-

Table 4.5: Involvement of final-year university students in their university's pre-graduation employment search activity by employment status upon graduation

Involvement in pre-graduation employment search activity	Employment status upon graduation		
	Full-time regular employment	Other casual employment	Not engaged
Male graduates			
Involved	94.8	82.2	69.0
Not involved	5.1	16.6	31.0
No response	0.2	1.2	0.0
Total	100.0	100.0	100.0
N	1,106	169	142
Female graduates			
Involved	95.4	83.1	77.0
Not involved	4.4	16.9	22.5
No response	0.2	0.9	0.6
Total	100.0	100.0	100.0
N	955	225	178

Source: Nihon Rodo Kenkyu Kiko (2001a), p. 56.

engaged had included persons looking in both directions. As the competition for those jobs in the public sector intensified in recent years, the pass rate dropped considerably for the civil service exam and for the exam taken by credentialled graduates wanting a teaching position. A good number of the unsuccessful are prepared to resit the exam the following year.

The middle columns in Table 4.6 show that graduates who became regular full-time employees were significantly more likely to have contacted a large number of prospective employers in their search for work. This measure probably provides a good index as to how earnestly prospective graduates went about looking for full-time regular employment upon graduation. This is even more apparent when the period of time over which the visits were made is considered. Those who were successful in finding a full-time regular job contacted nearly 22 companies over five months, an average of 4.4 companies per month. Those who found casual employment contacted 16 companies during an eight-month period for an average of 2 companies per month. The average for the non-engaged was closer to 1.5 companies. It is likely that personnel managers detect this difference in the level of intensity and hire accordingly.

Table 4.7 reveals other differences which set off those who were successful in this regard from those who were not. Those

Table 4.6: Involvement in pre-graduation employment placement activity of graduates by type of activity, gender and employment status upon graduation

Gender	Employment status upon graduation			Average for all graduates
	Full-time regular employment	Other casual employment	Not engaged	
Average number of months before graduation that activities started				
Male graduates	11.3	11.4	10.7	11.3
Female graduates	11.7	11.0	10.4	11.4
All graduates	11.5	11.1	10.5	11.4
Average number of companies contacted				
Male graduates	21.3	16.5	18.2	20.7
Female graduates	20.1	16.0	15.7	19.2
All graduates	21.5	16.2	17.3	20.0
Average duration of activity (in months)				
Male graduates	5.0	8.2	11.0	5.8
Female graduates	5.4	7.9	12.1	6.5
All graduates	5.2	8.1	11.6	6.1

Source: Nihon Rodo Kenkyu Kiko (2001a), p. 58.

Table 4.7: Type of pre-graduation employment search activity by gender and by employment outcome (%)

	Employment status upon graduation					
	Male graduates			Female graduates		
	Full-time regular employment	Casual employment	Not engaged	Full-time regular employment	Casual employment	Not engaged
Examined job offers from companies and applied to a firm	68.7	51.5	45.1	73.2	52.3	53.9
Used my tertiary institution's employment placement services	55.9	42.8	40.1	66.9	48.9	49.4
Sought help from the teaching staff at my tertiary institution	23.4	14.8	9.2	23.0	16.9	11.8
Involved a personal connection	18.5	18.9	20.4	20.8	21.8	11.2
Received a show of interest from a company	17.3	14.8	5.6	5.9	6.2	4.5
Used a private employment agency	13.0	11.2	7.0	14.0	11.1	5.1
Approached companies without knowledge about positions being offered	10.8	9.5	4.9	17.1	10.7	9.6
Contacted a public employment agency	9.3	10.1	16.2	13.4	12.0	23.6
N	1,106	169	142	955	225	178

Source: Nihon Rodo Kenkyu Kiko (2001a), p. 57

in the latter group were much less likely (a) to have studied the information provided by companies and to have responded, (b) to have consulted their university's placement office, or (c) to have sought advice from one of their professors. The data reveal that those who were non-engaged were likely to have sought advice from the government's Office for Employment Security (PESO). In all the other ways shown, the unsuccessful were less likely to seek advice or information. This too reflects a difference in the level of intensity with which work was sought. It is also likely that those who come through PESO come onto the labor market rather late after many employers have finalized their hiring.

This in turn leads us to refocus our attention on the ability of students to maintain their commitment to finding employment. The

1998 survey conducted under the auspices of the Japan Institute of Labor did not explicitly address this issue. However, the one-on-one interviews with *furiitaa* did provide some insight in this regard, with a good number of the interviewees saying either that they did not want a career inside a business firm or corporation or that they still did not know what they wanted to do and could thus not make a decision about taking on full-time regular employment. In this respect university graduates who became *furiitaa* were similar to senior high school graduates who became *furiitaa*. A major factor here is whether a student is able to commit to obtaining full-time regular employment.

Another factor affecting employment outcomes for university graduates is their use of the internet. Because Japan's tertiary students are increasingly left on their own by university placement offices, a good deal of their information about the labor market comes through the internet, the use of which connects back to the motivation and confidence students carry into the labor market.

Some limiting aspects related to use of the internet

The internet was not so widely used in the search for employment at the time of the Japan Institute of Labor Survey in 1998–1999. However, in the years that followed it became an important tool for a growing number of students. All major employers now have a home page, which allows prospective job candidates to know a good amount about a company before making contact with it. Even earlier, before showing an interest in particular companies, many students will sign-up with a company that supplies information on the job market for new university graduates. Through such agents students will receive various kinds of input and advice, including links to the home page of various employers. Once signed up, a student can receive information on a regular basis without much further effort.

Having obtained their information in this way, students can choose the employers in which they have an interest. They are then able to download any particular company's application forms, fill them in and return them. The internet allows this to be done without the student ever leaving his or her home. Students are now easily able to take the first step toward getting an interview with a prospective employer.

The consequences that flow from this use of the internet are several. First, information on each firm is supplied to an open market in a transparent manner. Everyone has equal access to the information. It is an effective means of recruitment in a market where individual students operate on their own. This stands in opposition to the old system whereby companies contracted designated professors or a set of selected universities, and the flow of information was restricted to a pre-ordained few. Although the old system continues to be an effective means of recruiting new graduates when the job requires a specific expertise that can be found only in a limited number of places, for generalist positions the open approach is now increasingly being taken by many Japanese firms. Nevertheless, the older approach offers greater certainty that an appropriate employee will be located by the firm, and a greater likelihood that the graduate will be placed in a position where he or she can most fully utilize skills acquired during their years in the education system.

At the same time, the openness of the internet approach generates its own challenges. The uninitiated student is often overwhelmed by the avalanche of information that is received off the internet. Included in the bombardment of information are many offers of employment by firms not able to hire a large number of new graduates as full-time regular employees. Many students are left with a huge number of job offers but have no criteria by which to sort through the offers so they can narrow the field to the most appropriate or most promising firms. One result is that many students simply select firms that are widely known because of their presence on TV or in other media. Such firms are overwhelmed by the responses they get and often end up having to cap the number of applications they will receive. Many become depressed as the "automatic" rejections from firms that have activated a cap mount. If they then withdraw altogether from the campaign to find permanent employment, graduation will soon be upon them, and their only recourse will be to work as a *furiitaa*.

Even when students know what they are looking for, it is hard for them to progress when the firms in which they might be interested do not provide clear guidelines or indicate how prospective employees ought to make an approach to a prospective employer for further information. In the past, meeting an alumnus from their own university who worked at one of the institution's designated employers allowed a final year student to gain a rather multi-dimensioned perspective of the firm in question and a broader outlook on the industry as a whole. Many of today's students rely heavily on web pages to obtain their information, ending up with lots of facts and figures on specific firms, but with much less of an understanding of work life and the overall ramifications of whatever choices they might make.

One conclusion might be that the role of the university's placement office and consultations with a close professor have conversely become even more important as the labor market evolves toward a more open approach whereby each individual has to act on their own behalf. The advice many students desperately need is about how to sort through the plethora of information they gather. They also require advice on how recruitment occurs "behind-the scenes", on broader trends and developments in a particular industry or professional area. This kind of information and insight is hard for firms or other bodies to put up on a home page or elsewhere on the internet. In the internet age the importance of the role which placement offices can play needs to be underlined.

Shifts in employment immediately after graduation

The final task of this chapter is to examine the progression of those who become *furiitaa* upon graduation over the first 44 months following graduation. Table 4.8 provides data showing how persons with different outcomes at graduation faired over that period. Nearly two thirds of the non-engaged males and half of the non-engaged females had become full-time regular employees over those 44 months. A fairly similar result was observed for those who had entered casual employment upon graduation. Among those who found permanent employment as *seishain*, 90 percent of the males and 75 percent of the females continued to be so employed over that 44-month period.

Table 4.8 also reveals a much lower level of unemployment for both males and females who had been fully employed on a full-time basis during the 44 months following graduation. How that period played out for those who were casually employed or non-engaged immediately after graduation has been assessed in two ways. The optimistic view is that graduates are still able to get full-time regular employment even though they may have ended up in casual employment or been non-engaged immediately after graduation. The pessimists, however, tend to focus on the fact that their unemployment rate is higher or on the fact that a sizeable number still do not get full-time regular employment.

To throw more light on the prospects facing graduates who choose to become *furiitaa*, we can examine responses to questions in the

Table 4.8: Employment status four years after graduation by gender and by employment outcome upon graduation (%)

Employment status 4 years after graduation	Employment status upon graduation							
	Male graduates				Female graduates			
	Full-time regular employment	Casual employment	Not engaged	All Males	Full-time regular employment	Casual employment	Not engaged	All females
In full-time regular employment	90.7	64.5	64.1	80.7	74.2	48.0	50.0	62.9
In other casual employment	2.6	19.5	18.3	6.2	9.1	26.7	25.8	14.9
Self-employed	0.6	3.6	2.8	1.5	0.8	1.3	2.8	2.2
Unemployed	3.1	4.7	6.3	3.5	3.4	4.0	8.4	3.8
In technical training	0.2	0.6	2.1	0.6	0.8	1.3	2.2	1.1
In postgraduate course	0.8	3.6	2.1	5.0	1.0	1.8	0.6	3.8
Housework/raising children	0.0	0.0	0.7	0.1	7.5	12.4	5.1	7.6
Other/no answer	2.0	3.6	3.5	2.5	3.0	4.4	5.1	3.7
Total	100.0	100.0	100.0	100.0	100.0	100.0	100.0	100.0
N	1,106	169	142	1,808	955	225	178	1,613

Source: Nihon Rodo Kenkyu Kiko (2001a), p. 64.

surveys that dealt with working life. In particular we are interested in the relationship between employment status and outcomes such as wages or hours of work. Should there not be much difference in the outcomes, we could then conclude that being a *furiitaa* need not be such a great social concern.

To carry out our analysis, the sample was divided into the following three groups based on the work experience of respondents over the preceding 44 months:

- the continuing *seishain*: those who were full-time permanent employees with the same employer throughout the period,
- the new *seishain*: those who were not engaged or were employed on a casual basis immediately after graduation, but who later found full-time regular employment, and
- the continuing casual: those graduates who started out as casual employees and who were still so employed 44 months later.

Among those in the sample, the largest number of males had remained as continuing *seishain* (category 1), whereas for females the largest group consisted of those who had remained in casual employment throughout the 44 months following graduation (category 3). By academic background those in category 2 were more likely to have graduated from a faculty of arts or a faculty of education. Males in the second category were also more likely to have graduated from a less prestigious university.

Tables 4.9 and 4.10 show how each grouping in the sample was spread across occupational categories and firm size. The most noticeable fact is that the continuing casuals (category 3) and those who changed to full-time regular employment (category 2) were much more likely to be employed in a small firm with fewer than thirty employees. They were also much less likely to be found in one of Japan's large firms with over 1000 employees. It should also be noted that the latecomers were considerably more likely to be employed in the public sector. A large number of the long-term casuals could be found in teaching. This no doubt reflects the fact that the examinations to become teachers and other civil servants are particularly hard to pass, requiring many applicants to sit several times before achieving success. Furthermore, these exams are open to persons into their late twenties. As a result, it may be the case that prospective applicants feel they can take their time and do other things before settling down to a career teaching or working elsewhere in the public service. This may also be one reason some students veer away from the private sector where firms are much

Table 4.9: Employer firm size (number of employees), by gender and by employment outcome (%)

	Employment status following graduation					
	Male graduates			Female graduates		
	Full-time regular employment	Late comer to full-time regular employment	Other casual employment	Full-time regular employment	Late comer to full-time regular employment	Other casual employment
–29	3.3	12.5	10.7	4.4	15.4	7.9
30–99	7.6	9.0	8.0	6.8	7.3	6.6
100–499	20.9	17.2	12.5	21.2	13.0	10.4
500–999	9.6	7.8	1.8	8.4	3.7	4.6
1,000–4,999	21.7	10.9	4.5	18.1	11.4	7.5
5,000–9,999	4.3	3.1	3.6	3.3	1.2	2.1
10,000+	9.6	5.5	0.9	6.8	2.0	4.6
Public service	19.8	29.3	26.8	24.8	37.8	25.3
Missing answer	3.1	4.7	31.3	6.4	8.1	31.1
Total	100.0	100.0	100.0	100.0	100.0	100.0
N	837	256	112	548	246	241

Source: Nihon Rodo Kenkyu Kiko (2001a), p. 69.

more conscious of age. Finally, we might note that over 10 percent of male graduates who remained in casual employment had been employed as factory workers.

Table 4.11 provides information on income and hours of work. The bottom row in the table shows income per hour worked. The italicized figures in the parentheses provide an index with the values for the continuously employed *seishain* set at 100.0. Because those in the second category ended up becoming *seishain* (in category 2), their hours of work are the same as those for the other *seishain* in category 1. However, the income of males in that category was 95 percent of that for the continuously employed *seishain*. The corresponding figure for the women was a bit lower at 90 percent. However, those continuously employed as casuals (category 3) worked hours that were considerably below those in the first two categories. Even so their income was even smaller proportionally, meaning the hourly income earned was some 91 percent (for males) to 76 percent (for females) of the incomes earned by their cohorts who were in full-time regular employment. For those who came late to full-time regular employment, the disadvantage seems negligible for males, though the gap is about ten percent for women.

Table 4.10: Employment paths by occupational category, by gender and by employment outcome (%)

	Employment status following graduation					
	Male graduates			Female graduates		
	Full-time regular employment	Late comer to full-time regular employment	Other casual employment	Full-time regular employment	Late comer to full-time regular employment	Other casual employment
Administration	5.4	5.9	4.5	3.3	2.8	0.0
Teaching	5.9	9.8	17.0	10.9	20.3	19.1
Profession other than teaching	28.6	23.4	15.2	21.5	21.1	15.4
Semi-professional	3.2	3.5	3.6	1.8	3.7	3.3
Clerical	24.3	28.1	15.2	39.8	38.6	32.8
Services and sales	23.4	17.2	14.3	14.4	5.3	10.8
Production, agriculture, fishing	3.3	6.3	11.6	1.3	1.2	2.5
Other	3.5	4.7	2.7	4.2	5.3	5.0
Missing Answer	2.5	1.2	16.1	2.7	1.6	11.2
Total	100.0	100.0	100.0	100.0	100.0	100.0
N	837	256	112	548	246	241

Source: Nihon Rodo Kenkyu Kiko (2001a), p. 69

For women who enter full-time regular employment immediately after graduation, other choices about career that are made soon after being employed also figure significantly when accounting for the long-term outcomes at work.

The data in Table 4.12 return us to considering the motivation to work. Overall, there seems to be a similar split among those who are long-term casuals and among those who come to full-time regular employment after casual employment. Some in each category seem to be much happier with their choices than many of the full-time regular employees in category 1, whereas others in each category seem much less happy (see the responses to Question C). The same split is seen in their response to the other two questions concerning the suitability of the work they are doing to their skill level and to their educational background. This perhaps reflects the fact that those coming late into permanent employment and those who remain in casual employment are likely to be in a wide range of jobs ranging from teaching and clerical work in large organizations to factory work for small subcontractors. Although the breakdown by occupation and firm size results in some categories having too few respondents for

Table 4.11: Pattern of transition into the labor force, income and hours of work

| | Employment status following graduation | | | | | |
| | Male graduates | | | Female graduates | | |
	Full-time regular employment	Late comer to full-time regular employment	Other casual employment	Full-time regular employment	Late comer to full-time regular employment	Other casual employment
Annual income	400.0	380.6	243.7	347.5	311.7	193.9
	(100)	(95)	(61)	(100)	(90)	(56)
Total hours of work per week	52.6	51.5	35.3	47.7	47.9	35.2
	(100)	(98)	(67)	(100)	(100)	(74)
Normal hours of work	40.3	40.6	31.3	40.0	40.4	31.9
	(100)	(101)	(78)	(100)	(101)	(80)
Average hourly wage rate	7.6	7.4	6.9	7.3	6.5	5.5
	(100)	(97)	(91)	(100)	(89)	(76)

Notes:

Annual income = JY10,000

Total hours of work per week = Normal hours + overtime

Average hourly wage rate = Annual income/weekly hours of work

The figures enclosed in parentheses serve as an index whereby persons in full-time regular employment are treated as the standard (*i.e.*, set at "100").

Source: Nihon Rodo Kenkyu Kiko (2001a), p. 69.

the results to be considered significant, they show that many teachers and other public sector employees provided favourable responses.

The above discussion leads us to conclude that the outcomes are varied for those who upon graduation remain un-engaged or accept casual employment. Those who use their time to acquire professional skills or who are able to enter the public service seem to end up happy in their work, and their experience shows that the period outside full-time regular employment can become an important step in the development of a career.

We can also conclude that the likelihood of entering a profession will be shaped to a considerable degree by the faculty in which an individual studies. Although students who majored in an artistic field, in education or in one of the health services are less likely to enter regular permanent employment immediately after graduation, they often have a professional goal to achieve. Whether it is passing an exam or passing through an informal apprenticeship or even a formal internship, many seem to be highly motivated to pursue

Table 4.12: Pattern of transition into the labor force and thoughts about the present job

| | Employment status 4 years after graduation | | | | | |
| | Male graduates | | | Female graduates | | |
	Full-time regular employment	Late comer to full-time regular employment	Other casual employment	Full-time regular employment	Late comer to full-time regular employment	Other casual employment
Question A: How suitable do you feel your present job is?						
Very suitable	8.8	12.9	11.6	13.9	18.7	9.1
Somewhat suitable	31.8	25.8	17.0	37.4	31.3	22.4
Can't really say	40.1	40.6	25.9	35.6	31.3	34.0
Not very suitable	12.9	12.5	18.8	11.5	13.0	16.2
Completely unsuitable	5.5	6.6	16.1	1.6	5.3	11.6
Missing answer	0.8	1.6	10.7	0.0	0.4	6.6
Question B: How often are you using knowledge and skills acquired during the course of your education?						
Very often	5.5	8.6	11.6	7.1	11.0	13.7
Fairly often	11.6	14.8	10.7	12.0	15.4	14.1
Every now and then	32.7	27.3	20.5	33.2	30.9	17.4
Not very often	34.6	30.5	15.2	30.3	23.6	23.7
Not at all	8.5	6.3	12.5	7.5	7.7	7.5
No relationship between my current job & my education	4.9	9.0	13.4	8.9	10.2	14.1
Missing answer	2.2	3.5	16.1	0.9	1.2	9.5
Question C: How satisfied are you at work?						
Very satisfied	7.2	14.1	7.1	7.5	8.5	10.0
Somewhat satisfied	36.0	33.6	28.6	42.5	46.7	37.8
Don't really know	25.3	23.4	28.6	22.3	21.1	25.7
Not very satisfied	24.1	20.7	17.9	22.6	17.9	17.8
Not satisfied at all	6.8	7.8	11.6	4.9	4.9	5.8
Missing answer	0.6	0.4	6.3	0.2	0.8	2.9

Source: Nihon Rodo Kenkyu Kiko (2001a), p. 71.

their chosen career. For those who were not in a specialist faculty attaining concrete occupational skills, the way forward is not as certain. Many end up doing work that is not directly related to the curriculum undertaken at university.

When considering the university graduate who ends up un-engaged or only casually employed upon graduation, it is important to distinguish between the two groups identified above. The group that requires immediate attention consists of students studying for generalist degrees. Upon graduation they either will not or cannot find permanent full-time regular employment, and become *arubaitaa* or part-time workers after functioning as white-collar workers. A career in a white-collar job in a private firm begins from the time one is employed. Those who delay entry into such firms once they have graduated face an up-hill struggle to catch up with others who started their careers immediately after graduating and have a head start up the career ladder.

5 The Failure to Make a "Smooth Transition"

The *furiitaa* and NEET phenomenon

Established placement processes characterize the school-to-work transition in postwar Japan. However, in recent years the number of students dropping out of that process is increasing. This chapter introduces some insights gleaned from interviews with 51 young people, and conveys in their words how they became derailed from the traditionally accepted path into the work force. The interviews were conducted after the interviews reported in the other chapters in this volume. The original research on *furiitaa* was conducted in 1999–2001, and concluded with a series of one-on-one interviews focused on the *furiitaa*. Following that research a second round of interviews was conducted with a fuller spectrum of students in order to understand better the context from which the *furiitaa* emerge. From one perspective, therefore, it makes sense chronologically that the findings from the follow-up interviews be provided after Chapter Six in this volume. However, for the reader to obtain a better narrative and an overall understanding of the *furiitaa,* that data is presented here in Chapter Five as a means of providing a broader context. The text for this chapter was first published as Chapter One in an edited volume by Kosugi *et al.* (2005), two years after the other chapters in this volume appeared as Kosugi (2003).

The term "smooth transition" is used in this chapter to refer to the overall journey of final-year senior high school students starting with the decision to seek employment. It follows the student through their school's placement program to employment immediately upon graduation. This fits in with the way work is organised in a typical Japanese firm with Japanese-style management. The standard pattern is for firms to hire young graduates directly out of school, to train them (partially covering the cost of training by initially paying them a low wage), and then to promote them and to increase their remuneration as their career progresses within the firm. The clear assumption is that the firm will utilize the skills each employee acquires through their training. Here we are also referring to the economics of becoming an adult in Japanese society – the process by which young people gain full-time regular employment and the financial security which goes with that status. This definition is somewhat narrower than that of those who use the term "transition" to include the experience of moving out of the parental home and establishing an independent household after years of dependence on various services supplied by their parents. Gaining permanent employment and thereby establishing one's economic independence is what those in the mainstream do in Japanese society.

In a macro-economic sense this Japanese-style transition into the labor market, and more broadly, into the economic life of the nation has come to be highly evaluated internationally. This is, however, the same system which is characterized by a huge gap between the world of the *seishain* (the full-time regular employee) and that of those who are not *seishain*. Moreover, once one is employed as a casual employee or non-*seishain*, it is very difficult to bridge the crevice which divides the two, and make one's way into regular full-time employment as a *seishain*.

The 51 young interviewees in our study had not made the transition from school to regular full-time employment. For one reason or another they had "fallen by the way side" at some point during their youth. Somehow they did not become *seishain*. This chapter tells their stories. Considering each case in a broader social context, I sketch some of the background factors contributing to the employment outcomes that characterize the lives of a growing number of Japanese young people.

Those in casual employment became derailed at one of several of several key junctions. For some, the "wheels came off" when they failed to commit to the placement program developed by their school or university. Others missed out when the introductions made possible through such programs did not pan out. A few achieved full-time regular employment upon graduation, but then found that things did not work out with their employer. They then resigned and fell back into the casual sector. Finally, there were those who failed to get back on track after dropping out of school or giving up their place in the permanent labor force. In the sections that follow I want to look at the influences that impinge on these young actors at each stage in the transition process. We will then consider the factors that tend to lock those young people into the secondary labor market. That discussion will focus on aspects related to the operation of the labor market, career trajectories and the work ethic.

Outside the school's placement program

A number of factors come into play that discourage young students from following through with the job placement procedures developed in their school. In this section several of those factors are discussed.

Abandoning further education beyond junior high

In recent years job offers for middle school graduates have dried up, and 97 percent of middle school graduates now continue to senior high school. Those without a senior high school diploma soon discover that the labor market does not offer them many options.

Early in his education one 24-year-old male middle school graduate came to see school as a repressive place. He gave no thought to going to senior high. He had help from his middle school to find a job pumping gas as a service station attendant. However, he felt the attitude of his supervisor was too strict and he quit that job after only six months.

Case 01: Male middle school graduate aged 24

There was something in me that felt chained down when I was at school...I'm not sure what it was, but there was something that made it hard for me to remain at school. I just did not want to go to school...I now don't know why, but at that time school was simply this place I didn't want to be at...

At the gasoline stand I had my first full-time regular job...There too small things got on my nerves. Maybe I was overly sensitive when the owner or other big wigs in the company got on my case. Even now some of it upsets me. I guess I was still a bit raw just after getting through middle school, and the challenge of dealing with that was just too much for me. It was a period when I blew up over even the smallest matter. But at the time I could not understand why these people had to make so much of every little thing, as though they could order me about simply because they set themselves up as being important. I looked for other employment, but sort of liked the idea of sleeping in each morning. Finally I ended up going from one short-term job to another.

The next example also involves an adolescent who did not want to be at school. He ended up attending a free school and working at a number of jobs as a *furiitaa*. At the urging of a friend he applied for full-time regular employment, but was not hired. He was still hoping to find permanent employment and become economically independent when we interviewed him. However, with a poor record at school and no real job experience, he had lost his self-confidence and was reluctant to apply for regular full-time employment.

Case 02: Male middle-school graduate aged 22
I was encouraged by my homeroom teacher to go to a correspondence school...However, I wanted to go to one of the free schools and to continue studying in that way...At the time I had a pretty "iffy" record at school. I knew nothing about the big world outside of school. So I didn't obtain any real guidance about these matters. All I knew was that I wanted to go to a free school and not a senior high school. I really did not think at all about the future.

I couldn't bring myself to become a *seishain* because I did not believe I had what it takes – like skills and the other stuff bosses want. If I at least had experience as a mature-aged working adult and felt I had some work-related skills, I would set about in a determined manner to gain regular full-time employment. However, as I have no skills to speak of, I do not have the confidence to apply for that kind of position...In order to get some work experience, I've got to go through the interview process, and involve myself in the activities generally associated with finding such a job. My biggest problem, however, is finding in myself something that will appeal to possible employers.

School drop-outs

Dropping out of senior high school is another way in which students fall off the employment-bound wagon. Among those who drop out are those such as Case 03 and Case 04. They find themselves not wanting to be at school; they are often late to school and simply walk out of school before classes finish. In other words, they have little interest in what is being taught at their school. They come to school only to see their friends, with whom they continue to socialize off the school grounds until late at night. To support that lifestyle, many do long hours of *arubaito*. Because the demands of *arubaito* often keep them out until late at night, each morning they struggle to get up in time for school. When they finally decide to drop out from school, few have thought much about their future in the labor force. Dropping out is seen by the individual mainly as a decision to remove themselves from the institutionalised repressiveness of their school.

Case 03: Male senior high school drop out aged 17
I took a year off from my studies. Once out of school it was easy to decide to drop out completely. I just felt stale and in need of a break…I was finding it hard to get up in the mornings. What point was there in having to get up in the morning to go to school…What a struggle to sit in class; the teaching was boring; I found it hard to focus in class because I was often out playing the night before. I found it hard to focus in class. In class I'd shift from one seat to another to talk to my friends, and completely ignored what the teacher was saying. Did teachers say anything? What could the teacher say? If they persisted, I'd just be rude and disrupt the class.

Case 04: Female senior high school drop out aged 20
I got along pretty well with my friends. However, there was an incident of rough play when we had a fight and one of the girls ended up with a good-sized bruise…She went to the nurse's room and told on us, giving our names, year and class to the authorities. Both parents were called in. It was not so serious that I was expelled, but I was told I would be suspended. In the end I was not suspended, but I'd had enough and quit school.

Our fifth case bore some similarities with the case that was just introduced. He felt out of place in the education system by the time he was in middle school. Although he continued on to an ordinary daytime senior high school, he felt there was little value in the secondary education he was receiving. However, that was partly because he had something he wanted to do (*yaritai koto*), and to pursue that interest he dropped out of senior high school. This decision was reinforced by the fact that he had to change schools when his father changed jobs. He found the ambience of the new school differed from that to which he had grown accustomed at his previous school. He felt the change added to his having to struggle at school each day. Unlike Cases 03 and 04, however, Case 05 did not have a circle of close friends with whom he socialized day and night.

Case 05: Male senior high school dropout aged 20
I formed a band. However, because we were in a rural area we could not get enough people together to make it work…Because I wagged middle school, I couldn't get into a normal high school…In the end, I was only six months into my first year in the new high school, in October it was, when I dropped out of school and made my way up to

Tokyo…At the time I was committed to doing the thing I most wanted to do. So I came to Tokyo quite determined to make it. At the same time, when I was in school I didn't hit it off very well with my teacher and felt I needed to be in a different place – somewhere that I could do my own thing, a place where I'd be motivated to succeed.

The sixth case did not really open up much. Nevertheless, it was clear that she too did not feel comfortable in her school's environment.

Case 06: Female senior high school dropout aged 20
I dropped out in my second year in a night high school. I don't remember exactly when that was; I sort of just faded from the scene at school. I was okay in the first two terms, but was missing a fair bit of school by the third term…At first I was going to class, but by the third term I was not going. It just got to be very hard having to go in to school every night.

Case 07 was a bit different. Through middle school this boy was always in the top group of students and enjoyed the competition among those vying to be at the very top of that group. As a result of his hard study, he was able to enter a select high school that was affiliated with a top university. However, his parents were Koreans who had not been naturalized Japanese citizens. As a stateless person, he would not be able to vote or to enjoy other benefits of citizenship. He would face various forms of discrimination and have tremendous difficulty getting full-time regular employment. These problems concerning his citizenship and ethnic identity affected his ability to concentrate on his studies, an outcome that caused him to worry about his psychological state.

Case 07: Male senior high school graduate aged 24 who dropped out and then re-enrolled to complete his secondary degree.
It was near the end of my third and last year in junior high school – over the December and January period. My ability to concentrate collapsed. I had been studying well up until then. But in senior high school I lost that desire to study. The sense of continuity was broken…That had a huge impact. I am a resident Korean; so are my parents. I hadn't known that, but just before I was to enter high school my mother told me about this. What a shock that was!…It sort of wiped out my future…The end result was that I decided to quit school. I progressed from my first year to the second year. In May of my second year, my mother had to be hospitalized on a permanent basis and we missed

her. I then spent a period treading water. For two and a half years, I
received counselling, and was taking sedatives and sleeping pills...At
that time I had been unable to make it from the second to third year,
and dropped out of school.

The first seven cases are summarized in Table 5.1. Among those
individuals, Case 03 seems to have been the most successful. He
left high school with his parents' permission on the condition he
would look for work. Doing *arubaito* arranged by an employment
support organization, he came to work in a *sushi* shop. He has been
asked by the *sushi* firm to consider becoming a *seishain*, but had
not made up his mind when we interviewed him.

Case 03: Male high school dropout aged 17
I've been encouraged to become a *seishain*. However, thinking only
for the short term the money is better as an *arubaitaa*. At the present
time *seishain* make slightly more income. However, you have to think
about the hours they work. Being an *arubaitaa*...in comparison a
seishain works from noon till late at night. In the worst case they
might have to work until dawn. That's the way things are: be there at
noon to prepare for opening the shop in the evening, serve customers
until midnight and close the shop, then clean up and get ready for the
next day...Can I do that every day for the next 4 or 5 years? I don't
know. I think I am better to wait until I'm sure...I think I should try
this job for a bit longer to see if I'm fit to do that.

Case 04 had centered her life on going out and being with her friends
each night. As a result she was unable to get up each morning until
noon. To enjoy herself each evening, she needed a certain income,
and to earn that she tried her hand at a variety of *arubaito*. However,
she had been unable to keep even that kind of job for a long period,
and had gone from one *arubaito* to another. At 17 she became an
unwed mother. With the help of her mother and grandmother she was
raising her child, and a year earlier her father had introduced her to
a part-time job with one of the publicly funded job creation schemes
that local governments establish in Japan's poorer neighbourhoods.
She had been working there for over one year and was hoping to
become a *seishain* when we interviewed her. She was aware that
she needs to get a high school diploma before she can do that, and
her parents have suggested that she return to school. She felt she
could do that, but wanted to wait for the child to be older. She was
thus struggling with the demands of motherhood, with the need

for more education, and with the requirements of holding down a full-time job.

Case 05 moved to Tokyo and entered a music school that did not require a high school diploma. At the same time, he joined a band, and put a lot of energy into making his music a success. Thinking it would be difficult to make it as a professional, he thought he should try something else. He passed the high school equivalence examination set by the Ministry of Education and Science and obtained the basic qualification required for entry to a university. He also became involved with an NPO that helped young people. In that way he earned a small income and tried to create opportunities that might connect him with the larger society. In other words, he was groping for a way forward without becoming fully independent economically.

Initially a very successful student, Case 07 had experienced personal trauma. Entering a good high school and then failing academically to qualify for his final year of studies, he re-enrolled in a night-time high school. Such schools pitch their curriculum much lower than that provided by a generalist academic school. Such schools tend to service dropouts from regular daytime schools. Few of his fellow students in that school would be thinking about going to university. However he did not have the confidence or desire necessary to participate in the school's job placement activities, and ended up doing a series of fixed-term jobs as an agricultural laborer. Without Japanese citizenship, he felt he had no hope of obtaining a secure position in Japanese society, affecting not only employment but also his chances in love and marriage. As a middle school student he had dreamed of going to a top university and then entering an elite company. However, when he learned that he did not have citizenship, he felt his efforts would be in vain, became depressed and gave up altogether.

Case 07: Male high school graduate aged 24 who had once dropped out and then enrolled in another school to complete his secondary education

Once I'd taken the high school entrance exam and been accepted, I lost it. From my point of view I was frightened. I was fragile. I simply could not come to grips with the emotions swelling up inside me. I became immobilized, unable to do anything. It was a form of melancholy, and I found that frightening. Moreover, that mental state has remained with me until the present time. Is it fear? In any case, it's taken hold of me. For that reason, I've struggled even in doing the jobs on lots of farms.

Table 5.1: Overview of cases 01–07

Case number	01	02	03	04	05	06	07
Demographic characteristics							
Age	29	22	17	20	20	20	24
Education	MSG	MSG	SHS-DO	SHS-DO	Special HS-DO	Special HS-DO	SHS-DO→ Special HSG
Gender	M	M	M	F	M	F	M
Geographic region	Kansai	C. reg.	Kansai	Kansai	C. reg.	Kansai	C. reg.
Present status	*arubaitaa*	*arubaitaa*	*arubaitaa*	*paatotaimaa*	NPO casual	not working	*arubaitaa*
Situation at the time of graduating from middle school							
Poor academic performance	○						
Participation in anti-school sub-culture	○						
Not fitting into school life/refusal to attend school		○			○		
Trouble with difficult interpersonal relationship	○						
Being late to school/difficulty in getting up in the morning						○	

Situation in senior high school when the decision to drop out was made

Taking a year off
Poor academic performance
Personal troubles
Lack of motivation to continue studies
Tardiness
Fighting with other students/staff
Difficulty in getting to night classes
Interested in things outside of school

Notes:
MSG = middle school graduate
SHS-DO = senior high school drop out
HS = high school
DO = drop out
M = male
F = female
Kansai = region including prefectures around the Osaka-Kobe-Kyoto area
C. reg. = Capital region = Tokyo metropolitan area and areas bordering on it

Tertiary dropouts

Table 5.2 provides an overview of Cases 08–13, all of whom gained entry into a tertiary institution and then dropped out part way through their studies. Again, the reasons for dropping out and the individual circumstances vary considerably.

Case 08: Male university dropout aged 24
I was in a faculty of engineering. In both semesters of my first year I took mostly general subjects that were part of the liberal arts curriculum for all students. In my second year I began my major in engineering in earnest. In both semesters I did not gain sufficient credit...The grading system was quite strict. For example, you were forced out if you were caught sleeping in class...Somehow it got to the point where I was no longer attending class...When I decided to drop out, my first reaction was that I would be starting all over...It brought a sense of relief.

Case 09: Male junior college dropout aged 22
I just believed I'd be all right as long as I was just scraping through with my assessments so that I'd be getting enough credit...I met some university students who were the same age. I then began to participate in events being organized at their university. I first got involved in the planning and organization of the events, and then into publicity and the setting up. I got to do lots of things...My own university was not a very good one; and I learned much more by being involved at the other university...From the point of view of what I was being taught in my major, I guess that was okay. However, the other facets of life at my university left a lot to be desired. It was boring to be on campus at my own university.

Case 10: Female university dropout aged 28
I wanted to study law. All my entrance exams were to enter a faculty of law – from my first choice university to my bottom choice university... Well, in the end I only got into my last choice...I was really interested in law even though I struggled academically. However, I was not interested in anything I was being taught...I studied the legislation. I tried hard, but nothing really grabbed me...It was hard going. I kept going to class, thinking I'd get something out of it, but I gradually became more and more depressed. I began to think, "I'm not trying hard enough." Or, "I am not one of those persons with enough drive to get ahead." Even now I wonder what I was doing. Somehow I just

Table 5.2: Overview of cases 08–13

Case number	08	09	10	11	12	13
Demographic characteristics						
Age	24	22	28	32	20	28
Education	UDO	UDO	UDO	UDO	STC-DO	UDO
Gender	M	M	F	M	F	F
Geographic region	C. reg.	C. reg.	C. reg.	C. reg.	Kansai	C. reg.
Present status	*arubaitaa*	not working	not working	*arubaitaa*	not working	*arubaitaa*
Appraisal of time spent at senior high school						
Strong reaction to school rules and restrictions	o				o	
Poor academic performance/taking a year out of school		o			o	
Unhappiness with the school curriculum		o				
More interested in things outside of school		o				
Illness			o			o
Not fitting into school life/refusal to attend school	o		o	o		

Notes:
UDO = university drop out
STC = specialized technical college
DO = drop out
M = male
F = female
Kansai = region including prefectures around the Osaka–Kobe–Kyoto area
C. reg. = Capital region = Tokyo metropolitan area and areas bordering on it

started to find it harder and harder to show up in class, and finally could
no longer bring myself to attend.

Case 11: Male university dropout aged 32
After two years as a *ronin* I managed to get into a bottom-choice
university...After my previous failed attempts to get into a better
university, I could only accept that as my fate in life. Simply put, I
went through the motions; it was a matter of wanting to do something
else. There was nothing left by the time I got to university. I did not
feel an obligation to be at university, and I went to almost none of my
classes. I went to some of the club activities for 2 or 3 years. But I
attended none of my classes.

Looking at Cases 08–11 we again see that something caused each
student to loose his or her interest in studying. Already in high school
Case 08 preferred arts over science. Even as a first-year high school
student he felt a bit uneasy when he entered the science classroom. It
was not a field of study he had chosen with any passion. Nevertheless,
his senior school allowed him to gain direct entry into university based
on his high school results, and he entered the department of mechanical
engineering without much thought. However, once into it he found it
difficult to get enthused about his field of study. Case 09 wanted to
become a flower arranger, and Case 10 had planned to become a lawyer.
However, they found their university and fellow students wanting, lost
interest in being at university, and subsequently dropped out.

Case 11 attended a large number of different schools in his primary
and secondary years owing to his father's frequent transfers within
his firm. For that reason he was unable to develop a network of close
friends. When his father was assigned to his firm's American office
and his family moved overseas, he entered a dormitory from which
he commuted to a preparatory school (*yobi gakko*) for two years.
He finally gained admission to a program of study in which he had
little interest. Not only did he fail to get excited about his studies, he
soon stopped attending university altogether and drifted into a life
of idleness. He soon dropped out completely. He lived by himself
without any adult guidance. Completely isolated from other people,
he lost all contact with others in society.

In contrast to Cases 08–11, Case 12 was exposed to excessive
restrictions and guidelines at school. She expected life at the specialized training college she entered to be the same as it was in her senior
high. However, she had trouble dealing with the relative freedom
given her and the concomitant expectations that she would take more

initiative by herself. In this regard she felt the college was remiss, and soon dropped out. It is difficult for many tertiary institutions to know how much support they should be giving such students.

Case 12: Female technical college dropout aged 20
I thought I should study hard to get into my nursing course, and took a fair bit of resolve with me to the college. However,...it was tough...If my hair was brown, they complained that it was dyed. If they were really concerned about educating nurses they wouldn't be worried about such things...I felt we were expected to ask questions that served only to show our ignorance. I thought maybe it was because the nurses felt they were really important, but whatever the reason I found it tiresome that they always pretended as though they knew everything...In any case, it got so I did not want to face those teachers. Before long it all got to be too much to bear. Soon I couldn't stand anything about the nursing college, I just started to come up with excuses for being absent from class. I just didn't want to go to the college any more. I got sick just looking at the faces.

In all of the cases considered so far, none of the students had considered the consequences in the labor market that would flow from their decision to drop out of their program of study. When students drop out of their school or university, they usually have only two options: to be unemployed or to do casual work. When they decide to be an *arubaitaa* they often say, "I won't be continuing in this job very long." Or, "I don't want to be saying, 'if I quit' very often." A good number like Case 11 thought they were boldly choosing to be *arubaitaa* only for a short period of time. Others like Case 09 thought they would first try out work as an *arubaitaa*, and then as a result moved from one casual job to another. Case 09 said he dropped out of university in order to join Japan's Self Defence Force (SDF), but in fact he had not passed enough units to earn the credit necessary to proceed in his university course. The SDF was an easy option, but he quit the Force after just one week. Rather than planning a careful shift to another career stream, he made an emotional on-the-spot decision to save face. By the time he had left the SDF, he had actually taken a step backwards. In reality he had fallen out of the labor market for permanent employees.

Case 11: Male university dropout aged 32
After leaving university, I've had a good variety of casual jobs...Only one or two lasted for any period of time. However, the ones I remember

most were all short-term ones...For example, at one job one of the bosses was my age. He was a despicable fellow and I quit within one week...I've quit about three *arubaito*. The other *arubaito* were all for a fixed term...In other words, when it became time to quit, I always found it difficult to know how best to say that I was quitting...For that reason I came to feel that a job with a predetermined contracted employment period was a good one. I soon got used to having all of my *arubaito* done that way.

Case 09: Male junior college dropout aged 22

I dropped out of my junior college so I could enter the Self Defence Force...It was precisely on September eleventh, the same day that New York experienced its ground zero. That's when I entered the SDF...I stayed with each of my jobs for various periods of time: the SDF, one week; as a security guard, one month; as a public bath attendant, three days; as a personal computer salesman, one month. I am now in my third year as a movie extra and in my second year as an entertainer.

In order to move to the next stage in their lives, many of these young people are going to some sort of school or agency (or planning to do so) to acquire a qualification or some sort of skill. The spring after dropping out of university Case 08 entered a school on how to edit manuscripts and had already graduated from that course by the time the interviewing for this study was underway. Case 10 had gone to several English schools. Case 12 had decided to pursue a new interest and had applied to become a child carer and was waiting to hear from a junior college to which he'd already submitted an application. Some of the young people in our sample, however, had not yet taken any steps in these regards. Case 11 was a bit vague in this regard, but was thinking of becoming a social worker and studying through NHK's university of the air. Case 13 wanted to become a counsellor, and planned over the coming year to save enough money to do that course. The overall impression was that tertiary level dropouts were more likely than secondary school dropouts to re-enrol with some other institution in order to gain a qualification that would lead to full-time permanent employment.

Among the secondary school dropouts some had sat for a high school equivalence examination or had returned to their studies by entering another high school. However, most of these students were already struggling academically back in their primary and middle school years. Furthermore, among those who had seen school largely as a place for socializing with their friends, few would return. Among those with this view of school only Case 04 felt a high school diploma would be necessary. However, even she had come around to seeing its importance after she had begun to see the possibility of working for one of the publicly funded bodies established in the poorer neighborhoods. When planning for some kind of program to help these young people obtain full-time regular employment, it is important to remember that some will want to acquire employable skills through some kind of schooling and others will not.

Even when young people attend a school to acquire such skills, it does not necessarily follow that they will find full-time regular employment. In the end, one's chances to become so employed will depend upon the balance of demand and supply for each skill combination that exists in the labor market. The education system not only provides a curriculum in the narrow sense. More importantly, perhaps are the opportunities it provides for obtaining career-relevant material, heightening one's motivation in their chosen field, and meeting a wider range of people who may have connections and ideas relevant to gaining employment in that field. For example, Case 08 began to feel the pinch in the labor market only after he had finished his course in editing and had started to look for on-going employment. Actually, he had stopped looking for work and then had come across an opportunity to prepare and to enter text onto the web page of a lecturer he had met by chance.

Those who do not look for work

Some students fail to become involved in their school's job placement activities, and simply become unemployed after graduating from their high school. This section introduces the comments of such students as to why they did not engage in such activities in the lead up to their graduation. Their cases are summarized in Table 5.3.

Case 14: Male senior high school graduate aged 19
I did absolutely nothing to secure employment upon graduation. From the start I had no interest in becoming employed. For the time being, I was skeptical as to whether looking for work was worth the effort...Even in April immediately following my graduation I had no drive to look for work.

Table 5.3: Overview of cases 14–19 and 07

Case number	14	15	16	17	07	18	19
Demographic characteristics							
Age	19	18	24	19	24	20	18
Education	SHSG	SHSG	SHSG	Special SHSG	Special SHSG	SHSG	SHSG
Gender	M	F	F	M	M	F	F
Geographic Region	Tohoku	Kansai	C. reg.	Kansai	C. reg.	Kansai	Tohoku
Present status	Unemployed	arubaitaa	arubaitaa	arubaitaa	arubaitaa	arubaitaa	arubaitaa
Views at the time of graduation							
Few positions on offer							○
Could not find desired job						○	
I don't know what I want to do		○		○		○	
Poor academic results and high absenteeism at school	○	○		○			
No advice taken on my future			○	○			
No drive to do anything	○		○		○		
Looking for arubaito outside of school			○	○			
I am happy to do arubaito							
I was put off by advice for job hunting which infringed on my persona						○	

Notes:
SHSG = senior high school graduate
M = male
F = female

Kansai = region including prefectures around the Osaka–Kobe–Kyoto area
C. reg. = Capital region = Tokyo metropolitan area and areas bordering on it
Tohoku = the six prefectures constituting Northeast Japan: Aomori, Iwata,
Akita, Yamagata and Morioka Prefectures

Case 15: Female senior high school graduate aged 18
I was always tardy or being absent from school. When everyone else was looking for work, I was again behind in getting going...I had no vision or awareness of the future...Even though I may have thought it was a good idea to join in, inside of me there was no real feeling: I still did not know if I would qualify to graduate...And then, just a month out in February, when school was already finished, I came to feel that I needed to do something...By the time I felt I wanted to do something, however, it was too late, and all I could do was become a *furiitaa*.

Case 16: Female senior high school graduate aged 24
I had not thought through very carefully about what I wanted to do after graduating, including the possibility of going on for more education...It just seemed to be too much trouble to think about a university. I just didn't want to spend my time commuting back and forth to university...it was all in the distance. I got tired thinking about it...Whatever else, I just didn't give it much thought at all. At best I simply thought I could think about it leisurely over a longer period of time.

Case 17: Male graduate of an alternative high school aged 19
I did absolutely nothing in terms of looking for a job placement upon graduation. I probably thought I would just continue on with the *arubaito* I was doing as a student. Even after graduating from school I still didn't think anything would change. None of the placements I did at school really appealed to me...If you talked to me about gaining regular employment, somehow I would already be thinking about leaving...Because the idea of gaining employment has that notion of always working, it just was not attractive...To suddenly agree to something long-term when I didn't know anything about it didn't catch my imagination...There was just nothing that made me feel, "Yes, this is what I want to do!"

Case 18: Female senior high school graduate aged 20
In thinking about what I wanted to do work-wise, I decided I wanted to work in a clothing store. I, my teacher and my parents all knew a long time before I graduated that that is what I would be doing when it came time to get employment. As a result I didn't do anything about looking for full-time regular employment. At the time even my father seemed happy with that. But before we knew it the time for doing placement activity had come. When I was told that I had to change my make-up and that the clothes I wore were unacceptable, it

turned me off. It made me decide that I didn't really want full-time
regular employment. When I mentioned that to my parents they didn't
give me any real guidance...I heard from another girl working for a
clothier that the clothing establishments would not be sending anyone
to recruit at schools.

Case 19: Female senior school graduate aged 18
When asked if there's any particular work I wanted to do, I answered
that it was to work in sales. I did not particularly want to be working
in a convenience store; a department store or supermarket would have
been fine. I can't remember whether my school was informed of any
positions,...I guess there was a time in high school when there was talk
about working in a convenience store. I can't remember the details.

Case 17 presented as someone who did not know what to do, someone who chose to do *arubaito* so that the hard decisions about career
direction could be postponed. Cases 18 and 19 were women who
wanted to find their own way without depending on their school's
placement procedures. Each had a clear idea as to the type of work
they wanted to do, and they were determined to find such work
regardless of whether or not it was as an *arubaitaa*. They were
rather reluctant to be drawn into having the school negotiate on their
behalf with a potential employer, but were quite willing to take the
initiative in looking for the type of work they wanted to be doing.

Among those who either made no move to gain full-time regular
employment or who from the start looked only for *arubaito*-type
employment were a few who wanted to spend a year or two focused
on study in order to resit a public service exam or an entrance
examination for the university of their choice. These paths that are
followed by "*ronin*" (young people still without an affiliation in
hand) are well known to Japanese. However, it is easy for those who
have supported themselves by doing *arubaito* to become *furiitaa*
when they fail to achieve their immediate goal – young persons who
might well be labelled the "lost *ronin*" (*ronin kuzure*).

In Table 5.4 are four cases that fit this category. Only one (Case
20) of the cases in Table 5.4, however, was actively studying to
resit an exam while also working as an *arubaitaa*. The other three
(Cases 21–23) had already decided to move away from the original
goal they had in mind when they first became *ronin*.

Case 21 grew up without the support of his parents. He had
received a scholarship from one of the newspapers so he could go to
a preparatory school (*yobi gakko*) in order to resit entrance exams.

Table 5.4: Overview of cases 20–23

Case Number	20	21	22	23
Demographic characteristics				
Age	18	31	19	21
Education	SHSG	SHSG	SHSG	SHSG
Gender	F	M	F	M
Geographic region	Kansai	C. reg.	Kansai	Kansai
Present status	*arubaitaa*	unemployed	*arubaitaa*	*arubaitaa*
Views at the time of graduation				
Unable to progress in education owing to family finances	○	○		
Poor academic results and high absenteeism at school			○	
Was not recommended for a placement by my school	○			
Working with plans to attend university	○	○		
Taking public service exam			○	○
Failed to get into a specialised technical college				
Looking for *arubaito* outside of school		○		
Change from being a ronin				
I want to do other things than study for an entrance exam				○
I am very busy with my *arubaito*		○	○	

Notes:
SHSG = senior high school graduate
M = male
F = female
Kansai = region including prefectures around the Osaka–Kobe–Kyoto area
C. reg. = Capital region = Tokyo metropolitan area and areas bordering on it

While studying he worked for the newspaper company delivering newspapers. In the end, his performance did not improve and he gave up. He then added his name to a list of casual employees who could be called in by a computer factory whenever it had busy bursts, and then held various short-term contracted jobs. Cases 22 and 23 shifted course and settled for casual employment as *arubaitaa*. Both were passive as *ronin* and gradually let *arubaito* become the core around which their lives revolved. At the same time one could detect a slightly positive note in his wanting to see what work doing a particular *arubaito* might involve. But in both cases, a definite decision had been made to become a *furiitaa*. In considering these cases it is important to see them not as failures, but as attempts to change course. Here we can see students who are attempting to work part-time while studying because their family's financial standing did not allow them to commit themselves fully to study. However, rather than give up outright, they decided to struggle as best they could to achieve a desired academic outcome. This commitment to struggle against the odds must also be recognized when trying to assess the *furiitaa* lifestyle.

Case 22: Female senior high graduate aged 19

After not being accepted into a nursing college, I thought I'd try to get into a course for becoming a nurse's aide. However, once I'd graduated I was pinched financially...I had to work every day. It was the first time to have my own money in hand. I was making more than 100,000 yen per month. That was great and had its own attraction...Yes, after graduation I enrolled in a preparatory school so I could sit an exam to become a nurse's aide. However, I got a small promotion where I did my *arubaito*. That meant a change in my working conditions, including the shift I worked. No matter how I tried, I could not receive enough time off for my studies. In the end, I quit the preparatory school.

Case 23: Male senior high graduate aged 21

My family circumstances meant I had to give up the idea of going to university. I decided to take the test to become a public servant, but did not pass. I became a casually employed lab assistant at a high school from which I graduated while studying to resit the examination, but again failed it...I then decided that the public service was not to be my calling in life...So one day I was in this store looking for a clothing brand I really liked. I got to talking with the store's owner. He thought I was a good talker and persuaded me that it was a good line of work to get into. I didn't think much further about it at the time, but later began to mull over the possibilities, thinking how much I liked clothing. I also liked talking to other people. I thought I should try out that kind of work as an *arubaitaa*...I thought I'd like the work, and decided to get into it.

As we have seen above, the number of tertiary graduates who do not look for full-time regular employment upon graduation has increased. However, in the sample of young people we interviewed there was only one university graduated *furiitaa* who had not looked for work. Case 44 had found her calling while studying at university, and had since embarked on a road to realizing her dream.

Case 44: Female university graduate aged 27
I did not participate in the final year search for employment...Cross-cultural communication was a most interesting area, and there is an interesting line of work known as "cross-cultural training". I thought I'd become a cross-cultural trainer. It's a job not found in a company. There was a problem in the department in which my final year seminar was located. I went to that teacher for advice. He showed me what he was doing. As a volunteer he had been to Bosnia. Shortly after I returned home the International Association for Cross-Cultural Communication held its international conference at my university. I was able to be involved for the week that conference ran, and I thought, 'That is it!'

Afterwards, she began working toward her goal, and came to have an interest in becoming a corporate counsellor. In order to prepare for the exam, she did not become a *seishain*, but she did take positive steps to achieve her goal of working in the area of cross-cultural communications. Although we had just this one case in our study, there is reason to believe there are others like this young woman who were making strides toward a career of their own that would be outside the world of corporate employment. One might even speculate that this approach to work will typify the world of work for many young persons in the next generation.

Many students who do not actively look for employment are quite passive when it comes to taking the initiative. Among our interviewees were many university graduates who had gone to one or more company presentations, but had then decided not to take the next step and apply for employment. We will look more carefully at this type of graduate next.

Drop-outs and graduates who did not look for employment

This chapter has so far considered a number of cases in which dropouts or even graduates had chosen not to become involved in activities that would lead to employment. What generalizations can be made about these students? To answer this question, it is important to remember that the research project involved more than just the interviews reported in this chapter. Those who have dropped out of high school can be sorted into one of three categories.

The first category consists of students who see little value in being at school beyond the opportunity it provides for socializing with friends. Some schools are more regimented than others and rigorously enforce behavioral norms which are seen by the school authorities as important to the teaching and learning environment. However, such schools are seen by this type of student as oppressive. These students rebel against their school and probably against schools in general; they are often seen by teachers as "disruptive". In the end they leave and have access to many other venues where they are able to socialize with their friends. Those in the second category are not able to develop friendship networks and somehow feel that school is an awkward place for them. The third category includes those who performed exceptionally well in school, but then ran into an unexpected hurdle that kept them from reaching their goal and resulted in their having to give up. The case involving citizenship is an example of the type.

After leaving school the first type quickly gets a job to earn spending money. The second and third types do not immediately enter the labor force. They spend time looking for work that will allow them to express themselves – some in music, some by working in agriculture, and some in yet other ways. Through that experience some come to be aware of themselves as having no real work experience and no real skills; they often feel a bit lost as to how best to proceed.

Among those in the tertiary sector as well, dropping out of their program of study is often accompanied by a decision not to seek regular full-time employment. It is often the case that tertiary students lose interest in the midst of the program and fail to pass the units they need to graduate. However, a look further back in their lives reveals that some had unresolved issues when they decided to continue their studies, choosing a tertiary course in which they had no interest or for which they were not suited. Others had a good idea of the career they wanted, and on that basis chose a university and the program of study they had truly wanted to enter, but into which they failed to gain entry. Having to go to a less prestigious university resulted in an overwhelming sense of disappointment and a subsequent loss of interest in their studies. The third type somewhere along the line became antagonistic to all forms of institutionalized activity and fought any attempt to regulate their lives. Most of the students who dropped out turned to short-term casual work as *arubaitaa*. The impression I received was that many took on such work with the aim of broadening their range of experiences and looking for a direction in which to go with their next job or with a move onto further education in order to gain a specific skill or qualification so they could make a new start.

In our sample, high school graduates seemed more likely than university graduates to have not looked for full-time regular employment. Some of these students had poor attendance records and appeared unlikely to obtain enough credits to graduate. The result is that they were often omitted from the placement activities organized by their school. They nevertheless managed somehow to graduate. They included the student who frequently missed class and performed poorly academically. Another group of students knew they would graduate, but were not sure what they should have been doing and made no plans for work or further education. With no thought for the future, they seemed to float through life without any concerns and then ended up doing casual work. Those in a third group had an idea about the work they wanted to do; quite independently from their school's placement program, they set about finding an *arubaito* that would lead them to the employment they desired. For example, firms in the retailing of clothing and apparel seldom come to schools looking for potential *seishain*. Rather, they tended to look closely at young people they had first employed on a casual basis to see how well they worked, choosing the most promising *arubaitaa* to be employed as *seishain*. Students wanting permanent employment in such firms sought alternative routes to realize their goal. In addition to these types were the *ronin*, young people engaged in casual work while studying to pass a public service examination or to enter a tertiary institution of their choice. However, a good number of these students would eventually be drawn further into casual work and give up such study altogether.

The inability to find employment upon graduation

The decline in job offers for high school graduates

Some students engage in the normal activities that should lead to employment, but still graduate without success. These students study the job offers, visit prospective employers and apply for jobs. However, the first reality that confronts them is the very significant drop in the demand for new high school graduates. Even in the rural prefectures of Northeastern Japan, where students regularly attend class on time and tardiness and absenteeism are below the national average, many good students go through their school's placement activities and still end up empty-handed upon graduation. Nineteen-year-old Case 24 claims she was told that the number of positions on offer had reached rock bottom and that she ought to think seriously of going on for more education.

Our supplementary interviews simply confirmed the view of educators in Japan's secondary schools that job offers for their graduates were at an all-time low at the turn of the century. Another young female graduate (Case 25) commented that "those responsible for our job placements sought to find positions that employers would be offering and formulated plans that did not include the kinds of jobs which would appeal to me." Here the suggestion is clearly that the school's placement officers were struggling in their efforts to formulate a suitable strategy to gain employment for their graduates.

Case 21: Female high school graduate aged 18
I went to interviews for 2 or 3 office positions, but in the end was unsuccessful. I would be happy with something in services or in information management. I also sat for the certificate tests for data management, word processing and bookkeeping. These were tests recommended by one of my teachers.

Case 24: Female high school graduate aged 19
In the summer nine months before I graduated I made a firm visit. They didn't say so directly, but I had the strong feeling that they were looking for male employees...Firms would say the employment they were considering would be different from normal office work, and then ask me to come in for a look around. So I went, and it was sort of different...After that my teacher introduced me to several other firms. However, those firms had some positions that were not focused

on office work. No one asked me directly if I'd be unhappy if it wasn't office work. It was left very unclear. Someone might have commented that the position required something different, or mumbled something about my not being able to do the work...That kind of treatment undermined my interest in looking for work.

Case 25 had graduated from a commercial arts high school, and held a number of skill certificates related to doing office work. For that reason the school's placement office had worked hard to get her employment as an office staff member. However, the student was not successful. Case 25 had a good academic record at her school, and had the school's solid support. It was her plan to apply for employment as a print operator. However, when she visited a prospective employer she found that she had been trained on a computer that did not use that employer's printing software. In the end she did not apply and gave up her search for regular full-time employment.

Among the other graduates introduced in Table 5.5, Case 26 also wanted employment upon graduation. However, her teacher did not think it very likely that she would be hired by the firm she wanted to enter. She was also told that she was not suited for the work she wanted to do. The teacher put a fair bit of time into working with that student. In the end the teacher recommended the student to a confection manufacturing firm. However, when the firm indicated it would not cover the commutation costs, the student lost interest and did not apply for the job. Without sitting for any firm's entrance examination the student graduated. Case 27 had wanted to work at a cake shop, but gave up when the school refused to recommend her to an employer in that line of business. She later applied to work in the hotel industry, but was not given an offer.

These were good students who regularly attended class, had solid academic records and evidence that they possessed practical skills and qualifications. They followed the advice given by their teachers. Even though they were fairly proactive, they were nevertheless unable to land a job. It seems likely that each of these young graduates was eager to work, but unfortunately came into a very tight labor market which offered new graduates few opportunities.

Case 28 was drawn from an urban area. She had originally planned to enter a specialist training school, and was late in deciding to look for employment. As a result she was behind in organizing letters of support and in applying for positions. By the time she

Table 5.5: Overview of cases 24–28 and 20

Case Number	24	25	26	27	28	20
Demographic characteristics						
Age	19	18	20	18	19	18
Education	SHSG	SHSG	SHSG	SHSG	SHSG	SHSG
Gender	F	F	F	F	F	F
Geographic region	Tohoku	Tohoku	Tohoku	Tohoku	Kansai	Kansai
Present status	not working	arubaitaa	paatotaimaa	not working	not working	arubaitaa
Situation upon graduation from senior high school						
Shortage of job offers	○	○	○	○		○
Financial situation at home made it hard to continue with education		○	○		○	
Desired career path required more education		○				
Little likelihood of getting into desired position	○		○	○	○	
No pressure to immediately start work					○	○
Poor performance record at school						
Failure to gain support/recommendation of school				○	○	
Had company interview but was not hired	○			○	○	
Not ready for employment and stopped looking				○		

Notes:
SHSG = senior high school graduate
M = male
F = female
Kansai = region including prefectures around the Osaka–Kobe–Kyoto area
Tohoku = the six prefectures constituting Northeast Japan: Aomori, Iwata, Akita, Yamagata and Morioka Prefectures

got into the swing of things, the number of unfilled positions had shrunk considerably.

Case 28 is a good example of how this happens. When a student and those looking after work placements at school cannot agree on a strategy, the teacher takes the student to a Hello Work office (*i.e.*, a Public Employment Security Office or PESO) and actually helps that person to look through the jobs on offer. The relationship between Hello Work offices and the schools varies from one geographic region to another, but the relationship seems to be closest in those areas where job offers are fewest.

Case 28: Female high school graduate aged 28
I really wanted to go to a specialist training school with a program in cooking. However, my parents opposed that. They thought it cost too much...If I really wanted to study cooking, they seemed to be telling me, I should work as a cook's apprentice and figure out a way to get certified as a cook...At the end of my last year I sort of gave up on cooking and changed my work preference. In January and February, just two months or so out from graduation, I was put in a group with other students who couldn't find work. We were all taken as a group to the Hello Work office.

These cases are similar in several regards. Case 25 answered the public advertisement of a hotel, and found *arubaito* there. She had wanted to work as a regular full-time employee, but at PESO she discovered that only a few permanent positions were on offer for those aged under 20. She thus resigned herself to working on a casual basis for the time being. In her final year at school Case 24 lost interest in looking for regular full-time employment: "There was nothing I felt passionate about doing. I had to find out what it is that I want to do. I was also thinking about some kind of course I could take." After graduation she felt the need to have a driver's licence for many jobs, and was taking driving lessons when she participated in this research. Case 26 was introduced by her school to an internship program run by her local government. Using that opportunity, she found work as a part-time office worker. Because she worked only five hours a day, she had her eyes open for other work. At the same time, she liked her work and was inclined to stay there for a while. Case 27 found *arubaito* in a small bakery, but found the early morning schedule too demanding and quit; she was looking for work when this research was conducted. Claiming that she would quit even a regular full-time job if she didn't like the work, Case 28 continued doing the *arubaito* she'd picked up when still in school – working for a *sushi* shop that served its food off a conveyer belt that wound its way along the counter in front of all the customers. Actually, because her mother was not well when we interviewed her, she had just resigned that job to spend more time at home doing housework and otherwise looking after her mother.

The women introduced in Table 5.5 were for the most part taking their *arubaito* seriously. Even Case 27, who had quit her job, was proactively looking for another position.

Case 27: Female high school graduate aged 18
Looking back on my *arubaito* experience, I found the relationships I developed at work to be really important. From when I first started, everyone was helpful and friendly. Although I was given all this work and was causing disruption for other employees, they were really understanding. Over time I came to feel a great responsibility not to let others down. That was a real positive that came out of that work experience.

Tertiary graduates not finding regular full-time employment

Our sample also included *furiitaa* with a tertiary degree who had looked unsuccessfully for regular full-time employment, but had been unsuccessful. Some of them are shown in Table 5.6. First are those in two-year technical colleges and junior colleges. Often their second and final year is taken up in various final year projects and they do not have the "free" time necessary to engage in placement activities. Some (such as Case 30) looked for work within a fairly confined domain defined largely in terms of the industry and occupational referents set by their course of study. She has continued her search for full-time regular employment after graduation: at the time of this study Case 30 was doing *arubaito* in the same field. This was clearly someone intent on a career as a specialist in a designated area.

Case 29: Female junior college graduate aged 24
All of us second-year junior college students were the same – none of us had any time to think about a placement upon graduation. We were just too busy. We all had a graduation project to complete. Because I'm in fashion, my project was to make a piece of apparel. We put on a big fashion show. It takes the whole year to get the production together. Some girls with leisure on their hands might have looked for

work, but it's a big "might". In any case, I wasn't able to get around to the placement activities.

Case 30: Female graduate from a technical college aged 24
We all had our graduation project to do. There was simply no time to think about placement activities and looking for full-time regular work. It wasn't that I didn't want to look for work; I just didn't have the time. As for the employment application form, we all completed one in a rushed manner and sent it off to one of the largest companies to see what would come of it. We all did that for one company. About my future? I occasionally give it passing thought, but nothing in a very careful way.

Case 31: Female junior college graduate aged 24
I was offered two positions while at my JC. I also sat for the public service examination, but I failed to make the grade in the second round. I'm not sure as to which direction I prefer – a private firm or the public service. In any case, it would be good to have a permanent position...I've not done the rounds of the firms. As for the two firms that offered me a position, I had simply responded to an advertisement. One was with an agricultural cooperative; another was for a local credit union.

Cases 29 and 30 found their specialist education program too demanding, the result being that the search for full-time regular employment was postponed. Case 31 was a junior college student, but she had majored in Japanese literature, a course that allowed her time to engage in the standard progression of placement activities. But her close friends at the time were not the type that went looking for work. "When I graduated," she confided, "none of the persons I knew had a full-time position lined up. They were all doing *arubaito*." She believed that would be the normal outcome for girls like herself. Asked about the future, she replied that she was not the type who would get married, have children, and then put them into childcare so that she could work full-time. Her choices would have been informed by this outlook on life, and by the options that similarly placed women would have in contemporary Japan.

Each of these interviewees reported that they were just like their friends in having no time and in not feeling a great sense of urgency to find employment. Basically, they and their friends made the same choices. Although this description might be provided for other graduates, it is clear that this type of young person is heavily

Table 5.6: Overview of cases 29–36

Case Number	29	30	31	32	33	34	35	36
Demographic characteristics								
Age	24	24	24	28	27	24	25	25
Education	JCG	STCG	JCG	UG	UG	UG	UG	UG
Gender	F	F	F	M	M	F	M	M
Geographic region	Kansai	C. reg.	C. reg.	C. reg.	C. reg.	C. reg.	C. reg.	C. reg.
Present status	*arubaitaa*	*arubaitaa*	not working	*arubaitaa*	contracted employee	*arubaitaa*	*arubaitaa*	not working
Situation upon graduation from a tertiary institution								
Decided on occupation and was looking for work		o		o	o	o	o	o
Had other things they wanted to do rather than look for work		o	o	o		o	o	o
Even if they apply, they felt they would not be hired	o	o						
Had personal issues to resolve	o							
Whatever else, did not want to be a salaried employee (*seishain*)			o			o	o	
Classmates are also not employed as *seishain* but are doing *arubaito*	o	o	o					
Too old because of being a *ronin* and taking a year off from university				o				
Taking public service exam			o	o	o			

Notes:
JCG = junior college graduate
STCG = specialized technical college graduate
UG = university graduate
M = male
F = female
Kansai = region including prefectures around the Osaka–Kobe–Kyoto area
C. reg. = Capital region = Tokyo metropolitan area and areas bordering on it

involved with friends and in patterns of mutual interaction which produce similar outcomes for everyone in their peer group.

The second set of graduates in Table 5.6 (Cases 32–36) shows that all have four-year university degrees. Although they engaged in placement activities, none was promised permanent employment. The interviewees claimed they were too selective in wanting to be in particular occupations in a designated industry, thereby seriously limiting their options. However, unlike the less educated tertiary graduates shown in the same table (Cases 29–31), they had not honed in on employment that was closely linked to their major. Rather they had aimed high, trying to enter the public service at a higher level or the Ministry of Foreign Affairs in the hope of seeing service oversees as a diplomat representing Japan. Others had applied to one or more publishing firms in an industry that attracted numerous applicants. The competition to land a position in such industries would obviously be quite tough, resulting in many graduates falling short of their goal (which was to obtain full-time permanent employment).

Case 32: Male university graduate aged 28

I took the Foreign Service exam as a senior in my fourth year at university. Mind you, it was for one of the non-career positions... While I was at uni I took a year off to study for exams. For that reason, I didn't then spend much time looking for a tenured position with a private firm...I was a bit disappointed when I failed to make the Foreign Service after two goes at the exam...Why did I want to become a diplomat? I thought I wanted to do something that would suit me; if I could not find any value in the work I was doing, I think it would be difficult to stick with it...I can think of lots of places I don't know much about; but, for example, take Africa. If I was sent to one of the African countries, wouldn't I be able to learn the language? Having that kind of specialized knowledge: for some reason that appeals to me.

Case 33: Male university graduate aged 27

As for a placement with a company, I thought I'd visit small publishers who made books for specialist audiences. That was my thinking in February or so at the end of my third year...In the end, I applied to about 40 companies all over the place. I had wanted to work in the public sector for a state owned enterprise – all of those enterprises – about 40 in all. Altogether I applied to about 80 companies...[In April I started my fourth and final year.] Throughout the following winter of that year I continued to look for suitable employment. And then in February – less than two months out from graduating – I was still without a job. Nothing! At that point I talked with one of the counsellors in the university's placement office. They got me to start thinking about being a civil servant...Once I had graduated, I started attending a preparatory school once a week in order to study for the public service exam. I knew nothing; I guess I studied there pretty well and then sat for the test to work for one of the local governments. I was considered until the final stage. But I didn't get through the interview. I tripped on the final hurdle.

Case 34: Female university graduate aged 24
I was interested in working for a number of publishers. Because they are so hard to get into, I also found two other positions to apply for – just ordinary administrative work...I thought working for a publisher would bring me into contact with various types of interesting people...It was really just a vague sense I had...I didn't really do much research on publishing firms; it was just that publishing seemed to come as a natural choice...The end result was that it was more like a fantasy that began rapidly to fade in the fall of my final year. Those who really wanted a career in publishing had started much earlier than I to prepare for the round of placement activities. They attended seminars on the publishing industry and studied hard, whereas I did none of those things. It made me wonder whether, compared to the others, I was really committed to having a career in a publishing firm.

Many cases, many reflections: there was, however, an unmistakable interest in finding a position in publishing and /or the public service. Case 32 had travelled overseas for six months while he was a university student. He then took off the entire year without earning any credit toward his degree. Moreover, he had spent two years as a *ronin* in order to pass the university entrance examination. His kind of resume with various interruptions makes it difficult for Case 32 to approach an established firm in the private sector. Case 33 spent a good deal of time thinking about how he could best find employment, which would link him with society. While broadening his outlook he diligently looked for suitable employment. He did not receive an offer because of his shyness and inability to express himself well in the interview. Reflecting on his disappointing performance, he recalled his inability to articulate his views during a discussion of gender-related issues. Although he felt he could sort out the various positions intellectually, he had felt confused emotionally and had clammed up.

Although Case 34 had felt an undefined interest in publishing she soon realized that she would have to compete against others with a more mature interest. Coming to a realization that she was under prepared for the competition, her interest waned and she dropped out of the placement game. She subsequently came to entertain various doubts about her ability to convert her own interests into a passion for a designated work domain.

With graduation and the expectation of work looming on the horizon, another type of student discovers a kind of work which is suited to their aptitude only to find no positions match the work. That type is able to think through their employment options rather carefully and then focus their sights on a defined range of positions in a set industry, but then finds that the jobs and career opportunities do not exist.

Case 35 was concerned with how he would find work that he would be happy doing. As a result, he defined his future options very narrowly during his years as a student. Although he could persuade himself that he was the appropriate person for a certain position, he found that potential employers could not easily be persuaded to hire someone with such narrowly defined interests. He eventually gave up searching for an "ideal" job, and ended up travelling overseas as a means of finding his true inner self.

Case 35: Male university graduate aged 25
My grandmother raised me, and after she died, I started to have this vague sense that I would have to work – to find some kind of permanent employment – once I'd graduated from university...I began to think of all kinds of grand possibilities. I did not feel that I had to enter a large prestigious corporation. I nevertheless began to rethink many of the assumptions I had held while studying at university. I began to think that it would be good to be permanently employed if I could find a position doing work I enjoyed doing. At the time I really liked movies and snowboarding. I sent expressions of interest to a film distributor and to a company selling sporting goods. But that's all I did...A bit later I did the same with a credit card company that provided employees with opportunities to study abroad...The outcome? They were all failures from the start – from when I first sent in my expression of interest. That's when I decided to withdraw from the hunt...I'm completely through looking for that type of employment.

At uni I guess I didn't get any information or advice from the placement office. I went and talked to some companies where some OBs from my university were employed, but I didn't really talk about my options with anyone in concrete terms. Once I lost my interest in finding full-time regular employment, as I mentioned, I looked to something overseas...In my third year or thereabout, I got this urge to travel abroad and spoke with my parents about doing that. If I were to go overseas, they advised, I should take a year off from my university and study in a proper program while abroad. They said something along those lines. I remember thinking, it can't be as easy as that...I began to think, however, that I would go after university. And so I graduated.

In each of these cases we can see young people that are squarely facing the task of making life decisions about their future life course and work career. In this regard, they are free from the pressures or other influences of a peer group. That they did not fully pursue employment by engaging in the various placement activities associated with their last year before graduation can be marked up to the seriousness with which they were confronting the challenges of late adolescence.

In contrast to those types are those who focus wholly on the specifics of the offer by employers: where they will be located geographically, the provisions for pensions and health insurance, the position of the labor union *etc.* They tend not to be concerned with the industry or occupational tasks *per se.* The next case is an example of this type.

Case 36: Male university graduate aged 25
I gained interviews at two companies. I told the head of my university's placement office that I'd be happy to sit for the examination at those two companies since someone in his office had gone to the trouble of making the arrangements on my behalf...As I'd soon be a new graduate, I said I was happy with whichever company they recommended to me. I said I had no real industrial or occupational preference. As I was graduating with a major in mechanical engineering, I was aware of some firms wanting to hire that type of graduate. However, those firms did not appeal to me...Thinking about the type of firm that would appeal to me, I thought first that I wanted a commitment that I could work in the Tokyo area...After that came various fringe benefits. It was important to me that there was a union. I was also concerned that the big four guarantees were in place – employment security, health insurance,

provisions for social welfare and a pension. I simply made tables to
compare working conditions at various firms and was surprised at the
number of firms that were wanting in those regards.

This person did not start placement activities in his third year
because he did not feel he would be ready to graduate at the end of
his fourth year. Instead, he took a year off and then, after returning,
did not approach the placement office until after he knew he would
have enough credits to graduate. Rather late to put up his hand, he
indicated a willingness to take whatever employment might be
available. In the end he was not offered employment by either of
the two companies that interviewed him, and he graduated without
having a position lined up. At that point he did not feel that "the
choice of a particular line of work was very important." Rather, he
decided to experience a range of work assignments as a means of
latching onto a type of work he would really enjoy. This outlook
led him to opt for a series of *arubaito*.

In all of these cases, university students were aware of the
importance of their first full-time regular employment. At the
same time, knowing how this would affect their future each
thought carefully about how to align a career with a broader set of
priorities in terms of their future life course. Because that process
of assessment and reassessment occurred at the same time as they
were engaged in placement activities, companies may have been
put off by what appeared to them to be a wavering commitment
to work.

Following graduation, Case 32 began to study for the exam to
become a certified social welfare consultant. Having achieved that
goal, he had gone to Tokyo to look for work. However, in the process
of looking for work he discovered that even with the qualification
employers felt that he was too old. He then decided to go to another
school and obtain a different qualification.

After graduation Case 33 passed the examination to become a
postal worker, and found work in a local post office. However, he
did not get along with one of his superiors and left after a short
stint. At the time of this study he was studying to become a public
servant while supporting himself by doing *arubaito* for a large
supermarket chain. The corporation had a system in place whereby
casual employees could become full-time regular employees, and
he was considering that as a possible option.

Case 34 had given up on gaining a placement even before she had
graduated, and had gravitated into *arubaito* at a television station

doing work which she thought was interesting. Life as a *furiitaa* was good, but she felt she was not getting enough work and had re-started the process of looking for permanent employment doing office work. Given that she had not found such employment by the time this study was conducted, she had begun to study bookkeeping. With the bookkeeping qualifications she got, she had visited a Hello Work Office hoping to find work. She told herself, "If it's something I really like doing, I'll be all right." At the same time she was still questioning herself as to the work she would really enjoy doing.

After graduation Case 35 saved money while working at a *pachinko* parlour. He then topped up his funds with a loan from his parents in order to go to New Zealand for one year on a working holiday visa. After returning to Japan he found *arubaito* in a restaurant. Although he felt apologetic towards his parents and thought he should be looking for some kind of full-time regular employment, he thought it best to proceed cautiously. "After all," he reasoned, " to rush into such employment and then to be unhappy six months or a year later would only make matters worse." He was still in the early stages of gathering information and assessing the labor market.

After graduating from university Case 36 did *arubaito* in a theme park for nine months. He then worked as a telephone consultant for an internet service provider, and did other odd jobs. Just one month short of his twenty sixth birthday at the time of this study, Case 36 was beginning to feel quite anxious about his future and had sought a permanent position through a Hello Work office set up for young people.

Some reasons for not landing permanent employment

We carefully examined the data for some of the common factors which might explain why students had failed to gain permanent employment even though they had engaged in placement activities at the time they graduated.

A number of high school graduates who had good attendance and solid academic records and who had participated in placement activities did not gain a position owing to the severe contraction in the number of positions available to such qualified graduates. Other students were simply too slow in joining the hunt. Around the time they graduated, some had gone to a Hello Work office only to find the job offers for young persons aged under twenty were very few in number and came with grossly inferior working conditions. Many of these students found *arubaito*, which offered many days of the week and had then continued to work in that job as an *arubaitaa*. There were also some who found work for a limited period in a publicly funded work scheme and who were able to use that experience as a springboard to other work. Many who had not found work after availing themselves of their school's placement program were well motivated to work and carried that willingness into whatever casual work they found.

Many students at junior colleges and specialized training schools with two-year tertiary diploma programs found that they could not complete their graduation project and make a serious effort to look for employment at the same time. Because they had a strong vocational orientation, upon graduation many of them looked for *arubaito* which would allow them to utilize the skills they had acquired, hoping that such work would provide experience leading to full-time regular employment. Others simply sought a full-time position doing office work. At this level, graduates seemed to be rather strongly influenced by the behavior and outlook of their peers. Many were planning eventually to become full-time housewives, and were happy with *arubaito* or other casual employment.

Students at four-year universities had to take much more initiative. Their first challenge had been to narrow their choice to a particular occupation in a specific industry. They know that timing is important because companies stick to a rather tight schedule in order to finish their hiring early each April along with all the other firms. Given the conveyer-like efficiency with which the placement process occurs, many students felt a certain pressure in having to meet the deadlines which punctuated that process while also trying to resolve various questions about their true aptitudes and to decide how best to meld work-life requirements with the other life-course values they had. In that process many lacked practical work experience that might inform their choice of an occupation and an industry in a larger labor market. A number of students were late to graduate and were quite conscious of their age and the questions or doubts employers would have with regard to the extra time they spent as *ronin* either studying to pass an entrance examination or taking a year off from their university studies to travel abroad or to have some other extra-curricular experience. Many in that situation opted to become public servants or to obtain a publicly recognized certificate for some particular occupation. Most were aware that they were seriously disadvantaged, particularly in terms of gaining employment with a good private firm once they had fallen behind in meeting one of the "deadlines" along the way in the employment placement cavalcade as it moved through the academic year toward the inevitable rounds of offers and then the hiring the next April following graduation.

Early separation

It is not unusual to hear about young graduates who get full-time regular employment only to quit their job shortly afterwards and then become either a *furiitaa* or someone who is unemployed. Some of the cases of this type are introduced in Table 5.7.

High school graduates who soon leave full-time regular employment

Lack of preparation for full-time regular employment

Case 37 is an extreme case. Although he found full-time regular employment, he claimed that he was not informed about the welcoming ceremony for new employees, and did not turn up for the event. He then decided not to work at that firm without even bothering to inform his prospective employer of the situation. Case 38 found the work too physically demanding and quit after only four days. Although we were not provided detailed information about the physical demands placed on her, she claimed that they were quite onerous and had prevented her from continuing the work. In both these cases the graduates had quit without really experiencing the work they would have been assigned. While these students certainly came across as being irresponsible, one could also say that their teachers had somehow failed to prepare them for work in the real world which lay beyond the school's gates. Case 37 later went to the Hello Work office, but was afterwards persuaded by her friends to take up work as an *arubaitaa* at a *karaoke* bar. Case 38 said he had "no strong feelings as to whether he did permanent or casual work," and asserted that the main thing is enjoying the work. If one finds work they like, they should consider themselves lucky." He alternated between sometimes actively looking for work and not looking at all.

> *Case 37: Male high school graduate aged 19*
> It's only on Saturday, Sunday and holidays; I chose my current *arubaito* because it is a stress-free happy option...I got into a company, you know! However, I never got the information on the welcoming ceremony. I think it must have been there somewhere, but I don't know.

Table 5.7: Overview of cases 37–46

Case Number	37	38	39	40	41	42	43	45	46
Demographic characteristics									
Age	19	18	19	19	22	24	20	24	19
Education	SHSG	SHSG	SHSG	SHSG	SHSG	SHSG	SHSG	SHSG	SHSG
Gender	M	F	F	M	M	M	M	M	F
Geographic region	Kansai	Kansai	Kansai	Kansai	Kansai	C. reg.	Tohoku	Kansai	Kansai
Present status	*arubaitaa*	not working	not working	*paatotaimaa*	*arubaitaa*	not working	not working	*arubaitaa*	*arubaitaa*
Previous employment as a seishain									
Company type	firm manufacturing machinery parts	printing company	metal wholesaler	Japanese restaurant	Japanese restaurant	construction firm	trucking firm	firm selling auto parts	beauty salon
Length of time with company (months)	less than one day	4 days	2	3	18	5	10	36	14
Reason for leaving full-time employment									
Half-heartedly accepting position at firm	○								
Long hours of work				○		○	○	○	○
Isolated work station				○		○			
Missing the company's entrance ceremony	○								
Conflict with a superior					○	○			
Physical abuse from a superior						○			
Unexpected change in the location of one's work station				○	○			○	○

Feeling that *arubaito* is more enjoyable

Variation in working conditions to what was promised

Excessively favourable treatment for university graduates

Inability to do the work assigned

Given work not suited to one's tastes

Not feeling well physically

Uncertainty regarding the firm's financial viability during a period of restructuring

Disillusionment with the industry as a whole

Notes:

SHSG = senior high school graduate

M = male

F = female

Kansai = region including prefectures around the Osaka–Kobe–Kyoto area

Tohoku = the six prefectures constituting Northeast Japan: Aomori, Iwata, Akita, Yamagata and Morioka Prefectures

C. reg. = Capital region = Tokyo metropolitan area and areas bordering on it

Did the school misplace it? Did I somehow misplace it? I guess there was a phone call from my school. One call from the school,...that was after the ceremony, suggesting that I go in and apologize. But what for? I told the school, "If the job depended on me apologizing for that kind of mix-up, what's the point of working there? If that's the situation and my missing the ceremony is so important, then I'll just quit outright. And I did just that. I quit the company.

Case 38: Female high school graduate aged 18
As graduation approached and then passed, I still had not settled on a job. So I went looking at a Hello Work office. And I found a position. However, once I started work I felt ill. I immediately had this uneasy feeling that I was not meant to be in that job. I started not as a regular employee (*seishain*) but as a trainee on some kind of probation. I would then be judged by someone in the company as being able to do the work or not being so able. I wanted to continue with that company, but somehow just knew it would not work out for me. So I quit and began the search for work all over again. Yes, that's how it was. I only lasted for four days in my first position. Just four days.

Cases where the job content was not appealing
The next case also tells us a story about a school placement that did not pan out. The graduate quit after just two months. Case 39 felt she could not motivate herself to work in an office job looking after sales activities. It is a mismatch that could have been avoided had she visited that kind of work place before agreeing to take the position.

Case 39: Female senior high school graduate aged 19
My job entailed general office work in the sales section...I worked with a computer and answered the phone. And then there were various forms to complete, dispatching merchandise. And lots more...My job was to look after customers...Once I had promised to look after things I could not just get up and leave. Let's face it: I had from early on decided the work was not for me...I told them I couldn't deal with customers – you know, on the phone and that sort of stuff. I said, "This work is stuff I cannot bring myself to do."

Workmates and a change in one's place of work
Case 40 also quit after a short period of work. He worked for three months at a privately owned restaurant. After he started he was shifted to another place of business and asked to look after the

company's live-in accommodation for single employees. He was particularly upset at being removed from his local friendships and having to break off ties he had just formed at work. His reaction to the change in working conditions was to quit. He had been moved to a workplace with few employees that was geographically removed from the close circle of friends he had formed while in school. For many young people such friends have come to be a tremendous source of support. The new place of work did not provide opportunities to develop such ties. From the perspective of many employers the emphasis placed on such friendships is seen as a distraction; many still believe they are free to command totally the hours of labor (including unpredictable overtime) they purchase when they employ a full-time regular employee. To some extent young people are not well prepared to immediately assume the professional posture associated with being a mature-aged skilled employee. At the same time, employers need to be understanding of young people who often feel socially isolated when suddenly thrown into a workplace without others of the same age cohort. This particular case had felt strongly motivated to become a cook since his days in middle school. After quitting the restaurant he found work as a "fish monger" in a large supermarket chain. He still dreams of owning his own eatery.

Case 41 also left his first position after being told he would be deployed to his firm's Nagoya operations. He had decided to apply for the position solely because the firm had a dormitory in which he could live. He worked for the firm for 18 months, but had not thought through the things most important to him. He would later reflect on that fact. When he was told to shift to Nagoya, he suddenly appreciated the freedom of his friends who were doing *arubaito* and still playing in a band. At that point he decided to leave the company. The deployment would have prevented him from seeing his friends. After quitting he was persuaded by a friend to work casually as a guard before again signing up as a *seishain* with a local employer. There he came to be anxious about that company's financial viability and resigned, returning once more to work casually as a guard. However, as his friends began to find full-time regular employment he again questioned his own direction and began for the third time to look for permanent employment.

Case 40: Male senior high school graduate aged 19
Why did I quit full-time regular employment? I was asked to work in the company's dormitory which was at another location...I was

not given a choice, but simply ordered to go...One day I was taken to the store with the lodgings and then simply told to start working there from that day onwards. I felt I was being treated like a piece of luggage. I was surprised and extremely upset...I would no longer be free to enjoy time with my close friends...I was simply told that I would need to break off with my friends. I was being told to go to the other store so that I'd be less distracted from work commitments by my friends. I could not live with that kind of treatment.

Case 41: Male senior high school graduate aged 41
We were told to go to our school on a day during the summer holidays. They said they would be finalizing the list of firms to which we students should be applying. On that day I forgot about the time and slept in past noon. I was phoned by my teacher, Mr. M, and asked what I planned to do...In my case I was told that I was to leave home once I got a full-time regular job. I was told to find employment with a firm that had a dormitory for single males like myself. I therefore told Mr. M that I'd be happy with a firm that had dormitory accommodation for its employees. I was thus assigned by the teachers to employment at a place that had a dorm...Why did I leave the restaurant after only 18 months? I was ordered to work at it's Nagoya shop. Once I verified that I would be transferred to Nagoya, I remember thinking how disagreeable all of that would be...My first permanent job after graduation – I had to think long and hard about it. I was aware that I'd been working there for 18 months. It was just a matter of the point in time that I was to be redeployed to Nagoya. When I was informed about the deployment I knew immediately that I could not go...At about that time I had met a friend whom I haven't seen for some time. He was doing casual work while also following his passionate interests. I thought how lucky he was. So when I was ordered to Nagoya I was extremely upset. My friend was doing *arubaito* and enjoying his life.

Bullying at work
Case 42 did not know what he wanted to do when he graduated from senior high school. Through a family connection he got a job with an engineering and construction firm. However, one of the labor bosses used physical force to discipline him, and that triggered his decision to quit. Also worth considering is the fact that he had no career direction in mind when he accepted the employment. By the time he left the damage had been done, and for a while he was unable to hold a job. Finally he settled into work as an *arubaitaa* in

a rental shop. Feeling he was having some difficulty in dealing with customers, he quit that job, then spent a further period unemployed before getting another casual job stocking shelves. However, he felt he was not getting enough hours of work, so he quit and was unemployed at the time this study was conducted.

Case 42: Male high school graduate aged 24
When people started talk about finding full-time regular employment, I still did not know what I wanted to do. I didn't know how to go about it...I sought advice from my dad, saying I was completely lost in these matters. Given the circumstances he took me around to a friend that ran an engineering company and I was hired...Well, I hung in there for five months. I expected it to be hard and physically draining because that is what work is. I could put up with that. All work is demanding. That's why one gets paid. However, one of the bosses assigned to show me the ropes was over the top. To put it bluntly, he spent a good part of each day beating me up. At times I was kicked. The treatment was beyond what a normal person could reasonably stand. At some point I just decided that I could no longer put up with it psychologically. I should not have to go to work in fear. Once I'd reached that realization, by myself I made the decision to quit.

Long hours of work and work intensification
The long hours of work expected of *seishain* in many of Japan's companies has often been mentioned in the media and by others critical of the way work is organized in Japan. As we can see in the orientation of many *furiitaa*, young people in Japan are finding such hours of work unnecessary. They often have other things they want to do with their time. The intensification of workloads is another matter of concern, and is a practice which young people also tend to view critically.

Case 43: Male senior high school graduate aged 20
I got my full-time regular position at a transport company thanks to the placement office at my school. The company's recruitment information said the position was from 8:30 in the morning until 5:30 in the evening. However, once I was employed they had me coming in from 7:00 until 5:30 or 6:00. As I learned the ropes, I was brought in at 6:00 in the morning...On some days I was required to work back until after midnight. Ten or eleven at night gradually became the norm. Everyday!...I was soon doing 100 hours of overtime each month...In the end, my body couldn't take it anymore, working late

and then getting up early the next day without enough rest. So I quit. Still, everyone else was working those hours so I put up with it as long as I could. But in the end I reached my limits.

The impact of the educational differential

Most work places employ persons who have achieved different levels of education. This is particularly true at firms which are trying to have a more educated labor force. Case 45 was a high school graduate who worked hard to establish himself in the firm. However, after he had gotten on top of his workload, the firm hired a university graduate and had that person do similar work. From the vantage point of Case 45, however, the university graduate was paid considerably more even though he was much less productive. He alleged this was done simply because the other employee had a degree. Case 45 felt this was very unfair. There may have been other factors in the background, but the injustice became a sticking point in this particular situation.

Case 45: Male senior high school graduate aged 24
After working for three years, I began to be acknowledged within the firm. I was promoted to be the assistant pit foreman in the repair shop. However, my pay did not go up accordingly...Maybe it was because of the recession that the firm found it could begin to hire university graduates. Because they could not get into a large prestigious firm, some graduates probably decided to come to work for the likes of our company. However, their monthly salary and the time they started work was quite different from that which us high school graduates got. I saw their payslips. I know. It was clear. They got us to work for a song...I'd worked there for three years. To some extent I'd picked up a number of important skills. I was a pit foreman. I think it's stupid the way they do that...I mentioned it to the head of operations, but he wouldn't talk about it. I talked to his assistant who would only tell me that's how things were. If that was to be my career, I did not want it and quit.

Disillusionment with the work place

There are many other reasons young people become disillusioned at work. Sometimes it is owing to interpersonal conflict among workmates; for others, it is the low level of technology and skill they find at their place of work. That kind of disappointment is not new; however, it is probably true that today more young people are demanding more of their work place and leave when their inferior working conditions fall below some minimum they have in mind.

Case 46: Female senior high school graduate aged 19

I found permanent employment with a beauty salon. I went to a training centre run by the man who ran the salon...I quit the job, but am still going to the training centre. As for the salon, many of the staff there complained that they did not know how things operated on a day-to-day basis, but it was the niggling between staff that made it an unpleasant place to work. In terms of the techniques being used, there was nothing to learn. Those who were there to supervise were full of talk, but when it came to showing us what to do there was very little guidance, and as younger girls we did not have a clue as to what we should be doing.

Tertiary graduates who soon leave permanent employment

The number of tertiary graduates who find permanent employment is also rising. The cases in Table 5.8 provide examples of the categories into which such graduates might be sorted.

An inability to do the work

From his school days Case 47 had wanted to work in the apparel industry, and had vigorously engaged in the full range of placement activities in order to find full-time regular employment. He was hired to work in a company's sales division. Although he threw himself into the work, for some reason he was unable to meet their performance expectations. He lost confidence in his ability to do the work, and resigned after 18 months on the job. It is a commonly accepted view that young employees are being loaded up with responsibilities and heavy workloads, probably a reflection of work intensification across the board, and Case 47 was bothered by the fact that he was inconveniencing his work mates.

Case 47: Male university graduate aged 26

I enjoyed my work, but it was often very difficult. In any case I needed to use all of my physical strength. And it was still hard work. Afterwards, there was just not enough time to sleep...I made mistakes and felt confused. Some of the mistakes resulted in the company losing money. I soon began to wonder why on earth I was doing this work. I'm sure I caused a lot of co-workers to lose sleep over my mistakes. This became a huge dilemma for me...Unable to take the minimal

Table 5.8: Overview of cases 47–51

Case Number	47	48	49	50	51
Demographic characteristics					
Age	26	24	26	25	22
Education	Uni	Uni	Uni	STC	STC
Gender	M	M	M	M	M
Geographic region	C. reg.	C. reg.	C. reg.	C. reg.	Kansai
Present status	*arubaitaa*	vocational training	not working	not working	*arubaitaa*
Previous employment as a seishain					
Company type	apparel trading company	producer of ball bearings	rentals	restaurant food supply company	drafting firm
Length of time with company (months)	12	5	30	4	3
Reason for leaving full-time employment					
Not getting on with a superior	○				
Physical abuse from a superior	○				
Having something else they would rather be doing	○				
Change in working conditions	○				
Inability to do the work assigned	○	○	○		

Given work not suited to one's tastes	○	○
If there is any work I can do I am happy to be employed	○	○

Notes:
UG = university graduate
STCG = specialized technical college graduate
M = male
F = female
Kansai = region including prefectures around the Osaka–Kobe–Kyoto area
C. reg. = Capital region = Tokyo metropolitan area and areas bordering on it

amount of responsibility for my work, I could not work as an adult in society, could I?...I had the feeling that others were conveying this kind of message to me. I too came to believe I could not do the work. I had come to believe I'd never be able to hold down a job. Saying I couldn't do the work meant that I was unsuited for that particular job. However, it got me to thinking that I couldn't do any type of work.

Critical work appraisals

The next case also quit after being severely reprimanded for poor work. More than a few university graduates share similar experiences. Case 48 had majored in engineering and had found permanent employment with a machine manufacturer. He was immediately placed on the shop floor where machines were being made. He knew he would be working there for about one year to gain experience at the bottom end of the organization. However, the graduate had never used machinery and felt a good deal of stress, as though he was a fish out of water. He lasted five months before resigning. It seemed that this employee and his management could not agree on the tasks he should be assigned or on how he should be nurtured within the company. There were obviously individual problems in coming to grips with the way he felt he was being treated on the shop floor. Nevertheless, this case most likely resigned as a result of his work continuously being harshly assessed.

Case 49 reported a similar experience. In other words, he did not measure up to the company's desired level of efficiency in doing the tasks he was assigned. He was berated for forgetting to draw a road on a diagram. He was told that as a regular employee he couldn't hold a light to the many casual employees hired in the same room with him. He was repeatedly warned that the company could not afford to carry full-time regular employees with his poor output and overall laziness. He was constantly reminded how much his salary was costing the firm. "A waste of money" he was told. Many of the young people who had the misfortunate of experiencing this kind of abuse in their first work experience lost the confidence or motivation to apply for further positions once they'd extricated themselves from such an unpleasant situation.

Case 48: Male university graduate aged 25
Although I majored in engineering at university, I had a certain weakness when I finally got hired. Drilling machines. Machining...At university I did research in related fields, but I had no hands-on experience with machines...I was told more things about the machines

than I could possibly remember. It caused me to panic a bit...In that regard I was assigned various types of work...It was hard, it really was. It got so I lost interest in doing anything...In the end I worked in that section for about six months. After only three months I was asked to do overtime. Among the new employees, I was told, I was the only one who refused to do overtime. "Aren't you embarrassed for yourself, letting all your workmates do your work all the time?"...I asked to be transferred to another section, you know...They then suggested that perhaps I wasn't suited for the company's work. It was the company president. At that point they involved my parents. They told my parents that I would eventually be fired if I continued as I was doing. That being the case, I resigned.

Conflict with one of the bosses and intimidation at work
In a number of these sorts of cases, young people came to accept as a reality of life that the less able employees could be physically abused at their place of work. Their only means of protest was to quit. The cases introduced here alleged that such abuse had occurred, and for that reason Case 50 seems to have regretted his decision to accept a position with his first employer. He did not look for another job after quitting; rather, he decided to obtain a different type of qualification.

The cases shown in Table 5.8 are all tertiary graduates who had a strong desire to become full-time regular employees. All were heavily involved in placement activity. Because he had not performed well academically, Case 50 had refrained from using the good offices of his specialized training school. He nevertheless decided to search for work on his own, happy to be a 'jack-of-all-trades' and to do whatever work he could find. The kinds of firm which hire this type of graduate are often firms that have not done so before. They include a range of companies that do not have in place the mechanisms necessary to integrate and nurture such graduates. Often they assign such employees to a section where that are few, if any, similarly educated individuals. It seems to be the situation that those responsible for the day-to-day running of such work sites have expectations of the new recruit which are at odds with those of the new employee himself, and there is often an assumption that those new to the firm should have to put up with overly harsh demands. Perhaps this is a generation gap. In any case, Japan has moved on, and its younger generation has grow up with an affluence and a world view which were unimaginable by those who are one or two generations older and now in positions of authority at the shop floor level.

Case 50: Male graduate of a specialized training school aged 25
I had three early offers of employment...I chose a firm in the
restaurant and outside functions industry – an area in which I'd
had experience doing *arubaito*. The work actually overlapped with
the work being done by *arubaitaa*...Every aspect of service was
imprinted on our minds, just as it was when I was doing *arubaito*...
We were thoroughly briefed on how to treat our customers and in
the preparation of food. In a general way we were exposed to all of
the firm's on-the-ground operations. However, I did not stay long.
The training part of my employment was quite satisfactory, but I felt
physically intimidated. The store manager used physical violence
against me whenever he felt I was not doing things properly. Those
higher up in the company used a kind of psychological strategy of
abuse to get me to believe or think in certain ways.

Insufficient mental preparation for work

Case 51 was also the graduate of a specialized training school
who had found permanent employment upon completion of his
studies. He too quit after only 2–3 months with the company. In his
case, however, the reason for quitting was not in workplace issues,
but in a more fundamental mismatch between the very activity of
work and the kind of lifestyle he imagined for himself. In other
words, before entering the labor force, he had not resolved within
himself a number of issues which would arise doing any job.

Case 51: Male graduate of a specialized training school aged 22
There was also the fact that the whole work scene was not my
thing. Thinking back, it was probably an immaturity on my part. In
addition, I am now in a band; I guess that is what I really wanted to
be doing. Somehow, being a *furiitaa* seemed to be a more natural or
convivial lifestyle for me. I first became involved in the band at the
end of my studies at the college. I guess there was no flexibility with
full-time regular employment. I could only have the one day off each
week – Saturdays. In these circumstances there was just not enough
free time to practise with the band.

Work became more and more of a burden, and a little voice inside
me kept saying 'Not yet!"...As graduation from my training school
grew nearer, I simply thought it would be all right to follow along with
everyone else and get a job. I guess I thought my music...would fit in
around it...But already I was wavering. Should I become a full-time
regular employee and keep to that employment, thereby being seen

as a fully fledged adult member of society? At the same time, I kept wondering, isn't there something I really WANT to being doing.

The driving force behind the early resignations

In the preceding sections the presentation highlighted a number of cases sorted by their level of education. Nevertheless, across the board there seems to have been an intensification of workloads in an increasingly competitive economy where many managements seem pressured to squeeze as much a possible from their workforce. (On this point, see *Rodo Seisaku Kenkyu-Kenshu Kiko* 2004b: 6). The number of young people who are leaving high pressure work situations is significant. When they lose confidence in their ability to work after being severely reprimanded or being exposed to the work habits of an older generation that had emerged from a tougher work oriented environment, they get the message from management and resign for ostensibly private reasons rather than being fired. They know that having a firing on their employment record would surely undermine any future efforts they might make to secure a better job.

Beyond education and permanent employment

After dropping out from an educational institution or after quitting their first full-time regular employment, many of the cases in this study do not attempt to secure permanent employment as *seishain*. Rather, they drop out of the labor force or they drift into casual employment. A closer look at such cases will provide further clues as to some of the barriers which make the school-to-work transition so hard for many young persons. The preceding sections conveyed a picture of why young people leave school and do not seek permanent employment. Here we shall consider the comments of those who quit full-time regular employment and do not seek such employment with another firm.

The limited number of positions for *seishain*

The first reason given for not attempting to find another position as *seishain* is that the number of such positions on offer has shrunk considerably since the bursting of the bubble and the onset of the Heisei Recession in the early 1990s. Many of the cases we interviewed believed they would never be hired, even if they tried. The reason they gave for having little chance of being so employed was that they did not have enough knowledge and/or experience.

The scarcity of job offers and the unlikelihood of being employed
Most of the interviewees stated that they had looked at fliers with job advertisements that had come in the newspapers and that they had been to a Hello Work office (*i.e.*, PESO). Often they reported that the conditions offered were not good enough or that they could not meet the desired standards. It appears that this is seen by these young people as being a barrier. In our study this was particularly so among new graduates from senior high schools in Japan's regional or rural areas.

Case 24: Female senior high school graduate aged 19
I'm not doing anything at the moment. I am, however, looking for work. Going to one of the Hello Work offices...Looking at a screen on a desktop computer, we go about looking for job offers.

Case 25: Female senior high school graduate aged 18
Although I didn't have a permanent position upon graduation, I did, however, find one shortly afterwards. I had gone around to the Hello Work office, and I could see that they wanted someone aged over 20...My parents had told me their view that it would be good if I could find a permanent position sometime before I turned 20.

Case 41:Male senior high school graduate aged 22
I was so surprised when my friend suddenly told me he'd found a position. I decided to go myself each day to the office for Employment Security. I thought I'd then and there be able to decide on one of the jobs being offered...I couldn't quit the next job I had. So I wanted permanent employment that would not be too taxing: something I could do for the nest of my life. Somewhere that I could be left to do my own thing. I'd worked in rather disciplined situations before. In those sort of big places, however, one needs qualifications. Even if I applied, I'd not get an interview.

Insufficient skill levels and inexperience
The first thing that firms look at on a resume is skills and experience. Case 45 had wanted to obtain a certificate for being an interior co-ordinator. Case 41 had thought of sitting for a license to drive large vehicles. However, both felt it would be hard to get the requisite

qualification, and both concluded that they'd find it hard to get work without experience even if they had the necessary certificates or licenses. Case 30, with a diploma from a specialized technical college, believed her age would count against her as a woman without any real experience working in an office environment.

Case 45: Male senior high school graduate aged 24
Well, for me it's sort of like wanting to be an interior co-ordinator. If I could do that I'd be sort of happy. I thought when I quit my first permanent job that I'd kind of move in that direction. However, because I wasn't licensed, the gap in my CV sort of stood out, and I couldn't get beyond that...And I had no relevant experience...Even me,...I could do the test to get certified as an internal co-ordinator. I guess I sort of regret it – I should have got the necessary qualifications much earlier...Something in furniture, something in that area. I thought I might have a go in manufacturing furniture...I went to several firms, but because I had never used any of the machinery or automated tools, I sort of didn't get past first base.

Case 41: Male senior high school graduate aged 22
In my situation I'd like to do something in the delivery business, even if it's a small firm. However, when I looked into things there was nothing. For the time being, I'm left looking at things in that way. I look at the work I want to do, but there's no positions. I've gradually come to accept that and continue to look. I'd like to get a license for driving large vehicles, but I don't have the necessary money. But even if I get the income to drive a large vehicle, it won't mean much without three years of experience. That means they won't hire you even for the larger vehicles unless you've got the experience.

Case 30: Female graduate of special technical college aged 24
I want to find work as a sound and image specialist. I've applied for over 30 jobs so far. I've been to an interview for less than 20 of those, but definitely over ten. The major reason that I've not been successful is that I have no experience. And then there's my age. For women, 23 or 24 is about it. I'm 24.

When it comes time to select a senior high school, Case 45 wanted to go to an industrial arts high school. However, his parents and teacher talked him into going to a generalist academic high school, and, upon graduation, he got a job he did not like. Unemployed at the time of this study, he felt that without any tangible skills he was facing a brick wall. He regretted his choice of a secondary school, and felt his life had ended on his first day in senior high school. All he was left with was a nagging appreciation of the importance of having a skill. Aware of how difficult it is to acquire new skills and regretting his past educational choice, he was finding it difficult to motivate himself at the time we interviewed him.

Mental preparation

Some of the cases mark up the failure of their employment applications for another position to inadequate mental preparation and to a failure of nerve.

Case 2: Male middle school graduate aged 22

I had wanted to work as a *seishain*. However, I did not have the necessary drive. I came to feel strongly that I was not cut out to be that type of person. I took up the suggestion of a relative to apply to a hotel chain and even got an interview. However, I was unable to convey the necessary amount of enthusiasm in the interview, and lost out at that stage in the hiring process...I don't think I'm a boring person, but I must come across in the interviews as a disinterested applicant. There is something missing – I just don't have that kind of fire or energy inside me. I guess I'm just not ready to work all-day and late at night like a *seishain*.

Long stints doing *arubaito* are seen by many as a minus

Some cases reported that their long experience as an *arubaitaa* had been evaluated negatively by prospective employers. The next case seemed to be thinking of working as a *seishain* doing office work, but believed her work experience in a coffee shop would be viewed negatively by most employers. She was swayed by those misgivings, and concluded she had no chance to become a *seishain*.

Case 29: Female junior college graduate aged 24

I want to be employed as a full-time regular employee. But that's not possible...The image associated with work in a coffee shop is not an altogether positive one when it comes to applying for permanent employment...Older people associate it with the sex industry. That's what people tell me. They say, "It's better not to mention that sort of work in your interview." That's what they say about *arubaito* in a coffee shop...Next is saying you've been a *furiitaa* for 4–5 years. If it's for one year or so, one can think of various reasons why one did such work, can't they?

Having no employment record as a *seishain*, having no tangible skills or practical experience, working as an *arubaitaa* – these traits are often negatively evaluated by prospective employers. Once the young people discussed in this section became aware of that fact, they concluded they would be severely disadvantaged in the labor market and gave up any hope of becoming a *seishain*.

Some positives about being a casual employee

Some young people see considerable merit in being casually employed, and for that reason do not apply for a permanent position. Here it is important to remember that casual employees and full-time employees often work side by side in Japan, and the former often come to have a good appreciation of what it means to be a *seishain*. First, they learn that *furiitaa* have work and an income. At the same time they also learn that they have much more free time with shorter hours of work, and that means they have much more opportunity to do the things they want to do. They often feel a certain lightness or cheerfulness at work with other casual employees. They can work hard all day knowing they will leave at 5:00 in the afternoon. Many can give examples of how they do better income-wise as well.

Having many job opportunities

There are many more openings for casual work than for full-time regular employment. In many cases, *furiitaa* learn of new job opportunities through their network of friends. Often they take up employment because a friend is also working for the new employer. Often the arrangements are made informally without a formal test or interview. Because their friend is already known to the employer, it is easy for the employer to go along with the advice of an employee who he already knows. The employer knows that he is free to let either go if they are unhappy with their performance. For the *furiitaa* as well, there is a sense of security in being able to work next to a friend without feeling the anxiety or stress that goes with entry into an unknown work place:

> *Case 37: Male senior high school graduate aged 19*
> When I was looking for work, I was persuaded by a friend to work as an *arubaitaa* with him. For the time being I am happy doing *arubaito*…It's now been four months doing *arubaito*, and I've decided to stay with it.

Case 41: Male senior high school graduate aged 22
For the first 3 or 4 months after quitting my first position, I sort of lounged around...Anyway I had this friend's phone number and rang him, I told him I was just cooling out a bit. He told me I should go work with him, which I did. As guardesmen we one day took a light truck and drove to X city. Should we have done it? Should we have not done it? But we did it; in a light truck.

Case 29: Female Junior college graduate aged 24
I got my *arubaito* through my friends. One friend asked me: "Do you know if there is someone to give us a hand?" That's about it. Every now and then a friend asks and sometimes I can help out.

For some entry into life as a *furiitaa* is just a natural extension of having on-going casual employment:

Case 17: Male graduate from a special high school aged 19
I did absolutely nothing to find full-time regular employment. I just thought I would go on with the *arubaito* I began while in school. I've kept at it even after finishing school.

Case 18: Female high school graduate aged 20
About half of my friends got full-time employment upon graduation... They simply stuck with the *arubaito* they'd been doing from long before while still in school. They didn't feel the need to do anything else.

For these young graduates who do not become employed as full-time regular employees, a range of employment opportunities exists. Local governments, schools and various other special bodies formed for that purpose assist them in finding work for the short-term. When these bodies are informed about such opportunities, they often pass on the information directly to the young people wanting more work. As these bodies are close to the ground, those who are *furiitaa* or want to be *furiitaa* feel little resistance to asking them for help. In this regard, there is the same sense of trust or security that is felt when these young people go to work with a friend. These types of organization are likely to continue into the future as important bridges into the labor force. However, to enhance the effectiveness of such organizations in helping young persons who shy away from publicly advertised positions, it would probably be useful for the relevant policy-making agencies of the government to take positive steps to assist these organizations in fulfilling their role.

Case 20: Female senior high school graduate aged 18
Y Senior High School has a program to support students who want to further their education. The teachers would find *arubaito* for you. If you did well at the *arubaito*, they'd think of you after you graduated. If a similar job became available, they'd let you know. As a result, I think it is easy to get stuck into *arubaito* on an on-going basis before realizing it.

Happy with *arubaito*

In opposition to the view of Case 20, others are quite positive about maintaining an *arubaito*-style approach to their life course. A number of those who participated in our study indicated that the kind of work they wanted to do was only available on a casual basis. They might argue that their chosen field was easier to enter from the casual labor market. Examples might be work in a theme park or in the fashion industry.

Male university graduate aged 36
I had wanted to work at S Theme Park ever since its establishment...I stopped looking for full-time regular employment because I was able to continue doing *arubaito* at the theme park. Actually there were two jobs I wanted to do that weighed up equally. While I wanted to do this job, I also wanted to do the other one. For that reason, I thought I should try out the other employer first before making up my mind...So, well, that's how it started. Basically I had extra time on my hands. Offered both positions, I figured I'd be able to fill up each day by doing both jobs. Even if there is other work to be done, at home for example, I'll stay with my *arubaito* because I've been doing it for some time.

Case 18: Female high school graduate aged 20
I liked the work I had done in clothing. In sales...Because I heard from another girl working in a clothing shop that the company she worked for would not come to my school to recruit students...so I went to that firm and asked if I could work there – not as a regular employee, but just as a casual while I was still young. That was about it.

Case 23: Male senior high school graduate aged 21
I wanted to work in the apparel industry. How can I put it? In a department store. Something like that. I wanted to do *arubaito* in that sort of place. I would like to work as a permanent employee, but I don't think that's possible. I guess I mainly just want an income. So

now I'm working in a shoe store, and looking for work somewhere in an apparel firm.

Enjoyable *arubaito* and a good income
Some of the young people in our study felt they were having a good time and earning sufficient income as an *arubaitaa*. Many young people know, or have heard from the media that this type of *arubaito* often puts one in an interesting or stimulating work situation. They know that they will be able to work alongside others of a similar age. They believe they will be able to work things out so they will be working with a friend. They know there's a good chance they will be doing work that they like doing. As for their wages, they know their total wage package will be smaller than that of the *seishain*, but they also know that they will work shorter hours and not be ordered to do overtime at the whim of some manager: overall the life of the *furiitaa* was not seen as a bad or excessively harsh way of getting on in the world.

Case 34: Female university graduate aged 24
When I started my *arubaito*, I thought I would for the time being become a *furiitaa*...I began my *arubaito* from January in my final year at university – just three months before I graduated. I did back-up work for a TV station. It was a bit of everything...Yes, it was an appealing job – the kind that many others would love to do. I even had the chance to meet some of the big talent stars. However, because I'm in charge of managing the flow of information to the media, I don't get to meet too many entertainers...It's a fun job!

Case 12: Female dropout from a specialized training school aged 20
I started doing my first *arubaito* at a restaurant. In the beginning I struggled to get along with everyone...But I hung in there. Once I got used to the work and the people, I came to understand how good the others who worked there really were, and I really began to enjoy working there...And from there it got even better. Even when I got really tired, I was able to push myself through the shift because the others were there supporting each other. I've not thought it was particularly hard work just because I'm an *arubaitaa*.

Case 03: Male senior high school dropout aged 17
I work as a casual for a *sushi* shop. Thinking only about the present, the money from my *arubaito* is good. To find a permanent position would mean slightly better wages, but if I continue as I'm doing and

the hourly wage rate improves, working as an *arubaitaa* is better. I get a bit less overall, but more on an hourly basis.

Case 22: Female senior high school graduate aged 19
Everyone keeps telling me, "If you're going to work, do it properly as a *seishain*. Work at a place where you are covered properly by the firm's insurance policy." However, if I were to be a *seishain*, I'd get 100,000 yen a month. As a *furiitaa* I'd receive over 200,000 yen and can pay for my own insurance. I tell all of those people that I'm happy just as I am.

A Future Career, Other Activities and *Arubaito*

Arubaito as a step to one's future career
Some young people choose to do *arubaito* not for the money or the lifestyle. It not only brings joy to one's present existence, but can also serve as an investment for the future. *Arubaito* is for many only a step on the way to achieving something grander. Case 33 aimed to sit for the public service exam and become a public servant, but has also taken an internal examination for promotion to the status of *seishain* at the supermarket where he is currently working. Case 44 wants to become an industrial consultant; to meet one of the criteria to be so certified he has purposely taken on casual work as a temp with a dispatch firm in order to gain office experience. In addition, he did other *arubaito* in order to save money so he could attend the necessary school to pass the written public service exam. In order to attain that kind of goal, many young people do *arubaito* and find employment that does not require them to become *seishain*.

Case 33: Male university graduate aged 27
I quit work only to fail the public service exam...Twenty-nine is the cut-off age for sitting the exam. I have two years to go and will do my best to pass it before I'm 29. In order to live, some kind of work is necessary. I am currently working at XYZ Company as a *paatotaimaa*...It would be great if I can make it into the ranks of the public service. That would be my most preferred outcome. However, even if I don't make it, I can still apply where I now work to be moved from my part-time status to that of a fully-fledged *seishain*...I have to take a test for that kind of promotion. It's an extremely fair system...If I fail that, I can always try again in six month's time. Taking two exams for that company each year, I reckon, it might take 3–4 years to get that kind of promotion, because people do fail that test each year.

Companies are doing things differently now, and the transition from a casual to a permanent labor status is increasingly being recognized. If I am successful in making that transition, my self-confidence will also be restored.

Case 44: Female university graduate aged 27
...at the time the only body approved by the Ministry of Labor to certify one as an industrial counsellor was the Industrial Counsellors Association (*Sangyo Kounseraa Kyokai*)...To gain its accreditation, some amount of experience as an adult member of society is necessary. At that time I didn't think of it as volunteer work; I believed that I'd have to be employed on a full-time basis to do things concerning psychology. I needed the money. While I was doing *arubaito* counselling at a cram school, I reached the point where I said I would obtain full-time regular employment. At that point I learned from a personnel manager's point of view that it would be difficult to convert my employment status from that of a casual to that of a permanent employee and that I'd need more experience in society. I thus decided for the time being that I would work as a temp with a personnel dispatch company. It also allowed me to save money, so I decided on the spot that I would do just that.

Some of the female participants in this study believed they would soon marry and become full-time housewives. They saw little merit in putting themselves through the hassle of securing full-time regular employment.

Case 18: Female senior high school graduate aged 20
I was also thinking that *arubaito* would be fine. I won't be working forever, I was thinking two years of *arubaito* and then marriage and work as a full-time wife.

Combining *arubaito* with other activity
Some cases choose to do *arubaito* because it allowed them to pursue other interests. For some like those who were able to be in a band, the other activities represented a future career choice. Others wanted a free go time-wise to care for other members in their family, such as an ill or elderly person.

Case 37: Male senior high school graduate aged 19
As I've been able to be in a band, avoiding full-time regular employment was a good choice for me.

Case 30: Female graduate of a special technical college aged 24
When my mother became ill and had to be hospitalised, out of the
blue my father told me to stop working...I left the workforce for about
one year during which time I did no work at all...My mother was not
in the hospital for such a long time, but it was stressful as she was
unable to work or to look after the household properly.

Attitudes toward permanent employment and work

Gaining occupational skills and certification
A good number of respondents felt they needed to acquire or further
upgrade their skills in order to be seriously considered for a *seishain*
position. In order to do so, many felt they needed to go to a specific
type of school or training centre.

Case 34: Female university graduate aged 24
Because I just couldn't firm up a position, I decided I needed to
acquire a specific skill, and started to study bookkeeping...I took
the second-level test, but failed. I then attempted both the first-level
and the second-level test together...I passed the first-level test, and
then thought I'd better look for work. At that point I went to a Hello
Work office.

Case 32: Male university graduate aged 28
I was not particularly interested in pensions when I decided to study
for becoming a social insurance and work consultant (*sharoshi*).
However, to become qualified as a lawyer one now needs to go to a
law school. I was told all about the ins and outs of doing that. I came
to feel that even the qualification to become a solicitor (*shiho shoshi*)
was beyond me, so I was easily led to conclude that becoming a work
and society adviser would be one way to proceed.

Case 02: Male middle school graduate aged 22
It was just when Ohira Mitsuyo's book[1]. appeared. [She was able to
leave behind her life amongst the yakuza and become a lawyer.] I
was so impressed by her book. I concluded that even without a very
impressive education I'd be able to work somewhere in the legal field if
I only obtained the right credentials. I then decided to pursue a career
in that direction...And so I started to study on my own while doing
arubaito. However, I could not continue the study. My parents told me
to get serious and get a job, and I had to give up that plan.

A period to recover one's confidence and rethink the options
For some the problem is not a lack of skills; rather it is the loss of confidence to front up and go through the rigors of applying for a position and then to be interviewed. Some in this category had previously been employed in a regular full-time position, but then had a psychologically damaging experience.

Case 42: Male senior high school graduate aged 24
There are several blanks in my employment record. For example, following my work with customers, I took some time out from working altogether. About 9 months I think...I did nothing. Let's see. What did I do during that period? I guess I just puttered about doing things at home...It was a period of self-doubt.

Case 47: Male university graduate aged 26
I guess my present situation evolved out of doing *arubaito*. I lost confidence that I'd be able to function as a *seishain*, and that's when I stated to do *arubaito*. At first I worked for two months in a factory. There was a sign-up system, and I was introduced to the factory where I did that *arubaito*. Anyway, I think it was about two months.

Case 07: A middle school male graduate aged 24 who had earlier dropped out and then managed to graduate from senior high school
I found an *arubaito* in the removal business through a flier that somehow came my way. Mansions and apartments. I did that *arubaito* for about one and a half years, maybe two...I saw it in *Furomu A* [a magazine listing employment opportunities]. I don't like being tied down, and was attracted to that *arubaito* because I could put together my own schedule...I liked being able to do the work by myself. I could think about all kinds of things while working. Thinking back on it, I am grateful for the opportunity it gave me to do that.

These cases told about lacking skills and confidence, and using the time as a *furiitaa* or in staying out of the labor force and spending a period of time to acquire a recognizable skill or to regain their confidence. The respondents saw this period of preparation as being necessary in terms of their effort to overcome the 'employment hurdle' and to think of becoming a *seishain* doing work that they themselves would feel comfortable doing. They all placed a value on working, but wanted to do work which would allow them to express their inner selves. Many, however, said they were not ready just yet to apply for permanent employment as *seishain*.

Indecision as to whether to do any work

Several cases fit into another category for persons who have a broader problem with work as a social activity. Their issue is not with finding a suitable position in terms of skills or confidence. It is not that they have stopped looking for work altogether, but their heart or full energy seems not to be in the effort. They seem lost and out of touch in some way. They are hesitant to move into the labor force, and it is as though they need a push from behind to get going.

Case 14: Male high school graduate aged 19
I have looked for work. I talked directly on the phone. It had something to do with roof repair...I liked the idea that the work was outside. I also applied to be a carpenter. However, without an apprentice's certificate, that was out of the question.

Case 31: Female junior college graduate aged 24
I am thinking that I want to work, but when it comes to the crunch, I just cannot do it...Is it something inside me? Is it breaking into a new situation that made me freeze? I just get so nervous about having to face those kinds of challenges. That's also true of going to a Hello Work office. I just can't get up even to applying for a job...I get scared just thinking about going to work...Because I've only had experience with *arubaito*, I simply could not manage a full-time regular position as a *seishain*.

Reasons for never becoming a *seishain*

We have looked at some of the reasons given for not seeking full-time regular employment after leaving school and/or permanent employment. One factor to consider is obviously the contraction in the number of permanent positions on offer. Even when positions are available, in a tighter labor market employers are more demanding, and the bar is often set at a level above that which many young aspirants can achieve. The hiring standard is set in terms of skills, technical knowledge and experience. There is also a perception that some young people do not have the right attitude, and a belief that time spent doing *arubaito* is seen as a negative by many employers.

There is, however, also the established view that the *arubaito* done by non-*seishain* contributes to the development of good work habits in at least two ways. First, because casual work opportunities are plentiful and hiring often occurs in a fairly informal manner, many young people can find work where friends will also be working. This and the relative absence of complicated application forms and interviews allows many to easily enter the labor force and to work without the burden of daily stress and other psychological pressures. Moreover, there now are a number of support organizations that can introduce young people to relatively short fixed-term positions. These are bodies that actively invite young people into the work force and then provide invaluable back-up support. A second consideration here is the range of available *arubaito* that allows many to work in the areas in which they want to be. Working in a theme park or experiencing the fashion industry are ready examples. A good many who find such work are then able to join their employer's permanent staff. With these benefits in the background, many *arubaitaa* find their work enjoyable and relatively stress free while also taking home a satisfactory income. Their joy at work often comes from the fact that their *arubaito* is in a work place that is cheerful and allows them to be with others from the same age group. Those in the mass communications industry often reported having the additional bonus of being able to meet interesting people and being in an intellectually stimulating situation. Many feel that their lower wages are offset by the fact that their hours of work fall far short of those worked by the *seishain* and that they had more control of the times they worked without sudden or unreasonable demands being put on them.

In addition, a good many *furiitaa* chose casual work as an intermediary and short-term means to a long-term goal, or as a flexible way of engaging in other activities that were also seen as being important. There were also some informants who still aspired to being *seishain*, and could be said to be "in waiting" as they sought to add to their profile of skills. Still others were recovering from a bad experience in their first position as a full-time regular employee. And there are a few who are agoraphobic or otherwise need to deal with a certain discomfort they feel in a social interaction that is required in most work situations and even in the process of finding and applying for work. They too need a bit more encouragement.

The variety of complications slowing the transition

This chapter has surveyed many factors affecting the transition of young people into permanent full-time employment. A few of these are mentioned in the remaining paragraphs of this chapter.

Leaving the education system

The first signs of difficulty facing many young people appear when they leave the school system without completing senior high school. Several factors increase the likelihood of this happening. First is the pull of an inner group of friends, some of whom may already be outside the school system. Peer pressure often shifts the student's attention from academic activity to socializing, often in ways that keep them out late at night and make it difficult for them to get up in time for school each morning. Along with this is an attitude that is resentful of the regulations imposed by many schools in Japan. For many young people dropping out or not progressing to senior high school is a way out, an "escape to freedom". Those who feel compelled to stay at school often underachieve. There is a second type consisting of those who do not develop such friendships, and remain at school as conspicuous loners. Finally, a small number of students perform well academically, but then find themselves unable to link that outstanding achievement to a viable image of the future.

After leaving school the first type often finds casual employment to earn the spending money they need for their socializing. Many find work through contacts that their friends have in the labor market. However, many of this type find even those work requirements overly binding and take up a relatively undisciplined lifestyle. Having time with their friends often becomes the focus of their life as they move from one casual job to another. School leavers in the other two categories often did not find work immediately. Many were intent on pursuing a focused interest – some in music, others in agriculture or in activities that will, in their eyes, allow them to realize their own potentialities. Often without experience and a clear-cut set of occupational skills, many are self-conscious and not confident as to how they should best make their way in the labor market.

Those who drop out of the tertiary education system also deviate from the normal path for transition. One type of tertiary dropout struggled in secondary school, and is probably not suited for further study. Nevertheless, for various reasons they may have felt compelled to go on. A second type had the clear expectation that they would progress through their tertiary studies, choose the right major, and then find full-time regular employment. However, after entering the tertiary system, they became disillusioned with the overall quality of their education or for other reasons lost interest in campus life and dropped out. Those in a third group come out of an overly regimented environment where the path has always been laid out before them. Out of that environment they have difficulty dealing with their newly found freedom and the relative absence of such structures for tertiary students.

After leaving their tertiary institutions, these former students often drift from one casual job to another. Many do *arubaito* with the view to trying a range of jobs and settling on one that might most appeal to them. A good number attend specialized schools to acquire new skills and start out in a new direction.

A large number of *furiitaa* in our study had graduated from a tertiary institution, but were not looking for permanent employment. Some had come to the realization that they would not have enough credit to graduate, and devoted their energies to getting those credits rather than to engaging in placement activities. With a less structured approach to placement at many tertiary institutions, many students were left not knowing how to take the initiative to find employment upon graduation. Some purposely chose to do *arubaito* because it offered the opportunities to work in an area of interest doing things of interest. Still others had decided to become *ronin* and study for examinations that would lead to further education or to a position in the public service, only to later change their minds and take up *arubaito* while they contemplated another direction.

Those not able to find a position

Some *furiitaa* had engaged in all the right placement activities only to end up without an offer of full-time regular employment when they graduated from their senior high school. Again, the declining number of job offers stands out in the background. This was particularly true in the prefectures of the Tohoku region in Northeast Japan. One interviewee had collected all of the relevant company data and had a solid academic record in information systems, but was nevertheless still unable to secure a position. The labor market in rural Japan has changed radically over the years. At the same time, urban markets have also tightened for new graduates, and those with poor academic records and many absences will also find that many doors to full-time regular employment are closed. Those who came late to placement activities or missed them completely in their efforts to pass an entrance examination for further education often found that there were few opportunities for full-time regular employment even at their local Hello Work office.

Similar cases at the tertiary level

Many students at two-year junior colleges and specialized training schools found the demands of doing a graduation project too demanding, leaving little time to participate adequately in placement activities. Most want to find employment that would allow them to utilize the skills they acquired at their college. They entered *arubaito* in an area in which they had training and continued to look for a more permanent position. Other students graduate from programs that do not provide good hands-on experience. Such graduates do not necessarily have a strong drive to do the specialized work for which they have been trained, and simply look for general office work. However, only a few are able to find full-time regular employment. These types seem to be heavily influenced by school friends and others in their peer group.

The situation at four-year universities is even looser, and tertiary students are much more on their own that secondary students when it comes to finding employment. Many find it difficult to link in concrete terms their rather abstract studies with on-the-ground employment. Many are aware of the importance of the employment round – a cycle which results in all firms going through roughly the same procedures at the same time. Students who become "out of sync" with the cycle often miss out altogether. For various reasons some students fall off the "placement wagon". At that point they may have a good idea of the occupation and industry toward which they want to gravitate. However, without the appropriate experience they are unable to navigate their way through the labor market. Some interviewees in our study felt they had disqualified themselves because they had "lingered" too long on the way to university graduation. "Lingering" included the extra year off qualifying for the university of their choice, and the year off from university studies to travel abroad. Some did both. By doing so some were just unlucky to have entered the labor market when it was most depressed, often finding that there had been more openings the year before.

Early retirement from one's first position

There is another type of *furiitaa* – those who make the transition into full-time regular employment upon graduation only to quit their company shortly afterwards. Senior high school graduates who did so included (i) those would not prepare adequately for the rigors of full-time regular employment, (ii) those who found they could not bring themselves to do the work required, (iii) those who felt they were unreasonably relocated to another office or factory in a less convenient location, and (iv) those who found the intensity of the work too great, or glaring inequalities in the work place and/or other shortcomings that would lead to an overall disillusionment with the place of work (or the industry overall).

Tertiary graduates often found they were unable to perform in line with their employer's expectations. Some were asked to resign by their employer. In some cases, the problem originated because a firm was not used to hiring such graduates and did so with expectations that they could be treated like other employees straight out of school. In other cases they expected them to be exceptionally different from their less educated workmates. Some tertiary graduates were asked to assume too much responsibility because the firm was unable to hire enough personnel overall and everyone was being pushed to the limit just to keep the operations going. Indications point to the fact that the output expected of all employees in Japan has risen over time as competition in the economy heightens in the wake of globalisation. This is, in a sense, a change which is beyond the control of young people coming into the market. Rising separation rates among recently employed staff is not a cause of this problem; rather, it is a symptom of a larger transformation that is under way at work. From the point of view of the individuals involved, the problem lies in how best to find another full-time regular position after they have lost confidence in their ability to do the work of the *seishain* employees.

Non-*seishain*

Some young people do not find employment as *seishain* and continue to live outside the labor force constituted by salaried employees. We can identify four reasons for this. First, reflecting larger structural changes, good positions for graduates are drying up, and the competition for the remaining positions is much stiffer than before. This is particularly true in Japan's rural areas. Second, once into an *arubaito*, some young people see the pluses of casual employment and lose interest in full-time regular employment even if such positions become available. Being a *furiitaa* gives one more opportunities to work with friends in a congenial atmosphere. Moreover, some forms of work – such as in a theme park or in selling fashion goods – come only as *arubaito*. In addition, the pay is not necessarily bad, especially on an hourly basis, and the work can be fun. Third, there is recognition that some casual employment can serve as a useful stepping stone to a future career – partly in terms of the experience it affords and partly in terms of the free time it allows casual employees to explore and to develop special interests. Fourth, casual employment provides the breathing space necessary for some to regather their psychological resources and come to grips with what will be the rigors of full-time regular employment. Some *furiitaa* need time to mature a bit more socially and then require a small push to get into the permanent labor force. The interlude as a *furiitaa* may also give them time to learn or enhance a skill needed for such employment.

The necessary policy initiatives

Several policy recommendations flow from the preceding discussion in this chapter. This study was based on interviews with a small sample of *furiitaa* or potential *furiitaa*, most of whom were engaged in some form of *arubaito*. Although it is hard to generalize from such a small sample, the researchers involved in the study were impressed by the extent to which each respondent's story differed from those of the others. The implications are that a multi-faceted approach will be needed.

The first suggestion is that secondary schools need to provide occupational education that is aimed at poor performers and others who seem to be "missing the boat" and not "getting on board" for their cohort's round of placement activities. In practical terms this means implementing educational strategies that will link the classroom to intern-type experience within firms. The aim would be to foster a greater appreciation of how content learned at school relates to work life and a greater interest in having a career and a healthy work life. Guidance and information is also needed for students so they will select friends who support, rather than undermine, their ambitions for permanent employment. Recognizing the barriers that prevent some students from joining in-house placement activities, other extra-curricular mechanisms need to be established to facilitate further the placement of the more difficult cases.

As for tertiary students, there is clearly a need for more guidance at the secondary level when they make decisions regarding further education. There is also a need for individually based consultations with each student shortly after they begin their tertiary education. While it may be hoped that such sessions would result in a heightened commitment to their studies, universities need to establish mechanisms that will facilitate the process of transferring from one major to another, from one faculty to another, or even from one university to another. Preventative steps should be taken long before students think about dropping out or not looking for permanent employment upon graduation. In other words, efforts should be made earlier to assist students in developing a vision for their life and work course.

It is also important to recognize that some students will engage in work on a trial basis for some period after leaving school or university. The broad experience they gain from such trial employment will help them to focus on a career. It is desirable that this occurs, and that support be given to such persons. Here too it is important to recognize that, on the one hand, there are ways to create employment opportunities for students planning to graduate but having no experience. Once young people are away from their educational institution and in the labor market on their own, the assumption is that they must then make their way in the different labor market that exists for mid-career employees. For those who are no longer students and have no work experience, the opportunities in that market for full-time regular employment are quite limited. Although entry into the casual labor force is extremely easy and straightforward for such persons, casual employment offers very limited prospects for a financially responsible future. As the number of young people who find themselves outside the traditional labor market for new graduates is increasing, along with the number who are not in regular full-time employment, careful consideration of the school-to-work transition and the treatment of casual employees is needed.

6 The Work and Skill Levels of the *Furiitaa*

The work performed by *furiitaa*

This volume has focused on young persons working as *arubaitaa* or *paatotaimaa* (as defined in Figure 1.1). Our working definition excluded full-time students and housewives. We also cite a number of surveys of young people that produced very similar findings with regard to their occupations and the working conditions of the *furiitaa*. We can thus comment with some confidence in these regards. Most *furiitaa* are employed five days a week and work eight hours a day. Their average monthly income is between JY100,000 and JY150,000. Hours of work do not appear to differ much from those of their counterparts who work as full-time regular employees. They are concentrated in running cash registers and stocking shelves at convenient stores and supermarkets, in working at fast food outlets, and in waiting on tables in restaurants. Compared to *seishain* they are more concentrated in retail sales and services.

We can verify these impressions by looking at the results of a recent survey on hours of work and income amongst young people aged 18 to 29 who were living in Tokyo. The survey on work styles among Japan's youth was administered in February 2001 to young people living in Tokyo who were aged 18–29 at the time. To obtain a sample of 2000 individuals, researchers visited selected homes and left the survey forms for each individual to complete, coming back later to collect the completed forms (for details see Nihon Rodo Kenkyu Kiko 2000a). One hundred administratively defined locations were randomly chosen, with returns from 20 individuals being collected using a stratified random sampling technique so the resultant sample would match the overall demographics of Tokyo. In February 2006 the same survey was administered using the same method of recruitment. (The details for that are given in Rodo Seisaku Kenkyu-Kenshu Kiko 2006.)

Results from that survey are fairly consistent with those derived from the other surveys (see Table 6.1). They show that in 2006 the *furiitaa* doing *arubaito* and *paatotaimu*-type jobs worked just under 40 hours a week, whereas those employed as *seishain*, contracted workers and the self-employee worked closer to 50 hours per week. The latter group of workers no doubt do 5–15 hours of overtime each week as a matter of course. *Furiitaa* tend to work only 7–8 hours a day, somewhat less than those in the other three categories. The income differentials show that the *seishain* earn considerably more, both in gross terms and on an hourly basis. The index in the right-hand column of Table 6.1 clearly shows on an hourly basis that those in casual employment earn about 70 percent of what full-time regular employees earn. This seems to hold for males and for females. The differential between tenured employee and those who are dispatched or on contract is only ten percent, the situation being slightly better for men than for women. In this regard it is interesting to note that for women the differential between those in tenured employment and those in entrepreneurial activity is only ten percent whereas it is about thirty percent for males. Overall, hours of work and total income levels for women are considerably below those associated with male employment. On an hourly basis, the differentials are smaller (or even reversed in two categories).

Work as *arubaitaa* and *paatotaimaa* is associated with low levels of pay and with little or no skill. Furthermore, it is seen as providing minimal opportunities to acquire skills through on-the-job experience. As we discuss below in Chapter Eight (*e.g.*, regarding Table 8.5), there is a tendency for differences in employment status to be a more significant factor for those with higher levels of education and for aged workers. This in turn reflects the fact that anyone can do tasks requiring minimal levels of skill. There is little reason for employers to reward highly educated or older employees for skills they are not using. Whereas pay increases on an upward trajectory along with skills acquired on the job as full-time regular employees age, skill and pay levels for casuals tend to remain at the same level, or at best to rise only marginally over time. This basic fact of life has been documented for most societies by those involved in the economics of education. The main conclusion is that those who position themselves in casual employment are unlikely over the long haul to be economically competitive in the labor market.

Skill acquisition and career trajectories

The greatest challenge facing *furiitaa* is in the difficulty they have acquiring the basic skills needed for a secure economic future.

Table 6.1: Weekly hours of work and the previous year's annual income by employment status

Employment status	A	B	C	D	E
For 2001					
Males					
Seishain	50.8	343.9	6.8	100	100
Arubaitaa and *paatotaimaa*	40.6	175.0	4.3	51	64
Dispatched and contracted workers	46.2	263.6	5.7	77	84
Self-employed and those who work out of home	52.5	240.4	4.6	70	68
Females					
Seishain	44.8	285.0	6.4	100	100
Arubaitaa and *paatotaimaa*	34.8	138.6	4.0	49	63
Dispatched and contracted workers	38.0	219.2	5.8	77	91
Self-employed and those who work out of home	34.8	197.1	5.7	69	89
For 2006					
Males					
Seishain	53.4	331.4	1.19	100	100
Arubaitaa and *paatotaimaa*	39.8	171.8	0.84	52	70
Dispatched and contracted workers	46.1	258.1	1.07	78	90
Self-employed and those who work out of home	58.0	313.9	1.07	95	87
Females					
Seishain	45.7	274.2	1.15	100	100
Arubaitaa and *paatotaimaa*	32.9	134.3	0.79	49	68
Dispatched and contracted workers	40.7	230.6	1.09	84	94
Self-employed and those who work out of home	-	-	-	-	-

Notes:

A: Hours of work during a recent week (hours)

B: Annual income earned during the previous year (JY10,000)

C: Annual income per hour worked per week (B/A) (JY1000)

D: Index of annual income with 'B' for *seishain* set at 100

E: Index based on hourly income with 'C' for the *seishain* set at 100

Source: For 2001, Hori (2001). For 2006, Rodo Seisaku Kenkyu-Kenshu Kiko (2006), p. 20.

Young workers are still impressionable. The period immediately after school or university is one when most new graduates are best able to acquire new knowledge and to master new skills and new ways of working. Those who enter full-time regular employment upon graduation are able immediately to learn at an accelerated pace through work experience and on-the-job training. Japanese firms function on the assumption that employees will remain with them for a long period of time, and that they will see returns when they invest heavily in the training of an employee. This period immediately after graduation is also important for individuals who by trail and error feel their way toward the career which they will find most pleasing and rewarding. This outlook is an important factor which firms need to consider when assessing the prospects of keeping a young person in casual work over a long period.

We tend to see the post-graduation years from the perspective of the individual, but we need also to remember that this period has a larger social significance. When the occupational training of a casual employee is deferred, the skill level of the entire nation falls. If the motivation to work is not properly instilled, the consequences for the national economy will be considerable. Thinking carefully about this period in a young person's life both as a time for experimentation and as an important time for acquiring critical skills, this is the developmental stage from which individuals emerge as full-fledged workers ready to contribute to the economic activity of the nation. Using empirical data from a report by the Japan Institute of Labor (Nihon Rodo Kenkyu Kiko 2000a), I comment in the paragraphs below on three aspects of career development.

One set of questions concerns the sense of direction young people have with regard to work. Many *furiitaa* indicated that they became *furiitaa* in order to have more time to think through career choices. They could be said to have placed a temporary moratorium on full-time regular employment, and having additional time to decide on a career was often mentioned as one of the merits associated with being a *furiitaa*. This begs a further question: did experience with casual employment foster better ideas as to how they might position themselves in the market for regular full-time employment?

A second set of concerns relates to skill formation and the acquisition of skills useful for regular full-time employment. On a concrete level one might inquire about the occupational skills that are actually learnt through casual employment. Although it is not likely that employers will take the initiative to train persons with whom they will not have a future relationship, it is nevertheless important for firms that use a lot of *arubaitaa* to think about how their casual work force might be exposed to as wide-ranging an experience as possible. It is also important for firms to be cognizant of ways in which casually employed staff can create their own opportunities to acquire new skills. Here it is important to ask questions about how skills are learnt and refined in rather restricted circumstances.

Many young people are challenged to develop skills in ways that will connect with the realities of the labor market and the future of the entire economy. Many have a "dream" that will remain a dream precisely because it is a vision that will be difficult to realize. The ability to link one's dream to reality depends upon one's ability to obtain information about the labor market and the longer-term economic trends shaping that market. Some have that ability, but most do not. Also important is the initiative individuals take to realize their dream, and the resilience with which they can readjust dreams that turn out to be unrealistic. Studies on how *furiitaa* grapple with their dreams will throw more light on the transition into full-time regular employment.

Exploring these questions further, the next section introduces some of the answers supplied by the *furiitaa* themselves. In doing so it uses data obtained by the Japan Institute of Labor (Nihon Rodo Kenkyu Kiko 2000a) based on interviews with about 100 persons who had in the past worked as *furiitaa*.

Finding one's career trajectory

Chapter One suggested that *furiitaa* could be divided into three groups based on their outlook regarding career choices when they first become *furiitaa*. This categorization provides a useful starting point in our research (see Nihon Rodo Kenkyu Kiko 2000a).

The first type was the "dream chaser". This was someone who started out having a fairly clear idea as to what they wanted to be doing in the future. Some of the *furiitaa* retained their dream; others felt compelled to alter their goals and move in new directions. Among those who retained their original dream, most were in the entertainment industry. Others became skeptical as to whether they would be able to "make it" in their chosen profession. A third group consisted of those who were able to "talk" their dream but had not progressed much in "doing the walk". They seemed to cling to the dream because it was fashionable to have a dream even though it could not be realized. The dream seemed to give day-to-day meaning to each individual in this category, and became a clear rationale for why they were employed as *furiitaa*. For this type, being a *furiitaa* was a source of pride – a status that earned them kudos among their peers. Below some of the comments made during the interviews are provided as indications of how these young people actually talked about themselves.

> There are not very many persons like me around. I work as a *furiitaa* in order to do something. You know, it's often said to me, "You're terrific – the way you stick at it to realize your dream." Or, "You are really brilliant for following your dream!" (Case 01 – Female high school graduate aged 23)

These comments were by someone who was in the midst of making her own CD. She was determined and could also say, "I am passionate about this. If I did not think I could ultimately make a future doing this type of work, I would not be able to continue as a *furiitaa*." She provided a good example of someone who was opening a path forward for herself. While she would be the first type of dream chaser mentioned above, she was aware of the risks and sometimes felt anxious about what was still an uncertain future.

Another example was provided by a male graduate who wanted to be a first class entertainer, and had continued with dance lessons and vocal training for over six years while maintaining himself on an income earned as a *furiitaa*.

> When I was twenty, I told myself that I would have to make a decision about work when I reached the age of 25...In any case, I now find that I have made it this far, and that must mean something. I'll just keep going for the time being. Really, I still don't know what I'll be doing in the future, but I am sure I'm not going to give up. (Case 02 – Male high school graduate aged 25)

The second type of dream chaser who changes the dream is less common. Two interviewees made particularly revealing comments:

> I've just come to realize that I don't know what I want to do. There are a lot of things to do in this life, and recently I've begun to feel that I want to try a number of different things before I settle down. Until now I've concentrated all my energy around singing, but in the future I want to branch out and try various new things. (Case 03 – Female high school graduate aged 20)

> How many times I thought I would quit acting...Some of my acquaint-ances have gotten married. Seeing how happy they are, I often wonder if I'm cut out for a career in acting. It's been my dream, and as a dream

I want to keep it alive and keep going. I'm torn in two directions; the feminine part of me wants to be happy, and that leads me to want to stay with acting if only as an amateur. To date I've spent a lot of time wrestling with this dilemma. (Case 04 – Female junior college graduate aged 27)

A good number of *furiitaa* gave up on their dreams and had actually started to prepare for a career in another direction or to commit to making the effort necessary to become a regular full-time employee:

Yes, recently I have definitely come around to thinking that I'd like full-time regular employment. I'd like to find such employment while maintaining my involvement in the band…Yes, in the final analysis I want a regular income. (Case 05 – Female high school graduate aged 20)

I've shifted my focus from being a band member to studying so I can become a beautician. It's taken some time, but so far I've done all right…At first I was attracted by the up-beat atmosphere which is associated with such work. I now know there is more to it than that. I plan to work hard like an ordinary person. Even if I don't attract a large number of customers, if I can come to earn the respect and the trust of customers and co-workers alike, I will have achieved a great deal…As for the future, maybe I could own my own shop. Yes, I'd like to own my own shop by the age of 30. (Case 06 – Male high school graduate aged 19)

Obviously many young persons will want to continue chasing their dream. However, the likelihood of failure is on the minds of many *furiitaa* as they pursue their dreams. They are probably aware of the risks involved in being a *furiitaa* in terms of the reduced chance to later obtain full-time regular employment in an area of interest. Nevertheless, some young people in the third category mentioned above have trouble linking their experience as *furiitaa* to a positive outcome in the labor market for full-time regular employment. The experience of working hard to realize a dream and then the pain that comes when an attractive vision is abandoned are only too real for many young people as they navigate through life toward a satisfactory occupational outcome.

I had once wanted to be a bar tender. However, I had lots of different experiences as a *furiitaa*. They included working for a dental firm, and dong things like selling and working at big events for a security firm. I am now thinking that I'd like to work in photography…For a while I want to continue working as a *furiitaa*. If you ask why, I would answer that I want to enjoy life. At night I can go out, but it's really only to have a good time. The ordinary company employee often goes out drinking, but has to report to work the next morning. There's no way I could put up with that. (Case 07 – Female high school graduate aged 19)

Many *furiitaa* did not feel they had any problem being a *furiitaa*, but were able to tell about other *furiitaa* who did have problems:

When talking about other *furiitaa* I know, there are some who go to school once a week to learn something like flower arranging or calligraphy, believing it would help them in obtaining a good job. However, many *furiitaa* don't have a dream. Some say they want to be a DJ. They say all kinds of things. Many of them don't come to grips with the fact that they have an unattainable dream. They think they will succeed simply by persisting. Still, because they are only 20 years old, they think, "There's still time. I'll be right." They want to continue to have a good time. That's how it is. (Case 08 – Female high school graduate aged 20)

Shifting our attention to the moratorium type who drifts into working as a *furiitaa* without any clear goal, we come across a different set of issues. Most graduates in this category are groping around, lost as to which career path they should take. Some of this type were planning to continue as moratorium beings. They included young people who were not happy with their current situation, but who were also taking no concrete steps to move beyond their life as *furiitaa*.

However, some years out from graduation some moratorium types were starting to think seriously about a career choice. One interviewee had previously been totally withdrawn into himself, but was earnestly taking concrete steps to find direction in his life at the time of the interview:

I am currently thinking of becoming a designer. I have headed off to enrol in a specialized training school to learn about clothing and apparel. I know it's a world in which it's difficult to be only halfway interested in work. It requires hard work. One of my parent's friends is a designer, and people like that have spoken to me about these matters…I've been in touch with a number of established schools…

> I've also had encouragement from people around me, and in the end
> I finally chose the school I'm now attending. (Case 09 – Male high
> school graduate aged 23)

Another moratorium type had been employed as a *seishain* before
quitting and circulating through a number of casual jobs. She had
only recently come to the conclusion that her high school dream
of becoming an illustrator could still be nurtured. Comments by
several *furiitaa* like this person were along the following lines:

> I want to be an illustrator. I had work for a while and seemed to be
> doing my job satisfactorily. However, that was because I was asked
> to help an acquaintance. Nevertheless, since childhood I used to
> draw a fair bit. I want to be working as an illustrator once I'm into
> my thirties. That's why I'm now working as a *furiitaa*. I'll keep at it.
> If you are working hard at something you like, there's little sense of
> hardship. You see, I really truly want to spend all my time drawing.
> (Case 10 – Female high school graduate aged 26)

For some who had not thought much about being in the labor force
while still in school, the time spent working as a *furiitaa* provided
them with the space they needed to think things through:

> I thought that for me the year spent working as a *furiitaa* was time well
> spent. In Japan today many young people are finishing high school
> and immediately entering some sort of university. Even among my
> friends, I know persons who have gone straight on without knowing
> what they want to do…I want to go on only after I know where I'm
> headed. Going to a school is so limiting. There are so many things one
> cannot do if one is in school every day all day long. My one year away
> from all of that has allowed me to think things through, considering
> where I've been in the past and where I want to go in the future. (Case
> 11 – Female high school graduate aged 19)

The next four examples represent another moratorium type. The
young man is typical of a number of young people who do not feel
anxious or pressured about their future. This type is quite positive
about their situation. There is, however, no sign that these young
people are advancing themselves career-wise:

> For a while there was nothing I really wanted to do. I was a bit aimless.
> I thought somewhere along the way I'd find some work I could do in

the future. That was my life, yah, there's no reason I should be overly worried. I'm not at all concerned about the future. No worries at all. (Case 12 – Male high school graduate aged 23)

I feel that I've something I want to do, but at the same time I don't know how to go about doing it. I want to make things. Anything contrary to mainstream thinking? I guess so. I have no strong feeling that continuing as a *furiitaa* would be the wrong thing to do. (Case 13 – Female high school graduate aged 18)

If someone told me that one has to get full-time regular employment, I would have absolutely no quarrels with him or her at all. They can keep saying those things, but as for the present I'm not going to change my mind. It's not that I dislike work, more of a thing of not having the interest in doing it. I guess I'm not interested in getting more money or material things. Maybe there'll be a time when I want that kind of life. That'll be okay, then, when it happens, but not now. (Case 14 – Male university graduate aged 26)

If possible, I'd like to become a full-time regular employee. However I like my life as it now is. Maybe that sounds too easy. Maybe I just do not want to take that first step. My gut feeling now is that I like the way I'm living. (Case 15 – Male high school graduate aged 19)

These voices seem to be pointing to an indifference that many *furiitaa* have concerning their employment status. As long as the work is not too demanding and they can maintain their lifestyle without being overly burdened by the demands of making a living, they seemed not to be concerned with whether they were a full-time regular employee or a *furiitaa*. They seem only to drift without being able to articulate clearly any goals in their lives. Repeating the claim that they want to be free to do "the things they want to do" (*yaritai koto*), they seemed not to have a clear vision of what they want to be doing. They nevertheless had a vague sense of things they do not want to do (*yaritakunai koto*). In some ways they are like the dream chasers; they differ in that their dream is very vague and not well defined.

As for work, if there's a job I enjoy doing I'll be happy to be employed. However, until I find the right job I'll not make up my mind about permanent employment. As long as I've not found the job for me, I'll continue as a *furiitaa*. Getting a regular full-time job at all costs is not my priority. (Case 16 – Female university dropout aged 20)

> As long as it's work I like to do, I'm happy. Whether it's as a regular
> full-time employee or as a *furiitaa* is not important to me. (Case
> 17 – Male university graduate aged 27)

For other *furiitaa* there was a sense of the inevitable. For some reason
beyond their control they felt they had to stop something else they
had been doing and then had to work as a *furiitaa*. Some were trying
hard to find full-time regular employment, but had been unsuccessful.
Although they had continued to look for such employment, they
also felt compelled to earn some income and had thus begun to
work as *furiitaa*. Doing so with a sense of disappointment, they fell
into a kind of depressed state as moratorium beings. Among these
youth some had lost all confidence about being able to find a job
that was "right". Some sought to deal with their "unemployability"
by working for a limited time as *furiitaa* while also pressing ahead
with a plan to further their education. Others, however, had more
difficulty with their setback. They seemed to loose their confidence
altogether. Believing they could not achieve their original goal, they
entered a moratorium state while looking for another direction or
purpose in life.

> Because I'm now 24. I think I am feeling a bit nervous or overwhelmed
> by the prospect of finding a full-time regular job. A part of me wants
> not to go out into the big world. At the same time, my parents have for
> some time been urging me to go out into that world and get a job with
> a proper firm. I too think it's important that I have that experience in
> life. However, whenever I contemplate doing that I keep coming back
> to the fact that I'm already 24. People will think I'm too old to be
> starting out. If I were only 20 or 21, I'd be okay, but now I'm already
> 24. I don't want to go through the testing and interviews again only to
> once more be rejected. What can I do? (Case 18 – Female university
> graduate aged 24)

The above are snapshots that throw light onto how *furiitaa* are
thinking. Most have some sense of a future career; they are
searching for a way forward and seeking to find a direction for
themselves. The *furiitaa* we interviewed were using their time as
furiitaa as a period for exploration, and moving through a process of
trial and error toward a fruitful outcome. However, there were also
those who wore their dreams like an accessory, having taken little
concrete action to achieve their goals. In the process they seemed
to have lost hope, continuing on as moratorium types or entering

that moratorium state for the first time. Aware of their own passivity with regard to the labor market, many in this state had put serious consideration of their economic future on hold.

Works as a *furiitaa* and skill formation

Another set of issues concerns the implications of being a *furiitaa* for the development and acquisition of career-relevant skills. Many of the interviewees commented that through their varied experiences in casual work they hoped to find work suited to their own needs. However, as we indicated in the last chapter, the types of work the *furiitaa* do are not that varied. This section considers the skills which the *furiitaa* actually acquire. Fifteen of the 97 *arubaitaa* we interviewed spoke of the link between their experience as *furiitaa* and the work they hoped they would be doing in the future. Table 6.2 lists the work done and the future work planned by each of those *furiitaa*.

The young people introduced in Table 6.2 were all casually employed as *arubaitaa*, and many are working in areas related to their career goal. Although this broadening process seemed to introduce casual workers to only the very basics, perhaps serving to do little more than whetting their appetite for more, and some, such as Case 04, had given thought to more than one field of work as a future possibility, overall each person's *arubaito* was seen by them as providing a range of experience related to their future in the workforce. In this regard, a number of interviewees mentioned ways in which contact with others was allowing them to develop important social skills. For many it is the first time they are socializing in a serious way outside the school and family environment:

> I've become accustomed to talking to other people. Before I found that I could not do that. Now I can talk with lots of people outside of where I'm working. There are lots of people out there. By talking to them one can learn a lot. (Case 19 – Male high school graduate aged 21)

> While working in a theme park, I've felt myself grow in some way. By dealing with a wide range of people, I've found that I can empathize with others much more. For example, when riding the train as a high school student, I would not get up and offer my seat to an older person; I would pretend that I didn't see them. Now I find it quite natural to stand up and offer my seat. (Case 20 – Female high school graduate aged 19)

Table 6.2: Linkages between the work experienced by furiitaa *and the work they want to be doing in the future*

Student	Work planned for the future	Current job as an *arubaitaa*	Student's background
01	Working as cook in a local restaurant	Cooking	Female high school graduate aged 20
02	Being a forestry worker or doing something in agriculture	Casual work in agriculture	Female university dropout aged 20
03	To open my own coffee shop once I've picked up enough knowledge from my *arubaito* to run my own shop	Casual work in a coffee shop	Female university dropout aged 20
04	To make a name for myself in photography and the performing arts	Casual work developing photographs	Female university dropout aged 20
05	I'd be happy being a make-up specialist…I am now looking for the right specialized training school	Working as a receptionist in a beauty salon	Female drop out from a specialized training school aged 20
06	I wanted to go to a specialized training school with a course on child care	Casual work at a child-care center	Female high school graduate aged 21
07	I'm most interested in drama and the theatre	Casual worker in the special effects section at a theatre	Female graduate of a specialized training school aged 20
08	Since my days at high school I wanted to be a bartender	Casual work as a bartender	Female dropout from a specialized training school aged 19
09	I definitely need a licence to work as a beautician and be a hair dresser	Casual work in a beauty parlour	Female dropout from a specialized training school aged 23
10	When I graduated in confectionery from a specialized training school, there were no good job offers	Casual work in a cake shop	Female graduate of a specialized training school aged 21
11	Something in education if I don't pass the public service exam	Casual work as a teacher in a cram school	Male university graduate aged 27
12	I want to work somewhere like in a department store	On call to do casual work in sales in clothing and apparel	Female graduate of a specialized training school aged 23
13	I want to be a coordinator for dispatched workers	Casual work as a temp (a dispatched worker)	Female graduate of a specialized training school aged 28
14	I want a career working in a hotel	Casual work in a restaurant greeting customers	Male dropout from university aged 23
15	I want to go to a specialized training school to study about the hotel industry	Casual work dealing with customers at a fast food outlet	Female high school graduate aged 21

Source: Nihon Rodo Kenkyu Kiko (2000a).

Somehow in the process of doing my casual job, I've learned how to skilfully fit into a work place and get on with others at work. (Case 21 – Male university drop out aged 23)

In addition to these accounts of work related skill acquisition, others told about how they had acquired useful information about work. From acquaintances made while working as a casual, some were able to obtain useful information about employment opportunities and the training needed for certification. This facet of the *furiitaa* experience I wish to consider further in the next section.

Opportunities that flow from casual work

The final task of this chapter is to consider the extent to which *furiitaa* actually avail themselves of useful information while casually employed. This kind of information includes ideas about how to acquire knowledge relevant to achieving work goals, how to prepare for a career, and how to fruitfully use one's remaining time as a *furiitaa*. Many also leave with a more realistic appraisal of the likelihood they will become regular full-time employees with their current attributes, and with insight into how career related skills are acquired. What they acquire is the discipline and the confidence needed for a career. If they actively avail themselves of these opportunities, they will probably get into a career without too much difficulty. Those without such a commitment are likely to continue working as *furiitaa* as the "easy way out". Young people who fail to utilize fully the limited opportunities provided by *furiitaa*-type employment are in danger. The next few cases indicate in an inarticulate way that *furiitaa* gained some idea about the world around them.

I want to be a nail artist. Even my high school teacher had not heard of that occupation. Still, if that's what I wanted to do, he wished me well and told me to go all out...However, when I got out of the school for nail artists, there were only two or three jobs on offer. Really! I didn't know the demand for nail artists was so small. (Case 22 – Female aged 21 who has graduated from a special training school)

I've got something I'd like to do. I just know it. I'd like to be a counsellor or do some similar type of work...I'd like to go to the sort of place that trains counsellors. I've seen mention of pamphlets in the newspapers. I'll get some when they come out. It takes one year plus fifty thousand yen, maybe 100,000 yen. It seems to cost something. I'll just keep looking. (Case 23 – Male high school graduate aged 25)

I wanted to learn Chinese medicine. At the present time, I am thinking of studying in China...In any case one should go at least once to China to be a real practitioner. Of course, I have to think about whether I could make ends meet over there. According to the stories I've heard, one can go there on a tourist visa, and then just continue living there and get qualified. (Case 24 – Male high school graduate aged 28)

Although some *furiitaa* were able to activate information gleaned from their experience as a *furiitaa* when making choices about their future, in some cases information came from other sources and parents may have played a big role. One young female *furiitaa* received good advice from one of the older workers to whom she had been introduced by her parents. There were also cases in which young persons talked with friends who were already employed in the industry they wanted to enter. Based on the information obtained from their friends, the *furiitaa* were better able to assess the available schools at which to study:

I wanted to be a make-up specialist. I thought make-up artists and beauticians were quite different. For that reason I went to a special school that taught only about make-up. Then I found out that it was not an officially recognized school that could give recognized certificates, and that one couldn't make a living by simply finishing that course and then doing only make-up. Make-up is not really a recognized occupation. At that point my parents began to worry and spoke to someone who was a beautician. The advice I got was first to become a beautician and then to go into make-up. I was told by someone in the business that it would be quite impossible to make a living only doing make up...When I undertook to choose a specialist school, I was again helped by my parents who did some investigating on my behalf. They wanted to make sure I went to the right school that would give me a certificate that was officially approved and would give me recognition in the industry. They were concerned that I didn't end up making another mistake...They seem to have spent a lot of time in this regard. (Case 25 – Female aged 20 who dropout out of a special school)

For some interviewees progress was made simply in coming to terms with the fact that their dream would have to remain a dream.

They were able to accept the fact that they would have to think of other more realistic options, even though they may have continued to work toward a dream they could not achieve. About one fifth of the *furiitaa* we interviewed had begun to prepare themselves mentally to shift. These young people were thinking of various occupations as future possibilities. One typical response was to work in the family business – either with a plan to eventually take it over or with the idea of helping out in some way. Another common response was to acquire computing skills and then seek employment as a regular full-time employee:

> My family has its own business, and I want to study how to manage the company. Really, I now want to be a company manager. It's only a small family business, but I want to build it up. I'm studying to do that. I want to branch into a new field. We've not yet got the technology, but if possible I'd like to save up so we can branch off in that direction. (Case 19 – Male high school graduate aged 21)

> I am looking for work. Perhaps a small licensed eatery. My family has been pushing in that direction…My parents want me to take over their place. That's okay. I don't mind them trying to persuade me to move in that direction. They often phone to check how I'm going, which is not brilliant, you know. I think I'll take them up on their offer. (Case 15 – Male high school graduate aged 19)

> I want to study computers, and somehow use the skills I acquire to get a regular full-time position. The desktop computer is the way to go, don't you think? After a while the computer becomes an extension of who you are, and it's an attribute that will open the way to the future. I've tried the internet, and I found that to be quite interesting. Even without going to a specialized school, there are a number of places where one can learn the necessary skills. It would take one month or maybe two months. Still, although it is cheaper than a certified school, it nevertheless will require some money to get going. Therefore, I'll get only the very basic necessary skills and buy my own computer. If I can do that, I think I'll then somehow be on my way. (Case 26 – Female high school graduate aged 24)

The last quote focuses attention on the need to have a skill and qualifications. One of the interviewees was involved in real estate and had taken concrete action to gain the necessary certification that would allow him to draw up contracts. He had a solid qualification that was recognized in the industry. However, in many cases, the attraction of computing had led the respondents to a simple belief that by going to a school several times each week they would be able to obtain the necessary skills and certification to become full-time regular employees. As one male high school graduate aged 27 commented, "I've not really investigated the types of computer skills that will be required in order to get full-time regular employment." In other words, a good many young people know they will need certain skills to gain permanent employment, but they remain fairly ignorant of what the labor market demands in concrete terms.

Most *furiitaa* have an age in mind by which time they hope they will have moved on to something else. They are aware that at a certain point in time age will begin to work against them in the labor market whether it is in terms of gaining full-time regular employment as a *seishain*, continuing in casual employment, or getting married.

> It's not as if I'm going to be working a long time as a part-timer after my mid-twenties. Since our customers are young, most being around twenty, you cannot stay in this job too long. Another two or three years, then I'll be thinking about some permanent employment. (Case 27 – Female high school graduate aged 21)

> I want to find some regular employment as soon as possible. I want to be in an industry I like and find something that fits into that sphere of economic activity. However, if after another year I don't find something along those lines, I may well think about working in an ordinary job in sales. (Case 28 – Male university graduate aged 25)

> When you get to my age, you can't still be working in a convenience store or a coffee shop. That *arubaito* is for high school students or other young persons. At my age one starts to worry about whether they can still interact with those youngsters. There are a number of ways in which this age-thing comes into play. (Case 23 – Male high school graduate aged 25)

As might be expected, there's an awareness that the chances of gaining full-time regular employment diminish considerably in one's late twenties. The result is that many individuals begin to feel a sense of urgency in their late twenties whenever they contemplate their prospects in the labor force over the coming five years or so:

> I don't plan to continue working as a *furiitaa*. I already feel a bit handicapped by my age. You'd have to be seen as being fairly resilient to cope with new work surroundings. For that reason nobody wants to hire you unless you're 25 years of age or younger. It starts to get tough when one turns 26. So, when you get to be 27 like me, you really feel the pressure. If I don't make a move now, it will become almost impossible to get into career-type employment. I am always thinking about it. If the opportunity arises I'll certainly be applying to work in a company. (Case 29 – Female graduate of a junior college with a recognized major, aged 27)

> I've looked into being a regular full-time employee. However, as a *furiitaa* I'm already getting too old. My chances are getting limited. Up to 25: that's the age! If you want to work in an accounting firm you need first to have a certificate in bookkeeping. That's what it's like out there today. They want someone who can do the work from day one. You know the test to be a tax accountant? To be an accountant you need to pass in five areas, but with just three passes one should be able to find some work in an accounting firm. My qualifications are higher than that of a bookkeeper. Firms won't hire you if you are only a bookkeeper. I've contacted some 30–40 companies. (Case 30 – Male university graduate aged 29)

When trying to get a foot into the labor market for full-time regular employment, many *furiitaa* face two barriers: age and the failure to have a recognized certificate or other proof that one has the required skills. For that reason, some *furiitaa* have begun to think about how they would fit into other labor markets. Some of the males have thought of opening a recycling shop dealing with white goods and home appliances or going into business making costumes for theatre companies. Many females seem less fussy about what they do because they are planning to get married and earn only a secondary income for their household:

> I never planned to work all out like a career woman. I planned to work until I got married. After that I was happy to stop working…If it were working as a master of ceremonies for weddings or an emcee doing something I liked, I'd be happy to work on Saturdays or other times

that fit into my own schedule. That would definitely be a possibility. (Case 18 – Female university graduate aged 24)

Because I'm female, I can always fall back on getting married. For that reason, I'll never have the feeling that I've been cornered or have to fight back...I am able to do what I want as an actress, and I plan to keep on as an actress up to a certain point. That seems to be my goal at the present time. (Case 31 – Female high school graduate aged 26)

Overcoming barriers to career-oriented skill acquisitions

A good many *furiitaa* become more conscious that work-related choices are career choices, and soon gain a clear vision of where in the future they want to be headed work-wise. Some *furiitaa* are slowly moving toward realizing a dream; others continue to grope for a way forward, often making the decision to pursue an avenue that was not originally envisaged. For those with a sense of direction, the time spent in casual work has been an important passage leading to full-time regular work.

On the other hand, there is still a large number of *furiitaa* who hold onto their dream even though they have not taken any concrete action that might move them closer to its realization. They seem intent on living with a dream, and for them talking about the dream is in itself a way of life. It is as though dream chasing is in vogue. Among those who have entered a moratorium on work, some may not be happy with their current situation in life, but nonetheless simply wish it would change without wanting to put in the hard work that is necessary for it actually to change. For this type, the period working as a *furiitaa* will add up to very little.

For most *furiitaa* very little, if any, skill development occurs. Although a few interviewees felt their basic social skills had improved, the simple fact for many is that they have very limited opportunities to interact socially while in high school. If the period as a *furiitaa* is short, it's unlikely that a young person will experience major difficulty getting permanent employment in the future. However, the longer they remain a *furiitaa*, the more likely it is that they will get further behind in developing work-place skills, and that should be a major concern.

As for enhancing the opportunities to make connections helpful in finding full-time regular employment, we were impressed by the extent to which many *furiitaa*, especially the older ones, felt unease regarding their future in the labor force. Most had not gathered much useful information about job prospects or the specialist schools they might attend to improve their array of skills. Many lamented the fact that they could not support a household with the income they were currently earning. Some were despondent about their poor chances at ever gaining proper employment. As informed observers we could only conclude that many *furiitaa* did not have a mature appreciation of the situation at work and had taken the easy option when it came to making choices related to their future in the labor force. In this regard it is important to remember that various schools for the adult population are run on a commercial basis and do not have any kind of official certification. Those running such schools are often not as interested, as they often claim to be in their brochures, in providing training based on a carefully developed curriculum that will be appropriately tailored to vocational requirements in the labor markets that their students are planning to enter. In some ways these schools contribute to an education industry that feeds on the dreams of less informed young people. Many of the students who attend such schools dream of being the one from among tens of thousands who become successful. This is particularly so among those who want to "make it big" in the entertainment industry. Given the slim possibility of success, there is ironically a certain logic in going all out to maximize one's chances. However, in our data there is also a warning: young people have to take pains to obtain accurate information before making major decisions about which careers to pursue or which schools to attend.

What steps can be taken to alleviate the problems faced by many of those who become *furiitaa*? First, it is important that the time as a *furiitaa* not be spent in extended idleness. Second, it is critical that this period be used to develop an awareness of career, and that young *furiitaa* think carefully about how they can acquire skills from their work experience. Third, specialist training courses should build in opportunities for on-the-job internships. Young people who work as *furiitaa* need real-to-life skill-building opportunities when they are learning a trade.

Finally, we can mention the need for accurate information and access to competent counselling. For organizations providing such services to function effectively, parents, teachers and other significant persons need to be actively involved. There are clearly limits to what young people can achieve on their own when it comes to obtaining adequate information about various careers. Part of the challenge is in how to acquire the judgement or discernment necessary to distinguish the good schools and the promising opportunities from those that are not. How to gather reliable information and how to assess the information which is obtained are two very important skills which we should all be trying to teach our young people. From a policy point of view, steps are needed to provide these kinds of services both within and outside the school system.

7 The Prevalence of *Furiitaa* Abroad

Beyond Japan

The first four chapters discussed the rapid increase in the number of *furiitaa* following the end of the bubble economy in the early 1990s. Chapters Five and Six introduced the voices of the *furiitaa* to convey some aspects of their lifestyle as a social problem. To the extent that such phenomena are connected to the Heisei recession of the 1990s, one might reasonably ask whether what the *furiitaa* represent is a peculiarly Japanese response to the times.

As explained at the outset in Chapter One, the term "*furiitaa*" is written in *katakana*, the Japanese script reserved mainly for foreign words which are transcribed into Japanese. However, the term is not a foreign word. It was created in Japan by combining the notion of being free (*furii*) to be one's own agent with the last syllable in the term "*arubaitaa*" which had been adopted some time ago in Japan from the German word "*arbeit*" (meaning "labor"). However, in Japan the term is not used to refer to work in general (as is the case in German). Rather, it is used to indicate an employment status whereby one is hired on a temporary or casual basis, and is now an *emic* term describing the employment of many young people in Japan, especially students at a secondary or tertiary institution. For this reason, "*furiitaa*" can be said to be a uniquely Japanese phenomenon. The basic assumption has been that students study full-time and assume full-time regular employment upon graduation. Over time, the number of young people who continue in *arubaito*-type employment after graduation has increased and today the term *arubaito* is used in a looser manner.

In this volume the term "*furiitaa*" is used in a rather restricted manner to refer to young people who are employed as *arubaitaa* or *paatotaimaa* and are neither housewives nor full-time students. "*Paatotaimaa*" or "part-timers" refers to those whose hours of work are shorter than those worked by persons who are regular full-time employees. "*Arubaitaa*" refers to those who are employed on a contract for a set period of some days or some months. When defined in this way, it is possible from government statistics to gain some idea as to the prevalence of this employment status abroad.

The *Labor White Paper* for 2000 (Rodo Sho 2000) contains a section which speculates about the situation abroad. Its analysis is based on data compiled by the OECD about part-time workers and those employed on fixed short-term contracts. An overview of the numbers is presented in Table 7.1. Here one should note that the Japanese and the European figures have been generated from surveys using slightly different methodologies. Japan's data comes from a survey of business firms with five or more employees which were asked to report on the proportion of all persons employed within the first year following their graduation (*i.e.*, between April and the following March) who were employed on a part-time basis. In the other OECD countries the unit of analysis is the individual, and on that basis one is able to calculate the percentage of employees who had graduated during the previous twelve months and were employed as part-timers. In Japan the questionnaire provided firms with only two categories: standard workers (*ippan rodosha*) and part-timers (*paatotaimu rodosha*), the latter being defined simply as those who worked less hours per day or per week than the standard worker. Using that definition, Japanese firms reported that 11 percent of their male employees and 15 percent of their female employees

Table 7.1: An international comparison of the percentage of graduates who became full-time regular employees in the late 1990s

Country	**Males**		**Females**	
	Employed for a fixed term	Employed part-time	Employed for a fixed term	Employed part-time
Japan		10.8		15.4
France	68.3	21.8	66.3	40.3
Germany	62.8	16.3	69.9	21.1
United Kingdom	27.3	45.3	25.7	54.1
United Sates		23.1		35.3
Average for all OECD countries	50.3	24.0	50.2	34.0

Notes:
1. The figures for Japan are for 1998; for Germany, 1995; for the other countries, 1996.
2. The figures for Japan are for those who are aged under 30 and who enter employment within one year of graduating. For the other OECD countries, the figures are for those aged 16–29 who enter employment within one year of graduating.

Source: Rodo Sho (2000), p. 402. The figures originally came from OECD and Japan's Ministry of Labor. .

were part-timers. This figure was lower than that derived for the other four OECD countries shown in Table 7.1.

Sixty to seventy percent of workers were hired on fixed term contracts in France and Germany. In the United Kingdom the figure was much lower, at below thirty percent, although the percentage of part-time employees was quite high at around fifty percent. In Japan, it is generally thought that the proportion of new graduates on fixed-term contracts is not as high as in the other OECD countries shown in Table 7.1. Other data not reported in the *Labor White Paper* for 2000 show that the percentage of young persons aged 15–24 who are not in school but are doing "*arubaito*" was 9.4 percent (for males) and 13.4 percent (for females) (Somu Sho Tokei Kyoku 2000a). Even though the statistics are not strictly comparable, most observers would agree that the percentage of young Japanese employed on a casual basis is lower than in the other major OECD countries. In other words, young people in Europe and North America are much more likely than their Japanese counterparts to be found in casual employment.

Having said that, however, it is also important to note that a term equivalent to "*furiitaa*" does not exist in the other countries. One does not hear of discussion in those countries which is focused on the casual employment of young people as a distinct issue.

In the 1970s and 1980s, the issue of high youth unemployment was raised as an endemic problem in many of the European and North American countries. A recent publication of the OECD (2000: 13) has noted that unemployment and casual employment seem to characterize the lifestyle of some youth, commenting that lowly paid part-time work, fixed-term employment and unemployment tend to create a crisis for many young people who are trying to make the transition into the permanent labor force. Still, the issue is taken up within frameworks commonly used for discussing unemployment more generally. Although the percentage of youth in fixed-term and/ or casual employment is much larger in those countries, the issue of such employment as a lifestyle has not been carefully considered in its own right.

How is the situation in Japan different? This chapter presents a careful comparison using empirical data, but I am left relying on the comparative data mentioned above in Chapter Four that emerged from the study carried out in eleven European countries and Japan. The study was limited to university graduates and focused on their situation four years after graduating. The study is interesting because the focus of attention in the other countries had previously been on young people with low levels of education (*e.g.*, middle school or high school graduates), whereas in Japan attention has shifted to the rapidly rising number of casually employed university graduates. Although Europe has a large number of young people overall in various forms of casual employment, there does not seem to have been as much concern as in Japan about university graduates who end up in casual employment. This chapter explores the reasons for that.

The employment situation immediately after graduation

Chapter Four reported that about 60 percent of all university graduates in Japan entered regular full-time employment immediately after their graduation. In Europe the employment status of many universities graduates after graduation is unclear. Questionnaires often asked only if graduates had found work, or, if they had changed jobs, simply asking them to describe the circumstances regarding their work. Moreover, the results were also difficult to interpret because many graduates in Europe often allow for a gap of several months before they take up employment. The European survey asked respondents to record their activities after graduation in chronological order. In Japan, most students graduate at the end of March and start work at the beginning of April. The survey was designed so that those not working during the first four months after graduation would be categorized as "unemployed". However, many of the European respondents simply left blank the space for the time between graduation and their first job. When the surveys were coded, the blank spaces were simply recorded as "Not Clear". One reason for the blank spaces may be that graduation in many European universities occurs just before the summer holidays. To capture those who graduated in Europe with a commitment to start work at the end of the summer, it made sense to redefine the "immediately after" period as being "up to six months".

Table 7.2 shows the activity in which Japanese graduates were involved during the first four months following graduation (which was six months in the European surveys). The findings show that 40 percent of the European sample was recorded as being "unclear" as to what they had been doing. However, looking at the remaining 60 percentage points; only 10 percent of the respondents reported that they had been in full-time regular employment. Just over 20 percent were non-engaged and 12 percent claimed they were in some kind of fixed-term casual position. In other words, in Europe

Table 7.2: The employment situation of university graduates in their fourth year after graduation (Japan and Europe)

Country	Regular full-time employment	Self-employed	Part-time employment for a fixed period	Further education	Occupational training	Not engaged	Other and missing answer	Total	N
Japan	61.5	1.5	12.8	12.0	3.2	6.4	2.5	100.0	3,421
All European countries (average)	10.4	1.6	11.5	9.9	3.2	20.7	42.7	100.0	33,276
UK	21.5	1.3	15.3	12.4	3.1	23.7	22.8	100.0	3,461
Czechoslovakia	21.1	2.0	8.1	11.1	1.0	12.7	44.1	100.0	3,093
Holland	18.4	2.5	23.1	10.0	1.7	21.3	22.9	100.0	3,087
Norway	17.5	0.8	21.7	6.2	1.7	19.3	32.8	100.0	3,329
Germany	9.2	2.7	7.7	9.5	2.0	27.0	41.9	100.0	3,506
Austria	7.6	3.4	9.4	7.8	5.7	26.8	39.4	100.0	2,312
France	4.3	0.1	3.9	33.1	6.9	18.3	33.4	100.0	3,050
Italy	3.0	2.7	7.1	2.6	4.2	35.5	45.0	100.0	3,102
Finland	2.5	0.4	10.7	5.5	0.7	9.9	70.2	100.0	2,675
Sweden	2.4	0.0	1.9	0.0	0.7	0.3	94.8	100.0	2,634
Spain	2.3	1.6	14.7	8.7	7.6	28.8	36.3	100.0	3,027

Source: Nihon Rodo Kenkyu Kiko (2001a), p. 50.

more graduates were in casual employment than in permanent full-time employment. From the United Kingdom to Norway, the non-engaged out numbered the fully employed regular employees in all countries except Czechoslovakia. In Holland and Norway, part-timers and others on fixed-term contracts were particularly numerous. In Czechoslovakia part-timers, others on fixed-term contracts and the non-engaged were relatively fewer in number, but even then the combined total for those three categories out numbered those in full-time regular employment. In Japan the proportion of full-time regular employees (*i.e.*, those employed as *seishain*) was three times the combined total in the other three categories.

The results of the comparative survey data confirm the impressions we formed by looking at the OECD data: in international terms the number of university graduates in part-time work and/or on fixed-term contracts in Japan is small. In saying that, a distinction is drawn between two categories: "full-time employees without a set period of employment" and "part-timers and others with a set period of employment". In reality we are referring to something that separates the two categories that is more than simply working shorter hours or simply being employed for a limited period of time. In Japan importance is attached to the distinction between being a "*seishain*" and being "something else" (including working as a *furiitaa*). For that reason when thinking about Japan it makes sense to combine together those with fixed terms and those with shorter hours of work and to differentiate them from those in full-time regular employment. In the various countries that constitute Europe it is usually the case that part-timers do not have a stipulated period of employment. In many countries they differ from full-time employees only in that their hours of work are shorter. In other respects, however, they are not differentiated in terms of the nature of their work or their rights in the workplace. In thinking about these matters, one has to be careful to keep (a) hours of work and (b) the fixing of a set term of employment as two distinctly different matters. When making international comparisons it is important to remember that there is a cultural element. When looking at Japan the term "*furiitaa*" is partly about having shorter hours of work, but it is even more importantly about a difference in employment status.

Employment in the fourth year after graduation

In the preceding discussion we emphasized the fact that Japan's university trained young people were much less involved in casual (non-*seishain*) employment than their counterparts in Europe. In Japan, well into the fourth year 81 percent of male university graduates and 63 percent of female graduates gain full-time regular employment; 6 percent of males and 15 percent of females gain other employment (Table 7.3). The unemployment rate for male and female graduates alike is about 4 percent. Compared with the period immediately after graduation, the percentage working as *seishain* increased over the three years leading up to the survey. The increase was particularly noticeable for male graduates. In Europe 59 percent of male university graduates and 44 percent of female graduates were employed full-time without being engaged for a set period. Both genders showed a marked increase in this form of employment. Those employed part-time or for a set period of time accounted for 16 percent of male graduates and 25 percent of female graduates, with only 3 percent of males and 4 percent of females being unemployed in their fourth year after graduation. By the end of the fourth year the difference between the European countries and Japan had greatly diminished.

In the UK, Sweden and Czechoslovakia the proportion of graduates in full-time employment without a time limitation was relatively high for both male and female university graduates. The low countries are Spain and Italy at below 40 percent. The other countries lie in between. In every country full-time regular employment is more prevalent for men than for women. In this regard, the difference between Japan and the various European countries in the four years after graduation is not very great.

Although the rate at which university graduates enter full-time regular employment is lower in all these countries than in Japan, the period of time required after graduation for a cohort to achieve those employment rates is much longer in Europe than in Japan. If we refer to those who are not in such employment as "*furiitaa*", we can conclude that the number of *furiitaa* in Europe surpasses the number in Japan by a huge amount.

As mentioned just above, a major similarity among all of these countries is the gender difference that exists when it comes to the transition from being a student to being employed on a regular full-time basis. Not only do fewer females make that transition; in most countries they are also more likely to be unemployed. This gender-based difference is tied to the fact that full-time employees are required to work longer hours and to the fact that there continues to be a division of labor based on gender, especially in terms of family life and the way families organize their domestic affairs.

Table 7.3: The employment situation of university graduates in their fourth year after graduation (males in Japan and Europe)

Country	Regular full-time employment	Part-time employment or for a fixed period	Self-employed	Unemployed	Special training	Graduate school	House wife	Other or no answer	Total	N
Japan	80.7	6.2	1.5	3.5	0.6	5.0	0.1	2.5	100.0	1,808
All European Countries (average)	58.6	16.3	7.8	2.5	1.4	5.0	0.2	8.3	100.0	14,886
Italy	38.7	15.5	23.4	2.3	4.9	7.6	0.0	7.6	100.0	1,453
Spain	24.0	26.1	9.1	8.2	1.3	3.1	0.1	28.1	100.0	1,291
France	64.7	9.4	1.7	4.0	3.9	12.0	0.0	4.3	100.0	1,380
Austria	59.0	22.1	8.0	2.5	1.3	2.4	0.2	4.3	100.0	1,206
Germany	59.1	16.0	8.2	2.1	1.3	3.5	0.2	9.6	100.0	1,960
Holland	66.6	20.4	6.4	1.3	0.0	1.2	0.1	4.0	100.0	1,350
UK	70.0	12.4	4.1	2.4	1.2	5.6	0.3	3.9	100.0	1,402
Finland	58.2	24.0	3.7	1.6	0.0	1.9	0.3	10.3	100.0	1,047
Sweden	69.1	8.0	3.7	0.5	1.2	7.9	0.4	9.1	100.0	1,151
Norway	66.7	13.6	4.2	0.8	0.0	5.1	0.1	9.4	100.0	1,344
Czechoslovakia	69.4	13.4	10.2	1.2	0.0	4.3	0.2	1.4	100.0	1,302

Source: Nihon Rodo Kenkyu Kiko (2001a), p. 73.

This expression of gender-based difference occurs in labor force behavior in all countries, but it seems to be considerably more pronounced in Japan than elsewhere.

Another difference between Japan and Europe is in labor turn-over. Although employees may be identified as "full-time regular employees" because they work full-time without a designated period, the number of firms at which these young people work is quite different in Japan and in Europe. Tables 7.4 and 7.5 show that among graduates who were full-time regular employees in their fourth year after graduation, 80 percent of males and 70 percent of females had worked for just the one company – their employer at the time they were surveyed. In Europe, however, the figure was close to 40 percent for both male and female graduates. In other words, the vast majority in the European countries had worked for two, three, four or more companies over the three years following graduation, and the European young people had experienced a variety of work situations before settling down to full-time regular employment.

Compared with their counterparts in the European countries, Japan's university graduates are much more likely to settle into a long-term career with the same company immediately following graduation. This is especially true for male graduates. The most likely explanations for this will have to do with the Japanese practice of the one-off hiring of university graduates in April each year and the commitment of Japanese firms to long-term employment.

Comparing the way graduates think about their careers

Given the fact that there are so many more *furiitaa* in the European countries, one might ask why such a fuss is made about the relatively few *furiitaa* in Japan. My view is that the answer may lie in the different way Japanese and the people in Europe think about part-time work and fixed-term employment. Until recently the lifecourse followed by most Japanese required them to immediately become a full-time regular employee upon gradation and then to work at the same firm for a long time as is commonly conceived when people speak of "life-time employment". In line with this approach, finding full-time regular employment was seen as the starting point for a life-long career in the labor force. This approach to work is quite different to what exists in Europe. Even though part-time workers and those on short-term contracts often experience a sense of uncertainty about the future, the way that employment status

Table 7.4: The employment situation of university graduates in their fourth year after graduation (females in Japan and Europe)

Country	Regular full-time employment	Part-time employment or for a fixed period	Self-employed	Unemployed	Special training	Graduate school	House wife	Other or no answer	Total	N
				Employment outcome						
Japan	62.9	14.9	2.2	3.8	1.1	3.8	7.6	3.7	100.0	1,613
Other European OECD countries	44.0	25.0	4.9	4.0	1.9	4.7	6.0	9.4	100.0	18,282
Italy	27.7	24.5	13.1	6.7	7.0	7.7	2.8	10.6	100.0	1,649
Spain	13.8	29.2	6.2	11.8	2.5	4.2	0.6	31.6	100.0	1,730
France	49.0	17.1	1.1	9.1	5.4	13.1	1.9	3.4	100.0	1,670
Austria	40.6	28.6	9.4	4.8	0.8	2.5	9.4	3.8	100.0	1,101
Germany	37.9	30.1	6.8	3.0	1.5	3.5	7.9	9.2	100.0	1,526
Holland	46.4	36.5	3.5	1.9	0.0	1.4	2.6	7.6	100.0	1,701
UK	61.6	17.9	3.9	2.0	2.0	6.0	2.7	4.0	100.0	2,034
Finland	41.2	34.7	2.9	1.3	1.0	2.3	5.3	12.3	100.0	1,617
Sweden	55.3	17.2	2.0	1.4	2.3	4.9	10.4	6.6	100.0	1,478
Norway	51.4	26.2	2.2	0.9	0.0	3.6	3.5	12.1	100.0	1,985
Czechoslovakia	53.8	15.6	4.9	2.0	0.0	2.0	21.6	0.2	100.0	1,791

Source: Nihon Rodo Kenkyu Kiko (2001a), p. 50.

Table 7.5: The number of firms at which graduates in full-time regular employment had worked during the 3–4 years following graduation (Japan and Europe)

	Male graduates		Female graduates	
Number of employers	Japan	Europe	Japan	Europe
At only 1 company	80.9	42.7	72.3	41.0
At 2–3 companies	13.2	33.1	18.3	30.8
At 4 or more companies	5.2	22.7	8.0	26.4
Total	100.0	100.0	100.0	100.0
N	1,459	8,707	1,014	8,040

Source: Nihon Rodo Kenkyu Kiko (2001a), p. 74.

articulates with an individual's future career is quite different in Europe and Japan. To reflect on those differences we might look further at some other results from the survey mentioned above to consider how part-time work and fixed-term employment are perceived in Japan and Europe.

Industry, firm size and occupation

Tables 7.6–7.8 show for the European countries and for Japan the breakdown of the labor force by gender for full-time employees without a fixed term of employment and for part-time and fixed-term workers. Table 7.6 incorporates industry as an additional variable. The distribution by industry is quite similar with the largest proportion of the male and the female labor force concentrated in educational activities both in Europe and in Japan. However, the second largest employer in Europe is welfare and medical services. Together those three industries in Europe employ 47 percent of male university graduates in part-time work and nearly 60 percent of their female counterparts. In Japan the second industry is "other services". Wholesaling, retailing and food/beverages also have a good number of males on a casual basis.

Another big difference is shown in Table 7.7. For this survey the public service was considered as its own category. In Europe over half of the university graduates in casual work were employed in the public service, whereas in Japan that figure is only one fourth. For male full-time employees, the difference between Europe and Japan is not so great. In the private sector university graduated *furiitaa* are concentrated a bit more in medium-sized firms with

Table 7.6: The distribution of university graduates in Europe and Japan by employment status, gender and industry

Industry	Male graduates				Female graduates			
	Full-time employment		Part-time or contract employment		Full-time employment		Part-time or contract employment	
	Japan	Europe	Japan	Europe	Japan	Europe	Japan	Europe
Mining, manufacturing and construction	27.6	27.9	9.8	10.9	16.1	13.2	7.1	5.4
Wholesaling, retailing and food/beverages	11.2	5.3	10.7	2.6	10.7	5.9	7.1	3.2
Finances & insurance	8.0	6.9	0.9	3.3	7.1	5.8	6.2	1.9
Administrative and special services	11.3	23.5	10.7	15.4	12.1	16.0	5.0	9.4
Education	6.3	6.9	17.9	29.5	14.2	19.0	24.1	32.3
Health and medical services	4.5	6.2	5.4	17.2	10.0	16.6	4.6	27.0
Other—public service	12.8	7.9	6.3	6.8	11.3	10.5	9.1	7.5
Other services	6.0	3.3	15.2	5.3	8.1	4.6	14.9	6.2
Other industries	8.1	8.1	4.5	4.2	5.4	4.8	9.1	2.3
No answer	4.2	4.0	18.8	4.8	5.0	3.6	12.9	4.7
Total	100.0	100.0	100.0	100.0	100.0	100.0	100.0	100.0
N	1,459	8,719	112	2,422	1,014	8,050	241	4,569

Source: Nihon Rodo Kenkyu Kiko (2001a), p. 75.

Table 7.7: The distribution of university graduates in Europe and Japan by employment status, gender and firm size

	Male graduates				Female graduates			
	Full-time employment		Part-time or contract employment		Full-time employment		Part-time or contract employment	
	Japan	Europe	Japan	Europe	Japan	Europe	Japan	Europe
Private sector (number of employees)								
1–29	8.4	11.1	25.5	19.7	16.4	13.7	17.3	24.0
30–99	10.5	11.3	19.1	11.3	12.4	12.1	15.4	16.2
100–499	26.2	19.9	29.8	24.5	28.5	21.8	24.0	23.5
500–999	11.6	8.1	4.3	8.2	8.8	7.8	10.6	9.1
1,000–4,999	24.7	19.7	10.6	18.5	21.8	20.5	17.3	15.5
5,000+	17.3	26.3	5.7	13.2	10.8	19.9	12.7	8.8
Public sector								
Public service	20.7	23.7	26.8	54.2	25.7	43.9	25.3	55.3
No answer	4.2	19.9	31.3	16.5	6.8	19.3	31.5	20.0
Total	100.0	100.0	100.0	100.0	100.0	100.0	100.0	100.0
N	1,459	8,719	112	2,422	1,014	8,050	214	4,569

Source: Nihon Rodo Kenkyu Kiko (2001a), p. 75.

100–499 employees, but overall the distributions in Europe and in Japan are not very different.

Table 7.8 shows a big difference in the distribution by occupation. Nearly eighty percent of males and females in Europe are in professional work or semi-professional work. In Japan the proportion is about half that in Europe, but a nearly similar proportion are in office work or in services and sales (about 30 percent of males and 40 percent of females).

Tables 7.6–7.8 allow us to consider how university graduates who work as full-time regular employees differ from those graduates who are casually employed. Both in Europe and in Japan the full-time regular male employees are concentrated more in the private sector in manufacturing and in larger scale firms. In Japan, about 40 percent of the male university graduates is in professional or semi-professional occupations, a figure considerably below the 73 percent recorded in Europe. In Japan a similar proportion of the population (another 42 percent) may be found in sales, services and office work (compared with only 3 percent in Europe). To some extent this may reflect the career approach taken in Japan's large firms which provide for new employees to work "on the ground" in clerical, sales and service positions for some time before being promoted upward into positions which are labelled "professional" or "semi-professional". In Europe the practice is for university graduates to be hired directly into such positions and in this regard their distribution across occupations is not too different from that for the casuals.

Tables 7.6–7.8 also provide data on females. In Japan and in Europe women university graduates in full-time regular employment tend to be less concentrated in education (14.2 and 19.0 percent respectively) than is the case for those in casual employment (24.1 and 32.3 percent). In Japan the most popular industry for regular full-time employees is manufacturing (16.1), whereas medical and health services also attract many European women in full-time regular employment (16.6 percent). The distribution across the public/private sector divide also reveals that a similar pattern exists for males and females in Europe where a high percentage of males (54.2 percent) and females (55.3 percent) in casual employment are employed in the public sector. Female university graduates in Europe are heavily concentrated in professional and semi-professional employment, though not quite to the extent of their male counterparts. Japanese women (at 37.7 percent) seem to follow the male pattern (at 35.5 percent) in Japan, but with the flows into

Table 7.8: The distribution of university graduates in Europe and Japan by employment status, gender and occupational grouping

Occupational grouping	Male graduates				Female graduates			
	Full-time employment		Part-time or contract employment		Full-time employment		Part-time or contract employment	
	Japan	Europe	Japan	Europe	Japan	Europe	Japan	Europe
Managerial	5.6	11.1	4.5	5.2	3.0	11.5	0.0	5.8
Professional	37.7	57.9	32.1	68.5	37.0	49.8	34.4	60.7
Semi-professional	3.7	15.2	3.6	11.4	3.1	20.8	3.3	17.3
Clerical	22.1	2.4	15.2	4.9	38.3	4.2	32.8	4.9
Services and sales	20.4	0.7	14.3	1.2	10.2	1.2	10.8	2.1
Manufacturing, farming, fishing	3.2	0.5	2.7	1.0	1.2	0.2	1.7	0.3
Other	1.1	1.1	1.1	1.1	1.1	1.1	1.1	1.1
No Answer	6.4	6.4	6.4	6.4	6.4	6.4	6.4	6.4
Total	100.0	100.0	100.0	100.0	100.0	100.0	100.0	100.0
N	1,459	8,719	112	2,422	1,014	8,050	214	4,569

Source: Nihon Rodo Kenkyu Kiko (2001a), p. 75.

the professional and semi-professional areas considerably below those in Europe.

Income and hours of work

Some comparisons of the hours of work, income and income per unit of time are provided in Table 7.9. This is done by presenting both an absolute value and an indexed value with the value for full-time regular employees set at 1.00. If we first compare full-time regular employees with casual employees, several facts emerge from the data. For males employment status seems to account for a larger difference in Europe than in Japan on an income-per-hour basis. This is owing mainly to the gap in total hours of work in Japan between full-time regular employees (52.04 hours) and the casually employed (35.30 hours). Employment status tends not to affect hours worked in Europe to the same extent; as a result the differential in gross hourly income is maintained at 77 percent whereas it is much narrower in Japan (at 91 percent).

The discussion in the preceding sections of this chapter might have led us to expect the differences based on employment status would be smaller in Europe. However, the differential in hourly remuneration was larger for male university graduates in Europe than in Japan. I imagine this may reflect the fact that in Europe many who are casually employed in the professions and in semi-professional occupations are actually seen as training. If so they would be paid less because they are seen as early career professionals on a longer-term trajectory that will eventually take them into full-time regular employment and remuneration in keeping with their future status as fully fledged professionals. It could also be that the larger income differentials in Japan are offset to a more marked degree by the large differential in hours worked, with males in full-time regular employment clocking up over 52 hours each week.

As for women, the gap between permanent and casual employees is larger in Japan than in Europe (50 percent as opposed to 79 percent). The gap in hours of work is also larger in Japan (74 to 84 percent for total hours of work and 79 to 83 percent for the standard work week). In this case the result is that a large gap also appears for Japan in the hourly earnings of women (79 to 91 percent).

The size of the gap seems also to vary by gender in a different way in Japan and in Europe. The difference in hourly earnings between permanent and casual employees is greater for women in

Table 7.9: Working conditions in Japan and Europe by gender and employment status

Employment status	A Annual income		B Hours of work		C Standard work week		D Annual income per hour each week	
	JY	Index	Hours	Index	Hours	Index	(A/B)	Index
Males								
Japan								
Full-time without fixed time period	393.1	100	52.04	100	40.31	100	7.55	100
Part-time or with fixed time period	243.4	62	35.30	68	31.31	78	6.9	91
Europe								
Full-time without fixed time period	398.8	100	46.65	100	39.28	100	8.55	100
Part-time or with fixed time period	292.4	73	44.67	96	35.22	90	6.55	77
Females								
Japan								
Full-time without fixed time period	335.5	100	47.83	100	40.18	100	7.01	100
Part-time or with fixed time period	194.8	58	35.21	74	31.92	79	5.53	79
Europe								
Full-time without fixed time period	315.1	100	43.54	100	37.81	100	7.24	100
Part-time or with fixed time period	248.8	79	37.90	87	31.29	83	6.56	91

Note: 1 Euro = JY122.7.

Source: Nihon Rodo Kenkyu Kiko (2001a), p. 77.

Japan whereas the reverse holds in Europe. This finding is difficult to explain apart from noting that hours worked by male and female casuals are about the same whereas a considerable gap exists in total income. The income gap between male and female casuals is smaller in Europe.

The consciousness of employees

Table 7.10 provides some findings from the comparative study on what employees thought about their work. The answers to Question A reveal that over two thirds of Europe's university graduates in both employment categories felt that the content of their work was very suitable to the work they were doing or somewhat suitable given their educational background. This was true both for male and for female graduates. This contrasted to Japan where only 40 percent of regular full-timers and just 30 percent of the casually employed felt that way. On the other hand, a high percentage of the Japanese sample felt their work did not match up with their educational qualifications, with the casually employed being more negative in this regard than regular full-time employees.

Related to this are the responses to Question B. As might be expected, they show that most of the European sample – males and females, full-time regular and part-time casuals – felt they were frequently using knowledge and skills acquired through their education. Congruent with the responses to Question A, many of the Japanese respondents felt they were not using skills and knowledge acquired in school. In this regard it is interesting to note that for the Japanese sample considerably more casually employed graduates were satisfied in this regard than were full-time regular employees.

When making the comparisons regarding Question B, we need to remember that the Japanese version of the questionnaire contained as one of the possible multiple choice answers the following category: "the content of the education I received at university was not relevant to the job I am *currently* doing". This complicates the comparison. At the time we were preparing the Japanese version of the survey, many of those involved felt the question world be hard for the Japanese respondents to grasp if we did not add this choice to the list. The idea that the generalist knowledge and skills imparted through a Japanese university education would have a direct relevance to one's work immediately after graduation was seen by the Japanese research team as foreign to the Japanese context.

Table 7.10: An evaluation of one's employment situation by employment status and gender – a Japan–Europe comparison

| | Male graduates | | | | Female graduates | | | |
| | Japan | | Europe | | Japan | | Europe | |
	Permanent	Casual	Permanent	Casual	Permanent	Casual	Permanent	Casual
Question A: To what extent is your employment and work appropriate to your level of education?								
Very appropriate	10.9	13.0	34.4	35.9	15.0	9.8	40.1	38.8
Rather appropriate	31.3	19.0	39.3	33.1	35.8	24.0	32.7	30.1
Can't really say	38.5	29.0	17.2	18.4	34.2	36.4	16.0	16.4
Not very suitable	13.9	21.0	7.1	8.3	11.9	17.3	8.2	9.6
Very inappropriate	5.5	18.0	2.2	4.3	3.1	12.4	3.1	5.2
(Average score)	3.3	2.9	4.0	3.9	3.5	3.0	4.0	3.9
Question B: To what extent do you use the knowledge and skills acquired in the course of study from which you graduated in 1994 or 1995?								
Very often	7.3	13.4	16.6	29.2	9.7	15.1	22.3	29.2
Fairly often	14.2	12.4	32.5	30.2	13.1	15.6	30.7	31.2
Every now and then	31.0	23.7	31.3	24.1	32.6	19.3	29.2	24.4
Not very often	33.2	17.5	17.0	12.6	28.0	26.1	14.6	11.9
Not at all	8.7	14.4	2.7	3.9	7.6	8.3	3.2	3.3
What was learned at university is not directly connected with my work	5.5	18.6	-	-	8.9	15.6	-	-
(Average score)	2.8	2.9	3.4	3.7	2.9	3.0	3.5	3.7

Question C: Altogether, to what extent are you satisfied with your current work?

Very satisfied	9.4	7.6	21.8	17.8	8.8	10.3	23.4	21.2
Somewhat satisfied	36.7	30.5	48.3	44.4	44.7	38.9	45.3	41.1
Don't really know	24.4	30.5	21.4	25.1	21.4	26.5	22.2	26.0
Not very satisfied	22.7	19.0	7.0	10.2	20.6	18.4	7.1	9.0
Very dissatisfied	6.8	12.4	1.6	2.4	4.5	6.0	2.0	2.7
(Average score)	3.2	3.0	3.8	3.7	3.3	3.3	3.8	3.7
Total	100.0	100.0	100.0	100.0	100.0	100.0	100.0	100.0
N	1,459	8,719	112	2,422	1,014	8,050	214	4,569

Notes:

1. When the question was not asked or there was no answer, the respondent was excluded from these tabulations. For this reason the totals vary and are not consistent from one column to another.

2. For each set of questions, the answers were scored in descending order, with the top receiving 5 points and the bottom answer receiving 1 point. Using that scale an overall average was calculated and given for each question for each sub-grouping identified across the top of the table.

3. The last choice for Question B was added only in the Japanese survey.

Source: Nihon Rodo Kenkyu Kiko (2001a), p. 78.

Many of the casually employed males in the Japanese sample chose this response. The averages suggest that the Japanese casuals felt a bit more reliant on what they learned in education system than did those who were in full-time regular employment.

Looking at the overall level of satisfaction (Question C), we can conclude from the averages that the Europeans were much happier with their work, although in both countries the full-time regular employees seem marginally more satisfied than those employed on a casual basis.

Challenges facing Japan's university graduated *furiitaa*

A major difference emerging from this chapter lies in the way study at university and employment articulate. In Europe the majority of graduates make their way into professional or technical occupations. This is why so many of the European respondents to the questionnaire were able to answer that in their work they were utilizing knowledge and skills acquired through their studies at university. In Japan, however, it is common for university graduates to start their career in sales or in doing routine office work, with those tasks forming the basis for their career within the firm. For most there is the assumption that they can stay on at the same firm indefinitely. In Japan's larger firms that assumption is bolstered by the existence of a fairly developed internal labor market. With the expectation that they will be promoted to other more rewarding work in the future, many of the graduates, as well as their employees, do not seem to be overly concerned with the exact nature of the education they received.

If this is the case and the difference in the transition from university to work life is as described above, the current situation in Japan is serious and will have long-term social consequences. At the beginning of the twenty first century over 100,000 university graduates are not finding regular full-time employment as *seishain*. Nor do these graduates continue to further study. In Europe many more graduates become unengaged or work as fixed-term casuals. Moreover, the percentage doing so even in their fourth year after graduation is higher in Europe than in Japan. However, in Europe graduates are able to connect to their career through a process that allows for casual work experience and periods of non-engagement. For this reason we can conclude that differences in the way employment status is defined can be said to have a huge impact on how careers are structured in Japan and in Europe.

In Japan the medical profession revolves around intern programs which put trainees to work on a casual basis. Graduates in medicine, education and many of the arts are numerous in Japan, and it is important to view their non-engagement and *furiitaa*-type work as preparation for their careers as distinct from that of those headed for full-time regular employment in white-collar positions. The peculiar status of *"seiki shain"* or *"seishain"* means that the transition from university to work has its own peculiarities for many university graduates in Japan.

Another issue concerns the way in which opportunities to acquire occupationally relevant knowledge and skills are made available to young people in Japan. Japanese firms have utilized on-the-job training and other practices linked to the work place, often starting white-collar employees in sales or other clerical tasks. Until now few firms seemed concerned about the specifics of each potential employee's education. For this reason, careful thought needs to be given to the relative lack of training and skill development for most graduates who do not become *seishain*. The above analysis and the comparison with Europe point to the need to rethink the curriculum all students are exposed to during their years in the university system.

The final issue to consider is the gender differential. We saw above that female graduates are more likely than male graduates to flow into *furiitaa*-type employment. Moreover, sizeable differentials exist in the working conditions between women in *furiitaa*-type employment and women in full-time regular employment. The predilection of women to be in casual employment is clearly a factor explaining male-female wage differentials that appear in aggregate data. To resolve this issue, fair rules are needed so that working conditions do not depend on gender, hours of work or the period of employment. Japan's policy makers need to explore the possibility of having part-time regular employment as *seishain* on a fractional appointment as a fully recognized and accepted employment status in Japan.

8 The Evolving Transition from School to Work

Changes in the recruitment of new graduates

The common practice in Japanese society has been for new graduates to assume permanent employment immediately following graduation. This has traditionally meant that each student's placement needed to be finalized before graduation occurred (i.e., while they were still a student in their last year of studies). Along with this came the expectation that Japan's large firms, the government, and its various bureaucracies and affiliated agencies would employ large numbers of new graduates as full-time regular employees (*seishain*) in the first week of April each year. In principle each employer structured their recruitment policy around the hiring and the training of new graduates. Employees were to be recruited from the open labor market only when special skills were needed or when an employer's needs for labor could not be met by hiring a new graduate (or by otherwise training up an existing employee).

The branches of the Public Employment Security Office (PESO) separates requests from firms for new graduates from their requests for persons with previous work experience. The Agency compiles different statistics on each group and separately calculates for each group the effective demand coefficient (the number of advertised positions divided by the number of job seekers). The effective demand coefficient for labor in 2001 was 0.59. This meant that there were only 59 positions on offer for every 100 persons who were seeking work. However, the coefficient in the market for new senior high school graduates in March 2002 was 1.32: 132 positions were on offer for every one hundred new graduates seeking work. On a per capita basis the demand for new graduates was twice that for persons with previous employment experience. This indicates the extent to which firms preferred to hire new graduates. Having said that, it is also important to note that the coefficient for new senior high graduates was over 3.0 in the early 1990s, after which the demand for such graduates relative to supply has dropped considerably since then.

Why has the demand for inexperienced graduates been stronger than for persons who already have experience in the labor market? It is commonly said that new graduates are in a certain sense "uncontaminated" and, therefore, easier to train in an employer's specific way of doing things. Moreover, as junior employees they command a lower wage. Given the lower rate of labor turnover associated with Japanese firms, it has made sense for them to hire employees who can be shaped in ways that will maximize their fit with the technology, skills and managerial culture of a specific firm. At many firms management believes it can afford to invest heavily in the training of its young employees because it assumes they will be with the firm for the long haul and be rewarded later in their careers as their seniority increases. Given that assumption, firms do not feel the need to tightly peg remuneration to output or productivity at each stage in the employee's career. It is within this broader context that employers value the newly graduated as an employee.

However, those practices have been changing. Change is perhaps best signalled in Nikkeiren's call in 1995 for a change from the currently practiced two-tiered approach to designating employment status to a three-tiered approach. The three categories it proposed for classifying employees were (i) the long-term career employee who would acquire many company-specific skills over a long period, (ii) those with highly professionalized technical skills, and (iii) all others who would constitute its labor force in areas where flexible adjustment needed to be made on a more frequent basis. The proposal was for each firm to devise a blueprint which would clearly stipulate its own requirements for each type of employee. The vision was that those in the first category would be recruited mainly from among new graduates as in the past. However, the proposal called for those in the second category to be recruited from among highly skilled experienced professionals and to be guaranteed an annual salary for a fixed term stretching over some years. Those in the final group were seen as being unskilled or semi-skilled at best, and were to be hired on a casual basis as *arubaitaa* or *paatotaimaa*. In the past those in the middle group tended to be hired as new graduates and trained in their firm's specific technologies. However, technologies, especially IT-related procedures, are more generic and widely available. In-house training is seen as being less necessary, and the aim of Nikkeiren's proposal was to provide firms with a means of obtaining greater flexibility in terms of their ability to adjust their labor force, thereby better matching aggregate labor costs and the overall level of output derived from each firm's labor force. It is in light of these changes that the demand for new graduates seeking full-time regular employment has declined while the demand for employees willing to work on a casual or part-time basis has increased.

The transition from school to work

The school-to-work transition involves a huge transformation. After spending most of everyday at school as an adolescent with one set of rules learned over twelve or more years, new graduates suddenly have to function much more on auto-pilot as an adult in an environment with a new set of rules. Until recently most young Japanese graduated in March and then immediately took up regular full-time employment at the beginning of April. The practice whereby firms employed large numbers of new graduates each April is about the transition from school to work. Over the past decade, however, the number of young people who do not make that transition has been increasing, a trend reflected in the increasing number of graduates who remain unemployed for some time after leaving school or who become *furiitaa*.

The Ministry of Education and Science has kept statistics which allows us to know where graduates go upon graduation. It provides breakdowns for senior high school and university graduates, including data on the number of students who drop out along the way. We can thus trace each age cohort as it leaves middle school and moves up through the various levels in the education system. This allows us to obtain a fairly reliable estimate of the number in each cohort who become employed upon graduation at each level of education along with the number who stay in the system and continue on to the next level of education. At the tertiary level figures exist for two-year junior colleges, for technical colleges (*senmon gakko*) and for four-year universities.

There is some slippage in the figures as some students temporarily leave the system to prepare for entrance at the next level. Accordingly, some students move down to a later cohort, and this distorts the figures ever so slightly. Of course, those that leave their original cohort are replaced by others in a previous cohort who have done the same thing. In addition we are also able to obtain similar statistics on the number who graduate from specialist training schools (*kakushu gakko*) for nursing. This gives us a fairly accurate picture of the numbers coming into the casual labor force from any particular cohort at each stage along the way.

By factoring out the number who either do not go on for more education or do not obtain full-time regular employment at each stage along the way, we can estimate the number in each cohort who have not followed the mainstream into regular full-time employment or into a graduate program by the time the cohort has reached the age of 22. We can refer to that figure as the pool of unemployed graduates. Using that estimate we can also calculate the size of that pool as a percentage of the cohort. Both the absolute number and the percentage estimates are given in Table 8.1 for each graduating cohort from 1974 onwards. As of 2000 the last cohort to reach the age of approximately 22 (which roughly would be the age when the more educated members of the cohort graduate from four-year universities with their bachelor's degrees) completed middle school in 1994. Until the cohort of 1988, the size of the cohort and the percentage of the cohort that deviated from the accepted path (*i.e.*, those that either gained full employment or continued their education) fluctuated together; there was a high correlation in the value of those two statistics. Beginning with the 1989 cohort, however, the number of middle school graduates (*i.e.*, the size of the cohort) begins to shrink, while the percentage of those in the cohort who dropped out along the way began to climb. Until the cohort of 1989 the percentage of drop-outs remained at about 20 percent. With each successive cohorts over the next seven years (from 1989 through 1994), however, that percentage steadily rose from around 20 percent to over 35 percent. In other words, one out of three in the 1994 cohort was by the age of 22 either unemployed or working as a *furiitaa*.

By the middle of the 1990s something had fundamentally changed in the way the labor market was behaving. By the time those in the 1994 cohort had entered their twenties, the world of work had been reorganized. Reflecting those changes, the transition from school to work also evolved as firms increased the percentage of casual or non-regular employees and mid-career entrants being hired. This meant that students now face a new situation with new rules for gaining employment. To be sure, two thirds of the 1994 cohort were successful in the old labor market. To understand how the new labor market in which the remaining one third found themselves functioned, we need to consider the path each student takes after leaving their last educational institution. In Chapter Four

Table 8.1: Middle school graduates obtaining employment outside the normal school placement procedures: 1974–1999

Year	Number of graduates	Percentage of young people outside the normal progression through school to work
1974	1,623,574	19.5
1975	1,580,495	18.5
1976	1,563,868	19.2
1977	1,579,953	19.3
1978	1,607,183	19.6
1979	1,635,460	19.8
1980	1,723,025	22.0
1981	1,677,764	21.1
1982	1,556,578	18.2
1983	1,850,694	22.2
1984	1,882,768	22.4
1985	1,882,034	21.6
1986	1,933,616	22.3
1987	2,005,425	23.7
1988	2,044,923	24.6
1989	2,049,471	27.0
1990	1,981,503	28.2
1991	1,860,300	28.8
1992	1,773,712	30.7
1993	1,732,437	33.0
1994	1,680,006	35.2
1995	1,622,198	35.3
1996	1,545,270	37.0
1997	1,510,994	38.1
1998	1,511,845	37.2
1999	1,502,711	36.1
2000	1,464,760	
2001	1,410,408	
2002	1,365,471	
2003	1,325,208	
2004	1,298,718	
2005	1,236,363	

Note: The percentages in Column B were calculated by subtracting from (a) the number of middle school graduates in a given year (b) the numbers who had (i) gained full-time regular employment in the same year, (ii) gained full-time regular employment following graduation from senior high school three years later, (iii) gained full-time regular employment following graduation from a two-year junior college, or specialized training college 5–7 years later, (iv) gained full-time regular employment following graduation from a four-year university 7 years later, (v) entered a postgraduate program following graduation from a four-year university 7 years later, and (vi) gained full-time regular employment following graduation from a junior nursing program or became nursing trainees two years later. The remaining number was then divided by the numbers which started the cohort when it graduated from middle school (given in Column A). Middle school graduation was the starting point for this exercise because it represents the last level of compulsory education in Japan.

Source: Mombu Kakagu Sho (The Ministry of Education and Science), *Gakko Kihon Chosa* (The Basic Survey of Schools in Japan), taken from the annual reports issued each year.

we looked at some survey data concerning university graduates who did not gain full-time regular employment (excluding those who continued onto postgraduate studies). The findings suggested that about two thirds of male university graduates and about half of female university graduates who had not found such employment upon graduation nevertheless found full-time regular employment within four years of graduating. The research also showed that many of those who found casual work connected to a career came to achieve outcomes quite different from the outcomes for those who did not find such work.

As Chapter One indicated, only ten percent of all *furiitaa* were university graduates. We thus need to consider more broadly the situation of all *furiitaa* whose ranks include many young people with low levels of education. To do so it is useful to look at data from a survey on Tokyo's youth which was described above in Chapter Four (see Nihon Rodo Kenkyu Kiko 2001b). Compared to their counterparts in the outer lying prefectures, youth in Japan's large cities are much more likely to become *furiitaa*. Although there are differences in the behavior of rural and urban youth, the percentage of urban young people in casual employment has rapidly increased across the board, and some might even argue that today's *furiitaa* are leading the nation's young people into new ways of working. For this reason, the survey of Tokyo's youth yields results which have a broader significance.

Empirical findings on the transition from school to work

The Tokyo survey targeted young persons aged 18–29 who were not studying at an educational institution. It found that 65 percent had become regular full-time employees immediately after leaving the education system (Table 8.2). This finding is consistent with the findings presented in Table 8.1. Looking at the breakdowns by level of education in Table 8.2, the extremely low percentage of school dropouts who become regular full-time employees is noteworthy. In general the percentage of graduates who become regular full-time employees is much higher than the figure attained by the drop-outs, but that figure varies inversely for both groups with the level of education attained.

Those who drop out from school at whatever level are excluded from the market for new graduates. They are also not able to avail themselves of the placement services offered by schools and the other institutes of education. This is a major reason why their rate of entry

Table 8.2: Percentage of students who became full-time regular employees upon leaving school in 2001 and 2006

Type of student	2001		2006	
	Number	Percentage	Number	Percentage
Senior high school graduate	450	57.8	663	40.6
Graduates from specialized training colleges and other vocational training institutions	302	72.4	392	61.0
Graduates of two-year junior colleges and other higher specialized				
Training colleges	175	79.5	194	65.2
Graduates from universities and/or graduate schools	337	77.2	491	68.0
Middle school graduates and/or senior high school drop-outs	76	29.1	164	12.8
Drop-outs from universities and other tertiary institutions	45	27.0	102	14.7
Totals for all females	704	62.0	1,038	49.8
Totals for all males	715	68.3	962	50.1
Total for all surveyed	1,419	65.2	2,000	50.0

Notes:

1. The numbers given in the 2001 data were reapportioned using data from the 1995 National Census and the 1997 Survey of Employment Status. A similar procedure was followed when adjusting the sample distribution derived from the 2006 survey.
2. Both surveys targeted young persons aged 18–29. In 2006 those aged 29 would have graduated from middle school in 1992, whereas those aged 18 would have finished senior high school in 2005.

Source: the 2001 data – Nihon Rodo Kenkyu Kiko (2001b), p. 42. The 2006 data – Rodo Seisaku Kenkyu-Kenshu Kiko (2006), p. 28

into full-time regular employment is so low. Because the age of the respondents when the survey was conducted in 2001 ranged between 18 and 29, we have a sample in which respondents were leaving the eduction system over more than a ten-year period. It also means we can use this data to view the outcomes for different age cohorts. Doing so we again find that the percentage of new graduates who enter regular full-time employment is lower in recent times. The results of the Tokyo survey simply confirm what other research has revealed and were followed up in a later survey in February 2006 (Rodo Seisaku Kenkyu-Kenshu Kiko 2006).

Table 8.3: The status of young persons immediately after leaving school (excluding those who proceed to further education or assume regular full-time employment): 2001 and 2006

Destination	2001			2006		
	Males	Females	Total	Males	Females	Total
Arubaito and part-time work	54.7	60.4	57.3	57.4	61.7	59.4
Temps assigned by labor dispatch firms and short-term contracted employees	9.3	10.8	10.0	10.6	16.9	13.6
Self-employment or family workers	10.3	5.7	8.2	7.5	1.3	4.5
Unemployed (looking for work, not sure what to do, doing nothing)	19.1	17.4	18.3	16.5	11.9	14.3
Others (preparing on own for examinations, preparing for marriage, no answer)	6.6	5.8	6.2	8.1	8.3	8.2
Total	100.0	100.0	100.0	100.0	100.0	100.0
N	268	226	494	521	480	1,001

Notes:
1. These figures are the result of retabulations done by the author. The figures given for 2001 were based on absolute numbers derived by reapportioning the sample distributions using data from the 1995 National Census and the 1997 Survey of Employment Status. A similar procedure was followed when adjusting the sample distribution derived from the 2006 survey.
2. Both surveys targeted young persons aged 18–29. In 2006 those aged 29 would have graduated from middle school in 1992, whereas those aged 18 would have finished senior high school in 2005.

Source: the 2001 data – Nihon Rodo Kenkyu Kiko (2001b), p. 42. The 2006 data – Rodo Seisaku Kenkyu-Kenshu Kiko (2006), p. 28

Table 8.3 shows the destination of those leaving the education system without full-time regular employment. About 60 percent were employed as *arabaitaa* or *paatotaimaa*; nearly a tenth worked as temporary help and another tenth became self-employed; about 20 percent remained unemployed. The patterns shown in Table 8.3 for males and females were similar, although slightly more males became self-employed. Not shown in Table 8.3 is the level of education. Male high school graduates were slightly more concentrated in self-employment while male graduates from junior colleges and specialized training colleges were more likely to become temporary help. Male university graduates were more likely than their female counterparts to be unemployed. For females less education correlated with a higher likelihood of being in *arubaito* or part-time work, and those with more education were more concentrated in jobs as temporary workers, dispatched workers or employees on fixed-term contracts.

The sample for the Tokyo survey included persons who had just graduated and others who had graduated more than ten years earlier. This differed from the survey of university graduates which was discussed above in Chapter Four. In that survey all of the respondents had graduated at the same time and belonged to the same cohort. In the Tokyo survey the time that had elapsed since their graduation becomes a critical variable. To control for that variable, we divided the respondents into three groups: (i) those who left the education system within the past three years, (ii) those who had been out of the system for 3–6 years, and (iii) those for whom 6–12 years had passed since leaving.

Table 8.4 shows for each group how those not in full-time regular employment when they left the education system were doing in 2001. For males, the proportion in regular full-time work increased the longer they had been out of the education system whereas the proportion in casual work dropped markedly. The same trends seem to occur for females, but they are not as pronounced. The drop in the percentage working as regular full-time employees drops for those in their late twenties as they become full-time housewives and experience childbirth. Not shown in the table is the fact that the movement of males into full-time employment is in one direction (from casual to permanent employment) whereas females shifted predominantly from full-time regular employment to other forms of work over the same period. This probably reflects gender differences in how the division of labor occurs once family life begins and males predominate as the main breadwinners.

The challenge of unemployment and working casually

About 80 percent of males who do not become full-time regular employees unpon graduation do so within 6–7 years of graduation. Some analysts believe this represents a new pattern in the transition of Japanese young people into the labor force. Another view is that the changes we have been discussing are not just about the transition into the labor force. Some argue that the decision to work on a casual basis represents a more fundamental change as an entirely new way of working emerges. Those who assume this view of work can readily point to a number of industries which depend fully on

Table 8.4: The progression through time of those not obtaining full-time regular employment upon graduation: 2006

Status in the labor market	Number of years after graduation					
	Males			Females		
	≤3 years	3–6 years	6–12 years	≤3 years	3–6 years	6–12 years
Full-time regular employee (*seishain*)	14.7	36.9	37.3	12.2	18.6	22.6
Arubaitaa or *paatotaimaa*	62.7	36.2	23.9	59.1	54.9	51.8
Dispatched worker or short-term contracted employee	8.0	11.4	12.7	17.0	18.6	15.3
Self-employed or family worker	2.7	10.7	19.7	1.3	2.7	4.4
Unemployed	4.9	2.7	4.9	4.3	1.8	2.2
Unemployed – involved in no activity	4.0	1.3	0.0	2.6	2.7	2.2
Unemployed – preparing for marriage or further education	2.7	0.7	0.0	2.6	0.9	1.5
Other, no answer	0.4	0.0	1.4	0.9	0.0	0.0
Total	100.0	100.0	100.0	100.0	100.0	100.0
N	225	149	142	230	113	13,139

Source: The figures presented ere were generated by the author from data used in Rodo Seisaku Kenkyu-Kenshu Kiko (2006).

the use of young casuals working as *arubaitaa* or as *paatotaimaa*. Along with this perspective comes the view that a new lifestyle is emerging among Japan's youth – the new graduates who are core participants in the new forms of Japanese popular culture that are now being exported around the world. This new culture includes Japanese m*anga*, various kinds of computer games, fashion and music. Some observers optimistically suggest that this new subset of the Japanese population will become not only a crucial component of the labor force supporting these export industries, but also consumers who will lead Japanese society in new directions.

I tend to agree with this latter assessment, and believe it is wrong to portray the *furiitaa* as a social problem. At the same time, it is important to recognize this alternative approach to work may not be as attractive as it first appears. Before drawing firm conclusions, it is necessary to study carefully the situation surrounding this previously overlooked segment of the labor force. The first step is to consider the social ramifications which flow from an increase in the number of *furiitaa*. Given the many challenges *furiitaaa* face when it comes to acquiring the skills necessary to establish a career trajectory, we also need to investigate in more detail how the process of acquiring skills differs for casuals and for full-time regular employees.

Firms are likely to invest differently in the skills of those who are employed directly out of school on the assumption that they will be employed on a long-term basis and in the skills of those who are doing *arubaito* or part-time work and are seen mostly as part of a temporary labor force which may be gone the next day. It is generally the case that management is much more likely to invest in training the former than in training the latter. In Japanese firms a good amount of training occurs on-the-job. Although it is difficult to assess accurately the difference in this regard as it relates to the work given to each group of employees, to some extent we can assess the level of sophistication associated with each type of work.

The data from Table 8.5 is from the 2006 survey of young people in Tokyo (whereas the data in Table 7.9 was from the 2001 survey). It compares the hourly income earned by full-time regular employees and that earned by casual employees. Column C shows that casually employed males on an average hourly basis earn only 70 percent of what full-time regular male employees earn; the figure is 68 percent for women (Column C). In other words, the reward for casual work is considerably below that earned by regular employees even when they are still in their twenties.

The table reveals two further sources of variation. First, as the level of education increases, the income differential widens. Second, with the exception of the men who graduated from junior colleges and specialized training colleges, the differential widens as cohorts age. It would seem that those in full-time permanent employment are likely to progress to more highly paid positions as they age. This would seem to be especially true for those with higher educational qualifications. On the other hand, those who are casually employed tend to continue in the same work throughout their working life regardless of their educational qualifications. They are likely to be repeatedly hired and rehired to perform the same unskilled work for which it is not necessary to accumulate skills or skill-related experience over the course of their career in the labor force. This no doubt varies from one employer to another. In some firms and industries casuals are able to develop their skills. However, the overall averages suggest that does not happen very often and that the effect is quite marginal when it does occur. In other words, casual

Table 8.5: *A comparison of the hourly remuneration to full-time regular employees and to those in* furiitaa-*type employment: 2006*

	Males			Females		
	A	B	C	A	B	C
SHS graduates aged 18–19	0.83	0.73	88	0.88	0.76	86
SHS graduates aged 20–24	1.07	0.87	81	1.19	0.82	69
SHS graduates aged 25–29	1.26	0.94	75	1.23	0.89	72
Junior college graduates aged under 25	0.93	0.87	93	0.96	0.74	77
Junior college graduates aged 25–29	1.18	0.96	81	1.21	0.79	66
University graduates aged under 25	1.17	0.73	62	1.20	0.96	80
University graduates aged 25–29	1.38	0.99	72	1.32	0.89	67
Entire sample, including school drop-outs	1.19	0.84	70	1.15	0.79	68
N	561	264		433	318	

Notes:
1. Table headings:
   A: Hourly remuneration of full-time regular employees
   B: Hourly remuneration of *arubaitaa* and *paatotaimaa*
   C: Ratio of hourly earnings (%) (100B/A)
2. SHS = senior high school
3. The hourly remuneration is calculated as follows:

$$\frac{\text{the annual income earned in the preceding tax year rounded to the nearest 10,000 yen}}{\text{weekly hours worked in a recent week}}$$

4. The hourly wage rates are given in 1000s of Japanese yen.

Source: Rodo Seisaku Kenkyu-Kenshu Kiko (2006), p. 26.

employment carries with it a certain risk that one will not receive adequate training for a career in the labor force.

Long transitions and the search for the right career

There is also the view that the casually employed and the unemployed might fruitfully be making an extended search for an appropriate career. This suggests that they might be looking for the work they really want to do. As we saw above, many young people who became *furiitaa* did so either because they did not know what they would ultimately want to do or because they wanted to do something other than being regularly employed full-time. Their having a different "dream" as mavericks is something that would appeal not only to the *furiitaa* themselves, but also to their acquaintances or significant others.

This outlook can also be seen in the number of young *furiitaa* who claimed that they would give priority to doing what they wanted to do while they were still young and that they would be happy with either casual or permanent employment as long as they could do what they "really" wanted to do: 17.1 percent of *seishain* and 27.8 percent of the *arubaitaa* indicated they subscribed to the first of those sentiments while 26.2 and 40.7 percent respectively indicated that they could identify with the second position. The results from the survey point to this concern with the freedom to do interesting things as a background factor accounting for the decision to accept work as a *furiitaa*.

Obviously, many *furiitaa* are not doing the work they want to do. Table 8.6 provides further data for 2006 that is broken down for male and female *furiitaa*. It shows the employment status they desired both at the time of the survey and at a time three years into the future. The survey indicated that 30–40 percent of male and female *furiitaa* would have preferred to be working as regular full-time employees in either the private or the public sector. In other words, they did not want to be *furiitaa*. Just under 50 percent wanted to continue working as *furiitaa*. Many wanting to be *furiitaa* were nevertheless consciously looking for a career to take up. To be more precise, their career search was conceived with a time limit clearly in mind. This can be seen in the fact that in contrast to their present situation few males (5.1 percent) (as against 29.6 percent of females) wanted to be

Table 8.6: Percentage distribution of males and females classified as furiitaa *in 2006 by the work outcome desired in three years' time*

Time Frame	Self-employed or family worker	*Arubaitaa* or *paatotaimaa*	Temp from a dispatching firm of short-term contract workers	Regular full-time employee	Other (including full-time housewives)
Position desired at present					
Males (N=225)	6.9	47.6	4.4	38.5	2.5
Females (N=335)	4.2	61.5	9.0	24.2	1.2
Position desired after 3 years					
Males (N=275)	23.6	5.1	2.5	64.0	4.7
Females (N=335)	9.6	29.6	6.6	46.0	8.4

Source: The figures presented here were generated by the author from data used in Rodo Seisaku Kenkyu-Kenshu Kiko (2006).

arubaitaa or *paatotaimaa* three years into the future. Only a further 2.5 and 6.6 percent respectively wanted to be contracted temps after three years. The reasoning is clear. For a set period of time many young Japanese are happy to follow their dream. However, they are also quick to discover that casual employment does not offer them much of a future. Many in the survey became *furiitaa* because they had few other options, but still saw it as a temporary measure and were persisting in seeing their time in the casual work force as a step toward finding a career.

Despite the optimism of many *furiitaa*, only 13 percent of the 514 *furiitaa* in the 2001 Tokyo survey actually felt they were acquiring useful career-relevant experience as a casual. Considering the reasons why young people left casual employment, only 19 percent claimed they had found what they wanted to do; 54 percent answered simply that they would be better off as a full-time regular employee. Another 41 percent claimed that it was appropriate at their age to move out of casual employment. Very few were able to state clearly that their stint in casual employment had real value for their future career.

Direct and indirect transitions

In addition to the acquisition of skills and the extent to which their work experience links to permanent employment, a third issue confronting the *furiitaa* is reflected in the differential in working condition which emerges as a result of the initial difference in their employment status immediately following graduation. It has already been noted that many young people work as *furiitaa* for a relatively short period before moving into the regular work force. Nonetheless, as we saw above in Tables 7.9 and 8.5, a difference could be detected in the wage rate between those who joined the ranks of the permanently employed immediately after graduation and those who first took a detour through casual employment. Table 8.7 compares the two cohort groups in terms of their attachment to their place of work and various working conditions. Compared to those who immediately became permanently employed upon graduation, the average age of those who later become *seishain* after a period as *furiitaa* is slightly higher. The proportion who are males is larger, and the *furriitaa* have lower educational qualifications. The *furiitaa* are more concentrated in service roles and in Japan's firms with fewer than 30 employees. Their hours of work are longer than those of the *seishain*, and their annual income is about ten percent lower.

Because gender and educational background account for huge differences in labor turnover, it is difficult to measure the direct impact of the two career paths on working conditions. To control for the effect of variables such as gender, age, and level of education, we must use multiple regression. By systematically experimenting with different weightings for each of the variables we can derive from the 2001 data on Tokyo's youth an overall model which shows the relative importance of each variable in accounting for the variation in each individual's income. This will give us a clue as to the relative importance of career path in determining the income of each type of regular full-time company employee.

The data in the last few rows of Table 8.7 provide us with a basic idea as to how the two sets of employees felt about their job as *seishain*. Four measures of satisfaction were used, and the results for each measure seem to correspond for each group. Here we should note that many males in the group with experience as *furiitaa* were much more anxious about their future than those who had not been *furiitaa*. It is possible that their relatively positive evaluation of their current job situation reflected the fact they had been able to avoid having an even longer stint in the casual labor force. This is mentioned to illustrate the fact that quantification is difficult even with regard to a key variable such as the level of satisfaction employees feel with regard to their work. Nevertheless, for those who have somehow made the transition from casual to permanent employment, in the short run there is very likely to be an added sense of satisfaction with whatever permanent employment they secure.

Young people likely to be long-term *furiitaa*

Everyone does not make the transition from casual to permanent employment. The stratification mosaic contains a class of people who are destined to remain in casual employment for most of their lives. These are the "hard-core *furiitaa*". As indicated above, a very high percentage of those who leave school without graduating become *furiitaa*. For financial reasons others are unable to continue their education to the next level following graduation and decide to become *furiitaa*. Table 8.8 shows that the respondents to our survey who became *furiitaa* saw their families as struggling financially.

Life on lower wages is possible for many *furiitaa* partly because they depend upon their parents for room and board. Put into perspective, however, it is likely that the vast majority of university students also do precisely that. Nevertheless, it is probably the case that many of the families of those who enter the labor force as *furiitaa* with only a high school education or less are at the lower end of the income scale, and that their families cannot easily provide such material support (*e.g.*, in the form of free accommodation).

We saw above that gender difference in the ability of young *furiitaa* to move beyond casual employment was significant. The survey of youth in the Tokyo Metropolitan area canvassed the young people who had experience as *furiitaa* about their current employment status. Table 8.9 shows the percentage of *furiitaa* who had at some point tried to become regular employees and the percentage of those who had actually succeeded. Not only were male respondents more likely to make the effort; a much higher proportion of the male attempts were successful. Nearly 55 percent (73% × 75%) of male *furiitaa* actually made the transition whereas only 25 percent of females (53% × 47%) did so.

At the same time, the survey's finding did not indicate that family and educational background were factors which significantly affected the decision of many *furiitaa* to move from casual to permanent employment.

The decision to become a *furiitaa* seems to be affected by those two variables, whereas the decision to move beyond casual employment to permanent employment seems to be affected largely by gender-linked considerations. The role these social factors play must be considered when discussing the best policies for society to take regarding the *furiitaa*.

Having mentioned gender as an important variable affecting the transition from casual to permanent employment, we can go a step further by using logistic regression analysis to examine for other factors that might impinge upon the process. Setting "success in making the transition to permanent employment" as the dependent variable, a range of independent variables were tested: gender, age, educational background, the length of time spent as a *furiitaa*, the individual's experience as a full-time regular employee, the extent to which the respondent was sympathetic to being a "*furiitaa*", the position or nature of the work performed while a *furiitaa*, the concrete steps or actions taken to make the transition, the reason for being a *furiitaa*, overall appraisals of the time spent as a *furiitaa*, the motivation behind the decision to make the transition, the parent's occupation and educational attainment, and their family's social-economic status.

Table 8.7: A comparison of those who became full-time regular employees immediately after graduation and those who did so after a stint as a furiitaa

	Those who became full-time regular employees	
	Immediately after graduation	**After a stint as a *furiitaa***
Gender		
Male	68.5	54.9
Female	31.5	45.1
Educational attainment		
Senior high school graduate	45.3	22.1
Junior college/specialized training college graduate	26.4	37.6
University graduate	8.9	35.8
Middle school graduate who drops out of senior high school	10.5	2.4
Tertiary level drop-out	7.3	1.2
Age		
18–19	3.2	3.1
20–24	29.2	37.6
25–29	67.6	59.3
Occupation		
Professional/technical	13.9	23.6
Administrative	20.3	34.3
Sales	20.1	18.6
Services	23.3	7.8
Manufacturing/construction/assembly	15.9	9.9
Transportation/communications/security	6.6	3.9
Firm Size (number of employees)		
–29	43.7	24.1
30–99	19.9	15.6
100–399	15.4	14.4
400–999	3.3	15.2
1,000+	10.8	26.0
public service	5.9	4.1
Working conditions		
Average number of hours worked per week	49.4	47.8
Average annual income in previous year in JY10,000	297.9	323.5

Views about current work situation[a]

I am doing work that I enjoy	73.4	75.0
I have superiors at work whom I respect	48.9	55.8
I do work which is suited to my character and ability	74.9	67.0
I want to be doing the same job in 3 years' time	48.9	53.9
Total in sample	100.0	100.0
Value of N	489	210

Note: a = Percentage of persons who agreed fully or partially with each of the four statements.

Source: The figures presented here were generated by the author from data used in Nihon Rodo Kenkyu-Kenshu Kiko (2001b).

Table 8.8: Percentage distribution of respondents according to their assessment of their own family's economic well-being (2006)

	Furiitaa	**Regular full-time employees**
My family is well-off	8.8	8.5
My family is somewhat well-off	40.0	48.7
My family is not very well-off	39.0	32.4
My family is not at all well-off	12.2	10.4
Total	100.0	100.0
N	879	533

Note:

1. The distribution is based on self assessments.

2. $p < 0.05$

Source: The figures presented here were generated by the author from data used in Rodo Seisaku Kenkyu-Kenshu Kiko (2006).

A proportionately large number of those who successfully made the transition had been *furiitaa* for less than one year, were employed in cleaning/sanitation work or on construction sites, and were motivated to make the switch by plans to marry. Many of those who were not successful in their attempt to obtain full-time permanent employment were those trying to change their employment simply because they had reached "the appropriate age". The successful also included a good number who had taken on casual employment in order to earn their school fees.

Part of the way the period as a *furiitaa* factored into the equation was owing to the perceptions which management had of *furiitaa*.

Table 8.9: The relative rate of success of male and female furiitaa
*in making the transition to full-time regular employment
(2006)*

	Males	**Females**	**Aggregate of males and females**
Percentage of *furitaa* who at one time wanted to become full-time regular employees	50.5	36.3	43.4
Percentage of *furitaa* who at one time wanted to become full-time regular employees that actually became full-time regular employees	29.7	19.4	24.5
N	499	499	998

Source: Rodo Seisaku Kenkyu Kenshu Kiko (2006), pp. 77 and 84.

According to the Survey of Employment Management (Koyo Kanri Chosa), management at nearly all firms negatively viewed the time young people spent working as a *furiitaa*. Although one year as a *furiitaa* tended to be seen by management simply as a year off from studies or a year as a "*ronin*" preparing for permanent work, that was not the case when the period was extended to two, three or four years. For that reason, the length of time spent as a *furiitaa* varied inversely with the likelihood of success in making the transition.

The next most influential set of factors revolved around the occupational content of the work performed as a casual, the reasons for taking on casual employment and the reasons for wanting to transfer to permanent employment. The type of work done as a casual to some extent reflected the individual's commitment to enhancing their income. So too did the decision of many males to move to permanent employment upon marriage. Behavior which reflected a desire for increased income would be seen favourably by many employers as a sign that one was ready to assume the responsibilities associated with full-time regular employment. From the perspective of many *furiitaa, furiitaa* in general could not afford to continue working as a casual. In other words, young people do respond to economic forces in their life and are willing to present themselves to a tightening labor market.

When considering the way life as a *furiitaa* was perceive by young people in the 2001 Tokyo survey Nihon Rodo Kenkyu Kiko 2001b), there is a big difference between those who make the transition (or want to make the transition) and those who stay on as *furiitaa*. However, a gender-linked difference exists. Among males who continue as *furiitaa* the image of being a *furiitaa* is generally positive. However, among those who had made the transition, there was generally a negative appraisal of the *furiitaa*. In this regard, their outlook does not vary much from that of other males who entered full-time permanent employment directly upon graduation. As for female respondents to our questionnaire, however, there was little variation between those who continued as *furiitaa* and those who made the transition. Both tended to see work as a *furiitaa* in a favourable light, and this meant that as a group they differed from women who entered full-time regular employment directly after graduation. This no doubt reflected the difficulty women have in making that transition.

In the previous chapter we noted that some *furiitaa* claimed they had a special goal to achieve, while others simply wanted the freedom that comes with casual employment. Although only a small number cited "freedom" as their first reason for becoming a *furiitaa*, it could be that those who choose "freedom" as a reason were those who wanted to avoid their social responsibility. In other words, they were young people who did not want to grow up and become adults in society. It is this outlook which will promote the *furiitaa* lifestyle, and is a main factor determining for whether many young *furiitaa* will to make the transition to full-time regular employment. However, in pointing to the attitudes of Japan's young people in this regard, it is important to consider the larger social milieu in which young people find themselves. Those with minimal educational qualifications are excluded from the labor market for permanent full-time employment. Moreover, educational outcomes are to a marked degree determined by socio-economic background. This means that some young people will not be able to stay in the educational system as long as they want or to the extent that they qualify academically. In such circumstances some students take positive steps to improve their lot by gaining employment as *furiitaa*. Young girls know that many mature-aged women work part-time so that they can fulfil their role as housewives. It is important to understand how such knowledge affects the decision of young people to become *furiitaa*. For these reasons, it would be fruitful to explore in more detail how views about work evolve and solidify in the minds of young people.

We must approach the task of policy formation from this broader social perspective when it comes to dealing with the long-term or hard-core *furiitaa*. There is room to speculate about the likelihood that young males will continue to make the transition from casual to permanent employment that appeared in the data introduced above. As we mentioned at the outset in Chapter One, the *furiitaa* phenomenon is spreading, and the number of *furiitaa* in their early thirties is increasing. Even in their late twenties and early thirties a growing number of *furiitaa* are not making the transition to permanent employment. In this trend there is ample reason to be concerned.

Toward appropriate policies

The process whereby young people make the transition from the educational system to work is changing fundamentally. More young people than before are seeking employment by going outside the established channels. In the Tokyo Metropolitan area, young male graduates are routing themselves through casual employment before finding regular full-time employment. Eighty percent taking that detour are able successfully to navigate the transition into permanent employment. In Japan this longer transition over a period of some years is a new phenomenon.

The new approach to the job market is not without its problems. First, the work available to the casual employee is often work which does not involve skill and provides few opportunities for skill development. Second, experience in the casual labor force does not very often result in the incumbent having a clearer idea as to what career they should pursue. As a result, many *furiitaa* shift to the permanent labor force simply because they want better working conditions and/or feel they have reached an age where it is socially unacceptable to continue as *furiitaa*. Third, the disadvantage of coming late to permanent employment tends to stay with an individual. The opportunities for "mid-career" entrants continue to be inferior to those for the employees who have come to their firm directly upon graduation. Fourth, in the background are factors related to an existing mosaic of social inequality. Those from economically disadvantaged households seem to be systematically disadvantaged. There is, of course, the importance of each individual's attitude and mental outlook. However, the judgment which bears on the choices one makes is shaped by the social realities surrounding each individual.

Fundamental changes are occurring in present day Japan as the unskilled and poorly paid work of the *arubaitaa* and the *paatotaimaa* comes to be removed from the workloads of regular full-time employees. Until recently Japanese-style management was conceived on the premise that new company employees would be allowed to cut their teeth by doing such work. That is decreasingly so these days. On the one hand, university graduates coming into the firm want to start with more challenging (and value-adding) tasks. On the other, management is increasingly concerned about the costs of training and the pressures to rationalize the way it acquires human resources. Accordingly, we must now ask ourselves where today's young people are learning their skills. It is time to think carefully about what can be done at a societal level to improve the support mechanisms which assist Japan's young people in their transition from the education system into regular full-time employment.

The transition to work is important not only in terms of the need to ensure we hire a skilled labor force. It is also important that the generation now finishing school be able to fulfil its social responsibility. The practice of hiring new graduates has worked in the past to give all young persons a meaningful position which guaranteed them a certain status within society. As a result young people were able to become full-fledged members of society. It was a system in which firms honoured an unwritten commitment to new graduates to integrate them into the placement procedures that were established in most schools and tertiary institutions. However, students who somehow did not make it to a job through that system were left by the wayside, and afterwards found it extremely difficult to get back on track. This was a major downside of that approach to transition. Today nearly two thirds of Japan's new graduates fall outside that system. I think it is time to realign labor markets so that these young people are not disadvantaged in terms of the opportunities they have to build a career at work. The future of these young people will be the future of our society. Their transition to work is about the way in which society looks after those who constitute its next generation. How we handle these matters will determine the nature of Japanese society in the not too distant future.

What are the requisites for a new system? First, educational institutions need to provide more information about work life and career choices. Second, there needs to be more support and guidance for those who can make the transition within the framework currently in place to provide regular full-time employment. Third, there need to be mechanisms which will facilitate the transition of *furiitaa* and other casually employed persons into the permanent full-time labor force.

Although the role of each school's placement activities in helping students find a career path has been the focus of on-going concern for many in society, the system has not functioned well in that regard. Because a job could be found for nearly all students and it appeared that each school had therefore fulfilled its responsibility to find employment for each graduate, a certain complacency may have set in. For that reason changes in the labor market and in society at large left many students uncertain as to their options, and they simply chose to be *furiitaa* almost by default. Moreover, in the past Japan's industries have been happy to leave occupational training and skills development to each individual firm to implement for each new graduate it hired. There has traditionally been very little expectation that the school system would do much more than provide a very basic generalist education. It was in such a milieu that the new type of young person emerged – one who became a *furiitaa* with no real job skills and little sense of how best to establish a career for themselves. As long as young people stick to the established path through school and graduation and then head directly into full-time regular employment, major problems are unlikely. But many young persons have a huge problem and face considerable difficulty when they cannot find a suitable job following graduation.

Given current trends in society and in the economy, it is probably necessary for today's schools to provide more career information, guidance and work experience which will assist students in thinking carefully about their future at work. Schools need also to place greater emphasis on giving students the skills and techniques that will be required of them once they join the labor force. In this regard it is crucial that schools work closely with management to coordinate their initiatives so that the requirements of industry are met. This is a call for the key stakeholders in society to transfer the responsibility for training and career development from individual firms to industry-wide bodies. Industries should organize their programs in league with the schools so that students can gain valuable work experience. With these changes in place, educational programs could be opened up to incorporate both students in work experience and *furiitaa* in casual employment. This would help to make the issue of occupational training a society-wide responsibility.

The established system of direct employment upon graduation results in a smooth school-to work transition. Few would argue that this is not a great strength of that system. Any proposal to alter the system at the secondary school level would need to be in some way attractive both for the students and for their potential employers.

At a minimum the current system would need to be reformed. For the system once again to serve all students the demand for new graduates would need to recover, and that is largely dependent on factors connected to the overall performance of the national economy – factors which are likely to play out over a longer period of time. Certainly for the foreseeable future the general prognosis is that the number of young people seeking to launch their career outside the confines of the established system is likely to increase. To better service young people who are looking for an alternative route into the full-time regular labor force, it is important that we uncover avenues which allow young people to independently establish themselves as vocationally capable: opportunities to acquire occupational skills, ways to provide work experience and strategies to deliver advice and information.

Regarding opportunities to acquire various skills, improved school programs and training facilities immediately come to mind. However, we need to go far beyond such infrastructure. For example, the government has put in place a framework whereby young people can gain work experience through a program of trial employment. This could in the future be developed further in ways that more fully enhance the opportunities for skill acquisition. *Furiitaa* could also use time spent doing casual work more creatively and thereby create new opportunities. This proposal might at first seem to be contradictory as it calls on employees to blur the distinction between casual and permanent employment. Although casual work by its very nature is often conceived as non-skilled work, there needs to be a greater appreciation of the attributes gained through such work. Whatever the skills acquired, their usefulness in developing a career needs to be highlighted both for employers and for the *furiitaa* themselves. We should change the culture in which the limiting aspects of *arubaito* are given undue attention and instead call for a more balanced assessment of that experience. When casuals are doing tasks integral in some way to the work done by regular employees at a company, there needs to be a way of listing that on the individual's curriculum vitae.

There has been a good deal of discussion about the possibility and desirability of regularizing part-time or short-term contracted employment. The idea is that part-timers gradually be given more demanding tasks that will allow them to gradually assume the workload and responsibilities associated with full-time regular employment. By doing that a means of moving between the two employment statuses is opened up.

Another strategy would be for young people seeking an alternative route to permanent employment. Working as a volunteer for a non-profit organization can open the way to form various social networks and to take on jobs which expand one's skills and chances for leadership. In an organizational context there are ample opportunities to learn about team work and to see through a specific project all on one's own. Because profit is not the main goal of NPOs, volunteers can also experience the joy of a job well done and see how the fruit of their labor contributes to the functioning of society as a whole. Through that process young people will come to see their own worth as fully-fledged members of society.

By rethinking the mechanisms which structure the school-to-work transition, steps will be taken to ensure that the next generation matures in ways that will sustain society in the future. To obtain the best results, the challenges cannot be left only to the schools, or to industry, or to the government or to the parents of Japan's growing number of *furiitaa*. It is now time to devise a strategy which will involve all of these groups cooperating together.

9 The *Furiitaa*: A New Social Class in Japan

The preceding chapters have looked at some empirical data on the increasing number of *furiitaa* in Japanese society and some of the realities that characterize their existence. A good deal has been written about this group within Japanese society, and I am often asked my views by policy makers and by other interested individuals. I have responded in various fora to these requests, and have occasionally set my ideas down in writing. This chapter consists of five essays penned for various media as shown in Table 9.1.

Choosing a job in a diversifying labor market

The proliferation of choices in the labor market

The situation facing Japan's university graduates
It would be incorrect to say that people have begun only recently to comment on the difficulties new graduates have finding their first job. Since the early 1990s many Japanese firms have shifted from (i) an approach according to which they sought to hire as many new graduates as possible and then sort through for the most promising to promote to (ii) an approach according to which they screened for a smaller number of quality graduates who were more certain to contribute to the future of the firm. Japan had gone through a period when new universities had been established to accommodate the growing number of young people who wanted to receive a university degree. By the 1990s there was an oversupply of university graduates coming onto the labor market.

In 1990 large firms with over 1000 employees were hiring over half of Japan's new university graduates. Over the next decade that figure would drop to about thirty percent. Behind the drop in the demand for new graduates was the Heisei Recession of the 1990s. Firms were also responding to a broad range of changes. One outcome was that they altered their profile of human resources by reducing

Table 9.1: The papers which constitute Chapter Nine

Title		Date of publication	Location
In Japanese	English rendition		
1. Kyoyo tayoka jidai no shigoto erabi	Choosing work in an increasingly diversified labor market	July 2002	*Nikkei Nabi* http://jjob.nikkei.co.jp/contents/oneself/find my job/index/html
2. Furiitaa kara no "hajime no ippo"	The first step away from being a *furiitaa*	2001	in *Furiitaa Naze? Dosuru? Furiitaa 200 Mannin Jidai ga Yatte Kita* (Why *Furiitaa* and How to Respond in an Age with Two Million *Furiitaa*)(Tokyo: Gakushu Kenkyusha), pp. 206–212.
3. Shigoto no sekai kara no messeiji o	A message from the world of work	October 2002	*Shinro Shido* (published by the Nihon Shinro Shido Kyokai), pp. 5–6.
4. Joshiki de nakunatta "shushoku"	Getting a job when the common sense has changed	Winter 2002	*Joho Kosa YuuYuu* (published by the Kanagawa Institute for the Study of Youth)
5. Kokosei no shushokunan e no taio	Some guidelines for students facing difficulty getting their first offer of employment	20 October 2002	*Nihon Keizai Shimbun*, morning edition, p. 16

their dependence on *seishain* (full-time regular employees). One key strategy was to use more dispatched workers and casual workers on short-term contracts. This meant an increase in the employment of *paatotaimaa* and *arubaitaa*. Another strategy was to out source more of the work previously done by *seishain*. Some firms have moved away from treating new graduates as a distinct labor force.

In 1990 18 percent of high school graduates were proceeding on to a four-year university; by 2001 that figure had doubled to 36 percent. Over the same period the percentage of high school graduates who entered full-time regular employment directly upon graduation fell by half from 35 to 18 percent. On the one hand, many universities had made entry much easier in order to maintain enrolments. On the other hand, the demand of firms for new high school graduates declined drastically over that same period, making it much more difficult for graduates to be successful in their plans to become employed. Reflecting these changes, firms today are more likely to hire graduates from four-year universities. Those who hold a university qualification or a certificate from junior colleges or specialized training colleges now account for about 70 percent of such hirings. Of course, over the years the meaning associated with having a higher educational qualification changed substantially as the number of graduates increased dramatically. It is important that all young graduates coming into this market fully understand these basic facts.

The proliferation of choice in the labor market

The rising level of education has meant that the "moratorium period" associated with late adolescence has lengthened. More people are continuing from junior high school to senior high school, and then from senior high to university and other tertiary institutions. They are taking positive steps to enhance the prospects that they will end up on a higher career trajectory. However, they are also postponing their entry into the real world of work. Today's university students have four choices as they approach graduation: (i) to look for full-time regular employment, (ii) to apply for post graduate study (*e.g.*, for an MA or a PhD candidature), (iii) to take a year off from their studies in Japan to study abroad, or (iv) to become a *furiitaa*. Among these there is a strong tendency for students to want to postpone their decision-making. Putting the choices in front of themselves, each student has to ask, "How will my choices affect my future? What will happen to me if I postpone my entry into regular full-time work?" Each faces the same set of choices, and each choice carries with it a set of several different possible outcomes which circumscribe the choices each student makes at the next level. Here an example might help.

Further education and the year off as easy options

Imagine choosing to continue in the tertiary sector and obtaining an MA. An MA in a science-related field would be recognized by management. However, an MA in the humanities is likely to be seen only as a training program for academic researchers, and few firms would see it as providing a concrete founding for life in the corporate world. Although the decision to study for a higher degree as part of a clearly formulated plan poses no problem, staying on as a student simply to postpone entry into the full-time regular labor force can result in a narrower range of career choices when one eventually enters the labor market for new graduates. While the number of university graduates going to graduate school has increased significantly, so too has the number of students who are taking time off from their studies to have an experience abroad before graduating.

In terms of getting a good job upon graduation, however, it is difficult to conclude that the time spent abroad will work to the student's advantage. One must ask hard questions about what is gained or actually learned as a result of studying abroad. The time commitment and the distance from the placement processes can only put prospective graduates at a disadvantage. If the student is not careful, the time spent away can even become a negative factor making it more difficult to secure a good position. I want everyone to think carefully about the fact that the extra time and money spent on overseas study or on postgraduate study will often not work to their advantage if the aim is primarily to "buy time" before having to enter full-time regular employment. I am asking those who are thinking of choosing one of those two options to rethink their decision before finalizing their plans. Ask honestly about what will be taken home from a year abroad. What more will be learned from an extra two years in a postgraduate program that will be of value to a future employer? This kind of self-examination can only assist every university student when it comes to choosing the best path for themselves upon graduation.

The *furiitaa* Lifestyle

The work of casual employees

The proportion of students who choose to become *furiitaa* is increasing. The preceding chapters have shown that students become *furiitaa* for a wide variety of reasons. Becoming a *furiitaa* is an easy choice for those who think they want to pursue a dream. Some want more time without commitments, living in a kind of extended moratorium. They do know, however, that they will not have time to freely ponder such matters once they are fully engaged as a regular employee. Others still do not know what they want to do career-wise

Some will exclaim, "It's not that I don't want to work, but that I don't want my life confined to just one line of work at just one firm." Or, "I don't want to be hemmed in by a large organization." Some *furiitaa* looked hard for permanent employment upon graduation, but did not receive an offer that was attractive enough. They then opted for life as a *furiitaa*. Many *furiitaa* would have had their own special circumstances to consider, and would have chosen their path only after careful consideration of all options.

I do not think that their choice was necessarily the wrong one. But I do worry that young people make that choice without fully considering the risk factors. To adequately assess the risks involved, one must first consider why firms are hiring *arubaitaa* and *paatotaimaa*.

Seishain (permanent company employees) work full-time with a kind of automatic tenure. *Arubaitaa* are contracted for a specific period of time. Part-timers work shorter hours than do *seishain*. *Arubaitaa* and *paatotaimaa* just out of school are likely to be assigned work that will bring an immediate return to the company. To yield a tangible outcome against each yen spent, such work must involve tasks that do not require additional training (*i.e.,* unskilled work). Obviously work that anyone off the street can do will not command much above the minimum wage.

As we saw above in Tables 8.5 and 7.9, the hourly rate of return to *furiitaa* is considerably below that paid to permanent company employees. The wage rate is about thirty percent lower for male and female university graduates aged 25–29. The individual's earnings serve as one measure of the skill level and job-relevant knowledge an employee possesses. Work is currently organized around two different types of workers: those who are employed on a long-term tenured basis and allowed to acquire skills within the firm (the *seishain*) and those who will continue to do the same level of work year in and year out on a casual basis (the *furiitaa*).

The risk that comes with life as a *furiitaa*

The *furiitaa* bears at least three risks. First, they risk going through life with no skills. The best time to acquire skills is when one is young. The basics learned when one is young have a big influence on what they can do later in life. The second risk is that work as a *furiitaa* will not lead to one's dream. Most *furiitaa* are left to work in "skill-restricted work sites" and have little opportunity to mix with others who can provide mentoring. However, few are able to refine and develop their dreams into realistic career plans. Our survey data, which has been introduced in the preceding chapters, clearly show that most *furiitaa* regard their time as *furiitaa* as lost time, or at least are aware that they must soon settle into some kind of work as a *seishain*. Very few come away having discovered what they really want to do.

The third risk is in the fact that even when a *furiitaa* is able to acquire good experience, it is difficult for prospective employers to fully recognize or appreciate the value of that experience. *Furiitaa* often find themselves in a kind of Catch 22 situation. If they try their hand at a variety of jobs to broaden their skill base, prospect employers will note their mobility and conclude that they don't have the fortitude to stick with a job and complete it. It is difficult for young *furiitaa* to impress those who make the decisions regarding the hiring of full-time regular employees. There is also data that show it is easier for those who have been *furiitaa* for less than one year to make the transition to full-time regular employment whereas those with experience of more than thirteen months become increasingly difficult for employers to utilize (Nihon Rodo Kenkyu Kiko 2001b: 111). Again, I want young people to properly understand the situation before they choose to become *furiitaa*.

There is a lot more to life than finding good full-time regular employment. At the present time there is a move to provide support to young persons who have a good idea, are looking for venture capital and want to start their own business. These innovative energetic entrepreneurs are the ones who are exporting fashion, music, games and *manga* to the world. Few of them have worked as *seishain*. Japan's future would indeed be bleak were it not for the energy generated by these young Japanese in pursuit of a dream.

Having said that, however, we have to realize that we are talking about a very small minority. Simply deciding to be a *furiitaa* and expending one's energy in that manner does not in very many cases lead to a release of the high level energy necessary to open the door leading to the realization of a big dream. It is quite a leap to the next stage, and few have the resolve to soar over the crevice that separates the two worlds of work. Most are more timid, and can only peer across that space and continue to wonder about where to go next.

I am most apprehensive about those who become *furiitaa* with nothing in mind that they really want to do. They are most likely to bear the full brunt of all three of the risks. Only talking in vague terms about what they want to do is not enough. To be successful in finding a career, one has to go several steps further – searching out meaningful work sites, obtaining information from reliable sources, and working with the key concept which underpins the dream. Many young persons do not know what they want to do; they need to think carefully about these matters before deciding to become a *furiitaa*. It is critical for success that young people very carefully take all of the risks into consideration. By seriously approaching life as a *furiitaa*, they can work with a realistic expectation that doors to a full career will open for then.

Changes to the way employment is structured

Working with increased choices

For those who do not become full-time regular employees, work as a *furiitaa* is not the only option in the labor market. One can work as a temp (*haken shain*) for a dispatch firm or as a contracted employee (*keiyaku shain*). Rather than employment as a *furiitaa* or as someone working at home, one could work in a firm's office as a sub-contracted operative (*gyomu itaku*). Until now there have been two major categories of employee: one was the full-time regular employee with tenure who enjoyed an on-going stable relationship with his or her employer. The other was for those in all other employment (*i.e.*, employment on a casual basis without any long-term certainty). This dichotomy was highlighted by the terms "*seiki koyosha*" (regular employee) and "*hiseiki koyosha*" (non-regular employee) or *hiseiki rodo* (non-regular work). The former status was associated with good working conditions; the latter, with inferior conditions. The term "*hiseiki koyosha*" has always had a negative connotation, implying that one was an inferior member of the labor force. In recent times the terms "*seiki*" and "*hiseiki*" have come to be replaced by "*tenkei*" (typical employment) and "*hitenkei*" (atypical employment), vocabulary which has less of the good/bad dichotomous judgement attached. This reflects the fact that the number of non-regular employees has skyrocketed in recent times, and that their working conditions are varied enough that it is now difficult to generalize that such employment can always be characterized as being decidedly inferior, disadvantaged or unstable. From the perspective of the individual wanting to supply their own labor to the labor market, one can say that the ways of working are much more diversified than in the past.

Diversified work ways and the *furiitaa*

The word '*furiitaa*" has been used by some to label those who
are in "atypical employment" (plus many who are temporarily
unemployed). I, however, try to keep the two terms separate by
using the term "*furiitaa*" for only a certain sub-group in "atypical
employment". Nearly all young people engaged in *arubaito*-type
work refer to themselves as "*furiitaa*". However, only about twenty
percent of those who are contracted employees or dispatched
workers do so. Very few of those who are self-employed – or who
are working as semi-entrepreneurs on a free-lance basis or within
their home – would identify themselves as "*furiitaa*". Furthermore,
most "*furiitaa*" would sense that they fill a supplementary role, a
temporary to help at the most busy times. For this reason most
furiitaa see their stint as a *furiiitaa* as a passing phase, as part of a
transition to other work and to a different lifestyle. Others who are
in atypical employment are likely to have a longer-term (or even
professional) interest in what they do for work. They work not
just to supplement someone else's operation, but also to develop a
specific skill base, and that outlook differentiates them from the
furiitaa in various ways.

The specialized work of contracted and dispatched workers

Another example of atypical employment can be found among those
who have developed a specific skill on their own, and who seek to
utilize it in the labor force on a long-term basis. In the IT industry,
for example, many persons in their thirties and forties are working
full-time as dispatchers or contracted employees.

These types prefer not to be tied down by a long-term commitment
to a single organization. One reason for their choice of an atypical
pattern of work is that they do not want to sit around waiting for
promotion in a typical Japanese firm where seniority is a major
(though not the only) consideration. Rather than waiting patiently
to learn skills on the job and then slowly progress upward in a large
organization, they prefer to polish their skills as one of the growing
number of narrowly defined, but highly prized, experts who are able
to market their skills as they see fit. We are beginning to see that some
of these experts have formed their own groups of similarly minded
professionals who collectively offer a package that is attractive to
firms wanting to outsource various technical requirements. To be
successful, however, these professionals have to be true masters over
the technologies they manage. In other words, they have to have a
solid basis on which to compete on an equal footing with experts

in Japan's large firms. This distinguishes them from many of the subcontracting firms in much of manufacturing. The decisive factor for these professionals is in the extent to which they can acquire and then further develop a specific set of skills. Although I continue to see full-time regular employment as the norm, it is important to remember that the existence of many firms is constantly being challenged as the national economy becomes subsumed within the global economy and competition is heightened even among firms within Japan. This means that the sureties associated with such employment are not as solidly given as in the past. As firms move to protect themselves by increasing their reliance on outsourcing, one might say that it is the individuals who have confidently built themselves a professional skill base that now have a greater sense of financial security in their own lives.

Working as a dispatchee and the avoidance of mismatching
Today the number of new graduates who find employment with a labor dispatching firm has increased. The attractiveness of doing so is now greater as a result of legislation which allows dispatching firms to serve as a kind of go-between in introducing their own employees as potential full-time regular employees to one of their client firms. This system of the dispatch with the prospect of employment (*shokai yotei haken*) allows client firms to contract for the services of a temp and then to observe the person at work before deciding whether to take them on as a *seiki shain*. This means that both the firm and the temp have a period of time (up to six months) to make sure they are happy with each other before entering into a relationship with longer-term commitments. This arrangement works to limit the amount of mismatching that occurs.

It is important in all of this to remember that the bottom line for dispatched workers, whether they work as prospective employees or not, is the extent to which they are able to acquire a solid skill base. Individuals cannot rely wholly on their employer to look after their own skill development. Even as a full-time regular employee one must still take the initiative to ensure that they end up with their own portable set of skills. This is especially true for women whose numbers among the dispatchees are rapidly rising. I say this because those who marry and have children are particularly vulnerable when they leave the labor force to take on childcare responsibilities. Many middle-aged and older women are still working, and they are likely to return to the labor force; it is important that they take positive steps to develop and then maintain their skills. For those wishing to look after their home while also developing a career, being a dispatched worker with highly developed professional skills may have a particular attraction.

Preparing to select the proper job

Taking the broad perspective
Choosing a job is to make a decision as to how one wants to interface with society at large. In a rigidly stratified society where tradition is important many individuals are not able to choose the work they will do. In today's world I think it is largely for the good that society allows individuals a much freer choice of lifestyles, working styles and occupation.

However, simply having to choose a company to work for as a regular full-time employee upon graduation can produce considerable stress in some students. How does one get onto the placement bandwagon? Still puzzled as to how best to proceed, one student mumbled that he could have decided on a firm if only he knew the standard test score each firm was looking for. In an abstract sense, the basics of choosing a job are fairly straightforward: know the world of work, know oneself, and then find a link between a specific kind of work and one's own predilections. For this student the standardized test score given to each high school student would have been his link. When one thinks of applying to a university, one can look at a table which shows the cut-off score for each university. When thinking about employment, however, firms seldom use such a simple quantifiable measuring stick which allows them to rank each applicant. For that reason, many students feel impelled to create their own stick against which to measure themselves. The measures used by firms include a variety of attitudes or values concerning a range of matters. Next on the list might be judgements about each applicant's aptitudes as they relate to the performance of various work-related tasks. The best way to deal with these kinds of expectations is to know oneself. In other words, it is important for students to engage in some introspection and to carefully analyze themselves.

To get a better understanding of themselves, many students take aptitude tests and get measured in other ways. This sort of self-examination or self-evaluation does not yield an absolute score; rather, the results are presented in relationship to the answers given by others who have taken the same test. These sorts of tests do not point to a specific occupational or employment choice; at best they can only provide hints or guidelines. The wise person will take a longer-term view of things and try to recall the way family and friends have viewed and advised them in the past.

Gathering information which is "alive"

Talking to other people has two positive outcomes: one is getting to know oneself better; the other is receiving information about the world of work. The latter type of knowledge often challenges us to think more carefully about how particular occupations or careers might appeal to us in our own circumstances. Knowing and thinking about work is one way of knowing ourselves better.

Many young people don't know what to ask others, and may find it useful to discover the types of work people do. They may also be able to observe the daily rhythms that punctuate the life of those they know, the activities that constitute an average day for someone doing a particular type of work. A further step would be to arrange to do some work experience. Actually experiencing work often highlights one's own values as they impinge on work. This in turn will help individuals to imagine how they might go in specific jobs. For this reason I would advise all young people to make the effort necessary to be part of an internship program. When choosing *arubaito*, young people should always do so with an eye on the types of information they might obtain that would be useful for a future career. Whatever the method used to obtain work experience, actually working at something will open one's eyes to new perspectives and a wider range of possibilities.

Once into a school's placement activities, final year students will be introduced to firms they can visit. Students can visit a firm and meet someone who has graduated recently from a university and can provide insight or advice concerning job hunting. To have privileged access to a work place can only result in an individual coming away with valuable insights.

In making these points, I wish to stress that students need to avoid relying too much on the internet as their main source of information. In the internet age, it is easy for students to conclude that they have obtained all the information they need simply by visiting a company's website. Today fewer students are visiting and consulting previous graduates (their "OBs" and "OGs"). Although one can download a huge amount of information from the internet in just seconds, much of that information has been carefully massaged by each firm for its own purposes. It is quite different to what one acquires with their own ears and eyes when visiting a firm or talking to someone who intimately knows the firm or the industry in question. Data from the internet provides only a useful starting point. It would be a mistake to conclude that a company's website provides sufficient information to make an informed decision about which career to pursue.

The importance of taking the initiative

For university students, there is an expectation that individuals will take more of the initiative in finding their own placement. Students who majored in one of the natural sciences have traditionally a more obvious occupational link, and it was common for those students to be placed in their first full-time regular position by a professor in their research section of the university. However, even in the natural sciences students are now taking more initiative on their own to find employment. This means increasingly that nothing happens for university students unless they themselves make the first move. Students are left to get their own information and to approach firms on their own. Even if they are a bit shy in moving beyond the confines of their lives as students, it is critical that they take the necessary steps on their own.

To do those things I believe that students need some training. To leave to others matters for which one needs to take responsibility will in the end not result in the individual finding direction in their life. Whether it is a club organized around activities in which one has an interest or is volunteer service with an NGO/NPO, one is doing it because one is motivated on their own. That is why I recommend that students look for opportunities to serve within such bodies. To expand one's range of possibilities, one has to find within oneself the motivation to become involved in various activities related to work and having a career.

The first step away from life as a *furiitaa*

Acquiring occupational skills

The common reasons given for becoming a *furiitaa* are (i) that one does not know what they want to do but must earn some income and (ii) that they want to experience a variety of things. While it is important to young people that they do work they feel passionate about doing, the fact is that many do not know what it is that they feel passionate about. For that reason, many think they will try their hand at a range of casual jobs, and thereby come across work that they are happy doing – work that fits their aptitudes and ignites their enthusiasm. They believe they would be happy doing that work regardless of whether they did it as a full-time regular employee or as a casual as long as the work gives them a strong sense of self-actualisation. If that is the case, we must inquire into the type of work they are actually doing as a casual employee. Most are employed to work at cash registers or to stock shelves in convenience stores or supermarkets, to wait on customers in restaurants, to make home deliveries for pizza shops or other retail outlets, or simply to sort things for delivery. Although they say they want to do various types of work, the fact is that they are often stuck with the rather narrow range of jobs that are on offer for *arubaitaa* – work that is poorly paid and requires few skills. When firms use casuals they do so precisely to hire people for work that requires no training, or only minimal training. Such work commands a very low wage rate and saves the firm from paying higher wages to its own more highly skilled permanent employees in whose training it has already invested.

One must then ask, where can the casual who is serious about work acquire occupational or vocational skills? Training is often classified as OJT (on-the-job training) or Off-JT (off-the-job training). OJT occurs when employees are given meaningful work experience from which they learn and acquire skills through actually being involved in production or other work. Off-JT occurs away from the actual place of work. Often this is in a classroom. Until recently, it was said that Japanese firms were highly committed to the skill development of their employees. However, that was primarily in terms of OJT. Firms thought carefully about how to rotate employees from one work place to another, mindful not only of where labor was needed, but also of the skill profile of each employee and the type of experience which would rather naturally come next in a longer-term vision for his or her growth and likely promotion within the firm. This long-term approach to educating an employee was predicated on assumptions about how long that person would be with the firm. Most firms would not consider it worthwhile to invest in someone who, like an *arubaitaa*, would only commit to the firm for a short period of time. The same calculation is also made regarding any Off-JT for which the firm would pay. If any such training were to be arranged for an *arubaitaa*, it would be for the minimal training needed so that person could do their job. It would not be an investment in the individual's future beyond the firm.

A major difference between casual and permanent employment is thus in the opportunities for training. The difference would be both in qualitative and in quantitative terms. Companies will make careful decisions about costs and benefits of providing training, developing over time views about the kind of training that makes money for the firm and the kind which does not. For this reason the *furiitaa* are on their own, and must themselves figure out how to acquire a profile of skills. The time one has as a young worker is precious. It is certainly the case that one can much more easily acquire skills when they are young. Young people need to think carefully about the skills they will acquire while they are still young.

Getting beyond fashionable dreams

For most *furiitaa*, being a *furiitaa* is a temporary stopover on the way to somewhere. On the one hand are the *furiitaa* who are looking for that somewhere. On the other are those who simply feel that wherever that somewhere may be it is not in the work they would be doing as a full-time regular employee. Among these *furiitaa* are a good number who want some kind of artistic work as a performer doing dance or playing in a band.

Some of these would-be artists attend the relevant special school; others have gotten together with high school classmates to form a band and are planning to cut a CD. Still others stand on street corners or around train stations and sing. Whether it is to become a musician, a writer or a painter, there is nothing new about such young people doing casual work to put food on their table while they try to reach a position in life where they can make ends meet as the artist they want to be. The two possibilities are to have parents who will be their unofficial patrons or to do casual work of one sort or another.

Those young people who have a dream and are working hard to realize it have a purpose in life. In interviews with *furiitaa* the one phrase that comes out repeatedly is "*yaritai koto*" (the thing I want to do). I think this is a generally used term to indicate the importance of having a dream – that something which one wants to do. Many of those who do not have such a dream are desperate to find it. Sometimes the dream is artificially created – the result of a mental exercise simply to set one's mind at ease. In these cases, some young people take hold of such dreams and spend each day trying to realize their dream. In other young people, however, there is no sign that steps are being taken to realize the dream. Having the dream is an expression of their "values". However, such values are like a cloak that is worn like an accessory. By saying the "right things" many young people are only mouthing that which they feel is fashionable – something that makes them feel as though they were "politically correct" and helps them to "fit in" psychologically. Beneath the veneer there is little that resembles in their behaviour a real commitment to the values being espoused.

As was mentioned just above, striving to realize a dream without full-time regular employment is not a new phenomenon. What is new is the large number of young people who are now doing so. In the past most people felt too pressed economically to give much weight to idealistic dreams; chasing such dreams was seen as a luxury by most ordinary Japanese. Today, however, parents in most average households can afford to support adult children and a growing number want to subsidize their children's pursuit of a dream. The idea of struggling to get ahead simply by working hard is more foreign today, and an increasing number of young people want to find some form of self-actualisation through their work. Many young people are pulled along by our consumerist culture. They are being tempted to spend now instead of investing in their own future. Celebrities in the entertainment world have come to be seen as representing the younger generation, and through the media their lifestyle seems to belong to the next door neighbour. As such it is a lifestyle that appears attainable by average Japanese. Our consumerist society plants the idea which becomes the dream, but from where comes the yarn actually needed to spin the dream?

The *furiitaa*'s financial fragility and the demands of civil society

In order to establish one's place in society and to be regarded by others as an adult both in economic and in social terms, one needs to be "occupationally independent" – to stand on their own two feet in the world of work. Working as a *furiitaa* leaves most young Japanese short of that goal. One could say that many *furiitaa* are socially delinquent, refusing to take responsibility as an adult member of society. For them, it is as though the very act of joining the ranks of a firm as a regular full-time employee is equivalent to giving up on the latent potential that is inside them – as though those who become *seishain* are seen as mindless individuals without a true soul or passion.

However, although this segment of the *furiitaa* population no doubt has difficulty accepting the proposition that everyone ought to become *sarariman*, it is likely that firms will continue to give priority to hiring a carefully selected group of new graduates each year, while also increasing the use of casuals. Wanting to achieve full-time regular employment, many young people turn to *arubaito*-type work. For many young people the sheer difficulty of finding work stands out from everything else. The previous generation had it relatively easy, growing up as they did in boom times. Good firms with good working conditions have become much more selective and are now much harder to enter. This kind of market probably leads to even more young people deciding to do their own thing. As society and the larger economic realities change, so too do the attitudes which young people have towards work.

Putting those considerations aside, as long as a young person has a clear goal around which their energies can be focused, and can make for themselves a place within society, I think it is fine that they spend some time doing *arubaito*. Problems arise for *furiitaa* when they don't know what it is that they want to do. When that is the case, casual work is no longer connected to a path that will lead to a realistic future. Then, whatever one puts forth as a dream or a goal will remain only as a fashion statement.

I feel that the schools in Japan have not educated students sufficiently in how to go forth into the labor market. Our schools see little need to prepare students for navigating the labor market. The assumption is that they will continue to go through the established placement channels established in each school. As long as each student progresses through those channels and keeps to "the plan", they will find that a place has been reserved for them somewhere in society. By following the traditional route that was already in place, one has in the past more-or-less automatically become a full-time regular employee. However, the times have changed and we have to rethink that approach.

How does a young *furiitaa* take the first step toward life as a fully fledged member of society? Most important in my view are moves that enhance the *furiitaa*'s understanding of the world of work. *Furiitaa* have to look inside themselves and understand what they want to do. Beyond that each *furiitaa* needs to start developing a concrete plan by observing how adults are working, how they are carving out a niche for themselves, and the relationships they develop with others. Although the work one is assigned as an *arubaitaa* is quite limited and fairly restricted, one can nevertheless use that opportunity to come in contact with a range of people. Young people need to talk with as many persons as possible.

Even though *arubaito* has been dismissed as a dead-end experience for many *furiitaa*, there are types of *arubaito* which do provide opportunities for skill acquisition. For example, being a waiter or waitress in a restaurant also has its professional side: remembering the order in which things go and are served, and the special requirements of some foods; knowing the origins of various foods; dealing with the peculiarities of certain patrons; and being informed about a wide range of wines and other alcoholic drinks. Those who master these aspects of the culinary arts no longer refer to themselves as *furiitaa*. To learn about these opportunities it is important for young people to meet as wide a range of working adults as possible, watching them work and talking to them about their work.

A message from the world of work

Attitudes toward work

A survey conducted among firms in Tokyo by the Nihon Kei-eisha Renmei and the Tokyo Kei-eisha Kyokai (2001), asked employers to assess the senior high school students who had applied for full-time regular employment. Forty six percent of the respondents claimed that they were unsatisfied or slightly disappointed in the attitudes of students concerning work or in the way they viewed work. Thirty four percent complained that their ability to communicate was insufficient. A similar proportion of employers found fault with their manners, level of politeness when talking, and general social outlook. With regard to the role of schools in the overall placement exercise, about sixty percent of employers felt that the school needed to do more to ensure that students had a fuller understanding of what the world of work entailed and a firmer grasp of what was needed at work.

Other signs also point to the existence of similar views. Managers frequently mention the declining work ethic. I myself feel that this reflects a concern that respect for work has been lost and that most students have a rather loose view of work-related matters. When it comes to making decisions about who to hire for full-time regular employment, the term "*soku senryoku jushi*" (instant fire power) is often heard. However, few firms expect to hire new graduates one day and then to extract significant value the next. The term more realistically refers to the expectation of management that it will be able to immediately set about training new recruits and then assign them meaningful work in the shortest time possible. What is importance is that new recruits are enthusiastic to learn new skills. It is an openness to what each new day might bring and to absorbing new information relevant to the running of the business. This is what managers are referring to when they mention the importance of attitudes toward work.

The orientation of high school students

In 2000 the Japan Institute of Labor conducted a survey of final year high school students in Japan's large cities just before they graduated (Nikon Rodo Kenkyu Kiko 2000 b: 110). About 12 percent of the sample of students was planning to work as *furiitaa*, and 23 percent of those students claimed they wanted to do things other than being a full-time regular employee. That was the most frequent reason given for deciding to become a *furiitaa*. Following that response came "I don't know what work best suits me", "I couldn't find a good place to work", and "further education was too expensive". To another question over 40 percent of respondents indicated that "for the time being I wanted income" and "I wanted to have the free use of my time rather than be a full-time regular employee". Factor analysis (principal component analysis) of the data revealed that these two responses were closely related, along with the view that "the interpersonal relations of the *seishain* are too stressful" and the wish to be able to change jobs freely. Taken as a cluster, these types of responses indicated that many *furiitaa* are looking for a happy and stress-free way to earn their living. When we interviewed those students, the most frequent reason given was having a "*yaritai koto*" (something they wanted to do) or a reason worded differently but pointing in that direction. Here too, however, the underlying themes were "freedom of choice" and "freedom from stress".

These responses suggest an orientation that is counter to what is sought by management. Many young people who become Japan's pool of *furiitaa* do not want to assume the responsibilities associated with looking after their employer's interests as faceless cogs in society. It seems to me that this is an approach to life in which there is little interest in preparing a position for themselves to live in adult society.

This is a typical trait of those who become *furiitaa*. It is probably an outlook that has a certain currency among many teenagers in today's Japan. It is not an outlook that has simply emerged over night. It has no doubt been fostered by Japan's relatively affluent lifestyle and has spread with successive improvements in the standard of living – change that has been reflected in the labor market over the past decade.

The role of schools

Japan's industrial leaders have the expectation that schools will play a fuller role in developing a positive, proactive approach to work in each student. They expect schools to somehow bridge the gap these young people feel between what or who they want to be and what is required to be a contributing member of society. This means that policy-makers concerned with these issues must somehow come to grips with the hesitation many students feel when thinking about becoming fully fledged adult member of society.

How should schools approach this task? It is hard for someone like myself, who does not have experience advising students, to make persuasive recommendations outside their field of expertise. However, my impression is that negative images of work predominate throughout society: the Heisei Recession, the bleak economic outlook held by many business leaders, the restructuring of work and concomitant lay-offs, and the decline of business ethics. We are not sending to our children positive messages about our hopes, expectations and passion that they will enjoy being permanently employed and be able to make positive contributions to society.

Our generation has grown up cultivating many interpersonal relationships through work. Through work we had opportunities to talk with a wide range of persons about various matters. Nearly all adults could talk about what they found interesting in their work, the joy of completing a piece of work, the sense of pride or fulfilment they derived from a job well-done, trust among one's friends and work mates, and the confidence which comes from being responsible. These are the positives we need to transmit to the next generation. There is a lot that is good about our society and about working in Japan, and we need to help students more fully appreciate that fact.

Toward new paradigms for thinking about work

The common view of getting a job upon graduation

Most Japanese have grown up believing that being a *seishain* in full-time and long-term employment was the natural progression for nearly all young people who did not seek further education. The reality, however, is somewhat different, as we saw above in Chapter Eight (*e.g.,* Table 8.1). Twenty percent of the 1985 cohort of middle school graduates did not follow the accepted path. Only ten years later about 35 percent of the 1994 cohort had taken alternative routes into the labor market.

Two points need to be made regarding that data. First, even in the 1980s the common view of the labor market for new graduates was held without any consideration for the substantial number of young people who were following alternative routes to full-time regular employment. Second, with the number of students in successive cohorts declining, especially after 1989, one might expect there to be a labor shortage which would in turn draw a larger portion of young people into permanent employment. However, the proportion of young people seeking employment outside the normal channels has grown over time. This reflected the fact that the demand for new graduates dropped by even more than the supply. In other words, something more fundamental was occurring in terms of how work was being organized. As a result, a good deal of public interest has been generated by those involved in developing unemployment policies for Japan's youth, by those providing support to assist them in their efforts to find permanent employment, and by those offering them career advice.

Reassessing direct entry into permanent employment

Young people would find it useful to have a social system in place that would protect them from being unemployed and allow them to slot smoothly into full-time regular employment on a long-term basis. With stability built into their employment, they would be able to take a long-term perspective at work and approach issues related to skill acquisition in a much more positive manner that would result in their actually acquiring skills. They would also be able to look to their employer to invest in their training. In a situation with a good measure of certainly they would be able to develop a good supportive network of interpersonal relationships, and then use the support to realize their own potential. Able to foresee wage increases over time, they would have a sense of economic independence and the wherewithal to plan for a household in the future. On the other hand, like all mass production systems, the efficiencies which would derive from having all young graduates processed in the same manner at the same time are offset by the very sameness such an approach produces. The emphasis on uniformity means that a good deal of individual variation and creative outlook are lost. Placed uncritically into jobs that don't "fit", many are quick to resign from their full-time regular employment.

The greatest demerit of such a system is in dealing with those who do not fit in. To begin with, society is left with a group of young people who have little hope of acquiring the skills necessary to gain full citizenship in the labor force. They are left wandering from one unskilled job to another. They soon age and lose the learning advantages which come from mental flexibility, physical fitness and freedom from family responsibility – all attributes commonly associated with youth. Second, young people who miss out on the mass migration into employment upon graduation are unable to secure for themselves a socially recognized status within their respective communities. The loss of status and having to exist in a non-recognized way can only lead to increased doubt concerning their identity. Without a firm base for surviving economically, it is difficult for those off the beaten path to create a vision for their own future. Even if they find work as *furiitaa*, they are left working for a minimal wage without much prospect that there will be a significant improvement in the future. Left in the casual labor force, they fall through many of the safety nets that are in place (*e.g.*, private pension schemes and health plans). It is difficult for individuals to overcome the hurdles mentioned here simply by gaining employment as a *furiitaa*. Among the *furiitaa* there are many who seek after their own goals and have "something they want to do". However, only a few are able to use their experience doing *arubaito* to realise their goals.

Cooperating to support *furiitaa* in finding a career

It is now time to formulate policies that will help young people who pursue an alternative route to overcome the barriers presently characterizing the system of mass employment for new graduates. At the same time policies are needed to augment the merits associated with the mass employment system. This can be done by better utilizing facilities which already exist in some schools and training institutions or by developing further the nascent system which allows for a kind of intern experience through trial periods of employment. The important thing is that young people continue to acquire appropriate occupational skills. Next is the placement of students into a work environment in which they can obtain information and insight concerning career possibilities. It is also important that industry send to these young people messages about the type of people they will employ and about the skills potential employees will need in the future. Opening the way for young people to become full-time regular employees by meeting the standards set by industry can only be a good thing because it minimizes the human resource costs involved in hiring, orienting and utilizing new labor.

Finally, I should underline the importance of cultivating an aptitude for work among students while they are still in school. To date the school's involvement has normally begun and ended with its program to place graduates in full-time regular employment. It is now time for schools to go a step further by arranging for work experience and for programs designed to inform students about various occupations and the role of work within society. Finally, there is need for counselling services which create a strong sense of worth and offer some idea about how to link individual aptitudes to a place in the labor force.

The above comments lead me to emphasize the importance of developing a coordinated approach too helping young people on their journey to adulthood – an approach involving families, schools, industry, various government bureaucracies, regional organizations and NPOs.

Overcoming the barriers facing senior high school graduates

The decline in the demand for high school graduates

The labor market for new graduates has been affected by two main forces. One is the business cycle, and the recent slump in demand owning to the Heisei Recession. The other is restructuring as firms reorganize themselves to maintain their competitiveness in an increasingly globalized economy.

According to another survey by the Nihon Kei-eisha Renmei and the Tokyo Keieisha Kyokai early in 2000 (reported in the *Nikkei Taimusu*, 24 February 2000, p. 2), three reasons surfaced to explain why firms were reluctant to hire high school graduates as permanent employees. One was the desire of many employers to hire more highly educated individuals. Second was the move of firms to hire more lowly skilled individuals on a casual basis rather than as *seishain*. Third was the effort being made by firms to further reduce their dependence on human resources by introducing more labor-saving procedures and machinery. Along with that is the export of labor-intensive processes oversees to countries where the labor costs are much lower. These factors add up to there being a significant drop in the opportunities for high school graduates to obtain full-time regular employment.

On the other hand, managers at many firms publicly lament what they claim is a decline in the work ethic and the absence of any feel for what is required to maintain a desirable lifestyle on the home front. In short, they would argue that "young people simply aren't what they used to be."

Internships

Hagiwara Shin-ichi, Head of the National Association to Provide Career Guidance to Senior High School Students (Zenkoku Kotogakko Shinro Shido Kyokai) has recently emphasized the importance of internships (Nihon Keizai Shimbun, morning edition, 13 October 2002, p. 16). By experiencing life within a company, young people learn about how the failure to complete a task at work impacts on others both inside and outside the firm, about what happens when customers change to other suppliers, and about the importance of what each employee does within the larger schema for a firm's overall operations. They are able to sense the enthusiasm with which people tackle their jobs and the satisfaction that comes from a job well done. This will contribute to them developing their own work ethic and an outlook which will enable them to link what they learn in school with a likely future in the work force. At the same time, one also needs to be realistic about the challenges that make the implementation of any intern program difficult.

Until recently, firms wanted schools to supply them with a blank page on which they could shape their own narratives according to requirements spelled out in their business plans. Now firms are beginning to ask that schools supply more sophisticated graduates – young people who already have character and a bit of their own narrative.

With higher eductional qualifications being the order of the day, students are staying at school longer. It seems that more time is required in adolescence, as young people now require more time to be acculturated in an increasingly sophisticated society. Young people seem to have matured more rapidly as fully fledged consumers, but have been slow to develop a full sense of their role as mature members of society. Students need to be in programs that will enhance their ability to fit into society, and that task cannot simply be left to schools. It is easy to be critical of young graduates, but we need to accept that there is a broader-based responsibility within society to provide students with a range of opportunities to experience life at work. I wish again to emphasize how important it is for the various sectors of our society to contribute to this process. Without such a cooperative effort, society will not be able to create the labor force it needs for the future.

The declining quality of high school graduates

The academic performance of students at all levels seems to be dropping. A bigger problem, however, is the reluctance of students to develop a sense of social responsibility. This means they are not developing as strong individuals with a sense of social obligation. In a certain sense they have been spoilt or given an easy ride with an affluent lifestyle. The kinds of life skills taken for granted in looking after oneself in the past now seem foreign to many of today's young people. Students now need to acquire and to be taught the life skills being promoted by the Ministry of Education and Science.

The growing number of graduates who become *furiitaa*

In Japan's large cities the number of high schools producing an abundance of *furiitaa* is increasing. Many teachers now accept this as inevitable. In schools where better outcomes are somehow being achieved despite the slack labor market, teachers have been highly motivated to come up with various strategies to assist their students in finding full-time regular employment. However, many claim there is little they can do to alleviate the problem. The more philosophical suggest that we do not need to worry about students who do nothing and end up without full-time regular employment.

The fact remains, nevertheless, that a lot of these adolescents are neither gaining lasting employment nor going on for further education. As things currently stand, the negative outcomes for one's career are conspicuous. If through some process they are able to find a direction for themselves, even if by a circuitous route determined by trial and error, that is probably okay. However, if they stay too long as a *furiitaa*, their chances of becoming a *seishain* are drastically reduced.

The unemployment rate and the proportion of graduates in casual employment vary inversely with the level of education. The number of university graduates who become unemployed or enter casual employment is increasing, but they still account for only about one tenth of all *furiitaa*. As those with less education are much more likely to remain as *furiitaa*, it is that group which is most urgently in need of policies to mitigate the problems they face when trying to enter the permanent labor force.

Secondary education at a crossroads

In 1992 there were about 1.67 million job offers for secondary school graduates. By 2001 this had fallen to just 240 thousand, one seventh the 1992 figure (as indicated in Table 1.4). Some business leaders are arguing that we need to maintain the current rate at which secondary school graduates enter the permanent labor force, and that schools need to make the effort required to commit themselves to ensuring that a steady stream of such graduates continues to come into the labor market in the future.

I would add that we need also to redesign our secondary school curriculum. To continue as a competitive society within the global context, Japan must become more knowledge or information intensive so its IT and service industries are at the forefront. At the same time technical skills must be kept at the highest standard possible. A demand exists for graduates who are trained in a trade and have work experience. However, for some time the number of generalist high schools has been increasing while the number of technical school has been declining. The generalist curriculum tends to be for students planning to continue further in the education system. Young students who want only a secondary school education deserve a more suitable education. They need to be educated in ways that give them a range of employment options upon graduation.

Even with a better curriculum in place for these students, young graduates should not be locked into the choices they may have made at the age of 15 or 18. If they cannot later change their direction, they will simply end up being stigmatized by a label placed on them when they make that early decision about work. Even while they are still in school some students will want to change direction as they mature. In such cases, students should be able to repeat their penultimate year at school if necessary. Simply keeping them in the same stream so that they will "automatically" flow into their final year in school may make it easier for school administrators to plan for student numbers in their classes, but the interests of students wanting a change will not be served. It makes more sense to create alternative progressions for such students. There is no overwhelming reason why all students have to complete their secondary school education in three years. We need to abandon the idea that one education formula fits all. Students should not be graduated from senior high school just because they are aged 18. They should be graduated because they have acquired skills associated with having a specific type of high school diploma. Schools need to assume more responsibility for the educational outcomes of their students.

In the past schools have tried to respond to student demand by offering subjects that would attract the most students. They seemed to be less responsive to the needs of business. If we are serious about diversifying the school curriculum, then more thought needs to be given to the views of industry and others who represent local interests. Now that a system of local school boards (*gakko hyogiin seido*) is being introduced, it is a good time to involve industry and local spokespersons more fully in the life of schools so that their views can be better incorporated into curriculum design at the local level. Through the frank exchange of opinions that would also allow for the wider community to have a better understanding of what educators are trying to accomplish.

Youth employment as a challenge in advanced economies

The practice of mass placements upon graduation has meant that youth unemployment has not traditionally been a problem in Japan. The relatively smooth/automatic transition of graduates into the labor force has been buttressed by firms taking the initiative through on-the-job training and other means. New employees straight out of school have been trained in ways that result in them becoming responsible and capable members of the labor force. However, over the last decade or so there has been a marked increase in the number of secondary school graduates who become either unemployed or only casually employed. One factor here is the view held by many youth that they can get by in life without assuming the responsibilities of adulthood. There has been a larger social change occurring in which the entire framework or set of assumptions that were crucial to the transformation of young people into adulthood has been altered.

At the macro level we are talking about our ability to give shape to the next generation of Japanese who will eventually steer our society into the future. If this next generation is not properly trained and given a sense of its destiny in taking society to its next stage, the society will lose its dynamism. After all, the next generation's future is the future of Japan. The issues we face in preparing our youth for a place in tomorrow's work force deserve our careful attention. The way in which we resolve those issues will have a considerable impact on how well Japan fares in the twenty-first century.

Notes

Chapter 1

1 The *"furiitaa* situation" was first considered in a labor white paper in 1991. The government had always considered youth (*"jakunen"* or *"seishonen"*) to be aged under 25, perhaps 30 at the most in some special circumstances. For the first time in 1991 the usage of these terms was extended to include persons aged up to 35. One aim of those preparing the white paper was to obtain an age profile for the *furiitaa* and it was felt that many in their early thirties would still be working in that way. This also fit with changes associated with the rise over time in the age at which "young" people were getting married.

Chapter 5

1 Case 02 is referring to Ohira's autobiography, *Dakara anata mo ikinuite* (You too can breath freely)(Tokyo: Kodansha 2000).

References

Furiitaa Kenkyukai (ed.) (2001), *Furiitaa ga wakaru hon* (A book all about the furiitaa) (Tokyo: Suken Shuppan).

Gakken (ed.) (2001), *Furiitaa – Naze? Dosuru? Furiitaa nihyakumannin jidai ga yatte kita* (The era of two million *furiitaa* – why they exist and what to do about them) (Tokyo: Gakushu Kenkyu Sha).

Genda, Yuji (2001), *Shigoto no naka no aimai na fuan – yureru wakamono no genzai* (The vague sense of uneasiness among young people: the uncertainty of youth in contemporary Japan) (Tokyo: Chuo Koron Shinsha).

Hori, Yukie (2001), '*Furiitaa* sekishutsu no haikei to *furiitaa* keiken ni taisuru hyoka' (Background to the appearance of the *furiitaa* and their experience – Toward an appraisal), in *Daitoshi no wakamono no shugyo kodo to ishiki – Hirogaru furiitaa keiken to kyokan* (Work life and consciousness of Japan's urban youth: The experience and outlook of *furiitaa* who are becoming more visible in Japan), JIL research report no. 146 (Tokyo: Nihon Rodo Kenkyu Kiko), pp. 78–101.

——————(2002), '*Furiitaa* de wa naze mazui no ka' (What is so bad about being a *furiitaa*?), *JIL Atto Waaku* (vol. 10: June), pp. 18–21.

Jiyu Jikan Dezain Kyokai (2002), *Jisedaigata raifu & waakusutairu ni kansuru chosa kenkyu hokokusho* (The lifestyle and approach to work of the next generation: a report on some survey results) (Tokyo: Jiyu Jikan Dezain Kyokai).

Kosei Rodo Sho Joho Bu Koyo Tokei Ka (2001), *Koyo kanari chosa* (The survey of employment strategies) (Tokyo: Kosei Rodo Sho Rokei Joho Bu).

Kosei Rodo Sho Shokugyo Antei Kyoku (every year a), *Shinsotsugyosha no rodo shijo* (The labor market for new graduates) (Tokyo: Kosei Rodo Sho Shokugyo Antei Kyoku).

——————(every year b), *Shinki sotsugyosha no shushoku naitei nado ni tsuite* (Informal commitments to employ new graduates) (Tokyo: Kosei Rodo Sho Shokugyo Antei Kyoku)

——————(every year c), *Daigakuto sotsugyo yoteisha naitei jokyo no chosa* (Survey of informal commitments to employ new university graduates) (Tokyo: Kosei Rodo Sho Shokugyo Antei Kyoku)

Kokosei no shushoku mondai ni kansuru kentokai (Committee to examine issues related to the employment of high school students) (2001), *Kokosei no shushoku mondai ni kansuru kentokai hokoku* (Report of the committee to examine issues related to the employment of high school students) (Tokyo: Monbu Kagaku Sho Shoto Chuto Kyoiku Kyoku Shokugyo Kyoiku Ka).

Kosugi, Reiko (2001a), 'Zoka suru jakunen hiseiki koyosha no jittai to sono mondaiten' (The increasing number of non-regular employees among our youth: the realities and major issues), *Nihon Rodo Kenkyu Zasshi* (no. 490: May), pp. 444–457.

———— (2001 b), 'Wakamono no shugyo kodo no henka to shinron shido – *furiitaa* o erabu kokosei no shokugyo ishiki wo chushin ni' (Changes in the employment of young people and career guidance – the career consciousness of high school students who choose to be *furiitaa*), in *Shokugyo kenkyu* (Research on occupations), edited by Koyo Mondai Kenkyukai (Tokyo: Koyo Mondai Kenkyukai), pp. 34–38.

———— (2003), *Furiitaa to iu ikikata* (Living as *furiitaa*) (Tokyo: Keiso Shobo).

Kosugi, Reiko (ed.), (2002), *Jiyu no daisho/furiitaa – gendai wakamono no shugyo ishiki to kodo* (*Furiitaa* and the cost of freedom – the behavior and consciousness of contemporary youth) (Tokyo: Nihon Rodo Kenkyu Kiko).

Kosugi, Reiko; Hori, Yukie; and Miyamoto, Michiko (eds) (2005), *Furiitaa to niito* (*Furiitaa* and the NEET) (Tokyo: Keiso Shobo).

Lead Writer, the Nikkeiren Taimusu (2002), 'Shucho' (My Say), *Nikkeiren Taimusu* (14 February 2002). Taken from http://db.go.jp/cgi-in/jntol?smode=dtldsp&detail=N20000224002.

Miyamoto, Michiko (2002), *Wakamono ga 'shakaiteki jakusha' ni tenraku suru* (Youth as the socially weak) (Tokyo: Yosen Sha).

Mombu Kagaku Sho, every year, *Gakko kihon chosa* (The basic survey of educational institutions) (Tokyo: Monbu Kagaku Sho)

Murakami, Ryu (ed.) (2001), *Jakunen rodosha no kiki – mirai no aru furiitaa mirai no nai furiitaa* (The danger facing young workers – *furiitaa* with a future and *furiitaa* without a future), Japan Mail Media no. 13 (Tokyo: Nihon Hoso Shuppan Kyokai), pp. 14–81.

Nihon Kei-eisha Renmei (The Japan Association of Employers) (1995), *Shinjidai no nihonteki kei-ei* (Japanese-style management for a new age) (Tokyo: Nikkeiren).

Nihon Kei-eisha Renmei and Tokyo Kei-eisha Renmei (2000), *Koko shin-sostsusha no saiyo ni kansuru ankeeto* (The questionnaire about the employment of new high school graduates) (Tokyo: Nihon Kei-eisha Renmei).

———— (2001), *Koko shinsostsusha no saiyo ni kansuru ankeeto* (The questionnaire about the employment of new high school graduates) (Tokyo: Nihon Kei-eisha Renmei).

Nihon Rodo Kenkyu Kiko (The Japan Institute of Labor) (ed.), (1992), *Kosotsu sannenme no kyaria to ishiki – shoki shokugyo keireki ni kansuru tsuiseki chosa (dai ni kai) yori* (The career and consciousness three years after graduation from senior high school – from the follow-up survey tracking their first job), JIL research report no. 28 (Tokyo: Nihon Rodo Kenkyu Kiko).

—————(1998), *Shinki kosotsu rodo shijo no henka to shokugyo e no iko no shien* (Changes in the labor market for new high school graduates and support for the transition to work), JIL research report no. 114 (Tokyo: Nihon Rodo Kenkyu Kiko).

—————(2000a), *Furiitaa no ishiki to jittai – kyujushichi-nin e no hiaringu chosa yori* (The realities and thoughts of the *furiitaa* – from interviews with ninety seven *furiitaa*), JIL research report no. 136 (Tokyo: Nihon Rodo Kenkyu Kiko).

—————(2000b), *Shinro kettei o meguru kokosei no ishiki to jittai – kosotsu 'furiitaa' zoka no jittai to haikei* (The reality and the consciousness of high school students as they decide what to do upon graduation – the increasing number of *furiitaa* among high school graduates), JIL research report no. 138 (Tokyo: Nihon Rodo Kenkyu Kiko).

—————(2001a), *Nichi-O no daigaku to shokugyo – koto kyoiku to shokugyo ni kansuru ju-nikakoku hikaku chosa kekka* (Results of the comparative study of higher education and work in twelve countries: reflections on universities and work in Japan and Europe), JIL research report no. 143 (Tokyo: Nihon Rodo Kenkyu Kiko).

—————(2001b), *Daitoshi no wakamono no shugyo kodo to ishiki – hirogaru furiitaa keiken to kyokan* (Work life and consciousness of Japan's urban youth: the experience and outlook of *furiitaa* who are becoming more visible in Japan), JIL research report no. 146 (Tokyo: Niho Rodo Kenkyu Kiko).

—————(2002a), *Wakamono no shugyo kodo ni kansuru deetabukku – shugyo kozo kihon chosa buseki yori* (A data book on the employment behavior of young Japanese: an analysis of data from the *Employment status survey*) (Tokyo: Nihon Rodo Kenkyu Kiko).

—————(2002b), *Jiyu no daisho – gendai wakamono no shugyo ishiki to kodo* (The cost of freedom – the behaviour and consciousness of today's youth regarding employment) (Tokyo: Nihon Rodo Kenkyu Kiko).

Okabe, Yukio (ed.), (2002) *Shinsotsu mugyo* (The unengaged new graduates) (Tokyo: Toyo Keizai Shimpo Sha).

Organisation for Economic Cooperation and Development (OECD) (2000a), *From Initial Education to Working Life – Making Transitions Work* (Paris: OECD).

Rengo Sogo Seikatsu Kaihatsu Kenkyujo (2000), *Jakunen rodosha no koyo ishiki – kodo no henka to roshi no torikumi ni kansuru chosa kenkyu hokokusho* (Report on the survey concerning the consciousness and behavior of young workers) (Tokyo: Rengo Sogo Seikatsu Kaihatsu Kenkyujo)

Rikuruuto Waakusu Kenkyujo (2000), *Furiitaa no shuro jokyo ni kansuru chosa kenkyu hokokusho* (A report on the survey research concerning the employment situation of *furiitaa*) (Tokyo: Rikuruuto Waakusu Kenkyujo).

————(2001), *Daisotsu kyujin bairitsu chosa* (Survey of the demand in the market for university graduates) (Tokyo: Rikuruuto Waakusu Kenkyujo).

Rodo Seisaku Kenkyu-Kenshu Kiko (The Japan Institute for Labour Policy and Training) (2004a), *Iko no kiki ni aru wakamono no jittai – mugyo/furiitaa no wakamono no intabyu chosa (chukan hokokusho)* (The situation of Japan's vulnerable youth struggling to make the transition into the labor force – an interim report) (Tokyo: Rodo Seisaku Kenkyu-Kenshu Kiko).

———— (2004b), *Daiikkai bijinesu-reebaa niita chosa – wakate seishain no sugata* (First business-labor NEET survey: a portrait of young company employees), available at www.jil.go.jp/press/jyakunen/index.html.

———— (2005), *Wakamono shugyo shien no genjo to kadai – Igirisu ni okeru shien no tenkai to Nihon no jittai bunseki kara* (Issues with the current state of support for youth employment: the development of support in England and an analysis of the situation in Japan) (Tokyo: Rodo Seisaku Kenkyu-Kenshu Kiko).

———— (2006), *Daitoshi no wakamono no shugyo kodo to iko katei – Hokatsuteki na iko shien ni mukete* (The employment behavior of urban youth and the transition to full-time regular employment – Toward a comprehensive system of support for the those facing the transition), Research report (Tokyo: Rodo Seisaku Kenkyu-Kenshu Kiko).

Rodo Sho (1991), *Rodo hakusho* (The labor whitepaper) (Tokyo: Nihon Rodo Kenkyu Kiko).

————(2000), *Rodo hakusho* (The labor whitepaper) (Tokyo: Nihon Rodo Kenkyu Kiko).

Somu Sho Tokei Kyoku (1997), *Shugyo kozo kihon chosa* (Employment status survey) (Tokyo: Somu Sho Tokei Kyoku).

Somu Sho Tokei Kyoku (every year a), *Rodoryoku chosa* (Labor force survey) (Tokyo: Somu Sho Tokei Kyoku).

———— (every year b), *Rodoryoku tokubetsu chosa hokoku* (The special survey of the labor force survey) (Tokyo: Somu Sho Tokei Kyoku). Data from these surveys may be obtained from www.stat.go.jp/english/index.htm.

Tanaka, Hirohide (1980), *Gendai koyo ron* (Current theories concerning employment) (Tokyo: Nihon Rodo Kyokai).

Uenishi, Mitsuko (ed.) (2001), '*Furiitaa* kara no ridatsu' (Beyond work as a *furiitaa*), in *Daitoshi no wakamono no shugyo kodo to ishiki – hirogaru furiitaa keiken to kyokan* (Work life and consciousness of Japan's urban youth: The experience and outlook of *furiitaa* who are becoming more visible in Japan), edited by the Nihon Rodo Kenkyu Kiko, JIL research report no. 146 (Tokyo: Nihon Rodo Kenkyu Kiko), pp. 102–130.

Index